Teacher's Manual

Regulation of Lawyers: Problems of Law and Ethics

Sixth Edition

by

Stephen Gillers
Vice Dean and Professor of Law
New York University School of Law

Aspen Law and Business
Aspen Publishers, Inc.
New York   Gaithersburg

ISBN 0 - 7355 - 2455 - 6

This manual is made available as a courtesy to law teachers with the understanding that it will not be reproduced, quoted or cited, except as where indicated. In the event that anyone would like to cite the manual for thoughts drawn from it, a reference to the relevant page number of the materials text (with the formula "suggested by") may be appropriate.

Copies of this manual are available on computer diskette. Teachers who have adopted the casebook may obtain a copy of the diskette, free of charge, by calling the Aspen Law & Business sales assistant at 1 – 800 – 950 – 5259.

Permissions
Aspen Law & Business
A Division of Aspen Publishers, Inc.
1185 Avenue of the Americas
New York, NY 10036

1 2 3 4 5

TABLE OF CONTENTS

---

* The Preface contains information on changes in the sixth edition and suggestions for coverage.

PREFACE

WHY WRITE A TEACHER'S MANUAL?
(And an Overview of the Sixth Edition)

Why write a Teacher's Manual? Why indeed? After all, it's not an art form that gets a whole lot of respect in academic circles, is it now? No one cites teacher's manuals. No one openly discusses them. They appear on few if any resumes. Maybe you are not quick to admit that you read teacher's manuals. So why bother?

Cynics and publishers will say that it's because they help sell books. Or at the least that they <u>might</u> help sell books. Or, at the very, very least, that not having one will <u>decrease</u> the number of books sold if competing books <u>do</u> have them (which in this case, I cannot tell a lie, they do). As often, cynics and publishers have a point, especially cynics. But only a point. While their point may or may not make a teacher's manual a necessity, the daughter of necessity is still invention. And that's where we have opportunity for a little fun.

Look at it this way. A teacher's manual, if you're going to do one -- note that even I say "do" one, not "write" one, as though it were manufactured if you are going to <u>write</u> one, why not push the medium to the limits of its possibilities, why not invent or reinvent it? Surely, things can be done in a TM that the rules of traditional academic publishing venues do not tolerate. We can be frisky, adventurous, colloquial, personal, anecdotal, in short, human. No reason why this endeavor cannot be enjoyable for both of us. A conversation if you will.

Of course, only I get to talk, but you get to talk back in your mind, and I get to anticipate your responses. You can also write to me once in a while -- it wouldn't hurt -- or even ring up for a chat. (212) 998-6264. My E-Mail address is:

stephen.gillers@nyu.edu

Much of what I'll say here -- and much of the new material in the SIXTH edition -- responds to letters and conversations I've had from and with many of you. If you see a gap in the book, or excess coverage, or inadequate coverage, please let me know. If you have a question, please let me know. After all, it's in my interest (and the interest of those who use the books, students and teachers) to make it as clear and helpful as possible. And, incidentally, if there is material absent from this edition but present in earlier editions that you think I should not have excluded and which you wish to use, faculty adopting the sixth edition of the casebook have permission to copy and distribute material from prior editions.

All that being said, and publishers aside, there's a good (*i.e.*, non-commercial) reason to have a teacher's manual for a book used in a course like legal ethics (a term I'll use as a shorthand although the course is no longer called that in most places and rightly so). The reason is that there is great variety in the focus of legal ethics courses and in the books edited for them, much more so than for other standard law school courses. The study of legal ethics -- what we mean to teach our students, how we hope to do it -- has been evolving sharply and in several directions. The course is, in short, rather idiosyncratic when compared to others in the curriculum. We have more choices about what to cover, what materials to use, and how to teach than do most of our colleagues. And we exercise those choices in diverse ways.

So a teacher's manual is an especially useful adjunct to a legal ethics casebook because, given the diversity within the genre, it explains the authors' point of view, their orientation toward the materials, and how it all fits together in their minds, or doesn't, as the case may be. You know, the vision thing.

Complementing this circumstance is the fact that the course conventionally called "legal ethics" is continuously evolving. Remember that scene in the film "The Graduate" in which a friend of Dustin Hoffman's parents, trying to help him make the right career choice, whispers "plastics?" A decade ago (and even today) he might have whispered "legal ethics."

If you dig out an old AALS Directory, one from a quarter century ago, and turn to the list of teachers under "Legal Profession," you will see perhaps a quarter or a third of the number listed in the current AALS Directory. Not only is the course offered more often more places, but more of us are making it our primary area of study. My own proprietary interests keep me constantly aware of the number of casebooks and problem books that an instructor may adopt for a legal ethics course. Thirty years ago, perhaps two books dominated the field. Now there are more than a half dozen to choose from.

Increased academic interest in the subject is also reflected both in the profession and in the popular culture. We didn't need the S&L debacle, O.J. Simpson, Jones v. Clinton, or Kenneth Starr to spark public and professional interest in what lawyers do and how they do it. But it sure helped. Add the tobacco and other high profile litigation and headline stories in which the law of lawyering, lawyers, and legal institutions all have principal parts, and you know that this subject will be popular and debated for quite some time.

On the other hand, legal ethics does not yet have the same level of coherence as, say, contracts, or torts, or even criminal law. It doesn't have the well-formed history of those traditional subjects. One might say that its heyday, its formative period, is right now. And we are part of it. The past is still prologue.

But can a teacher's manual make order out of this chaos? You bet. Or it can at least offer "ordered chaos." Read on.

ON TEACHING "LEGAL ETHICS"

I doubt there are as many ways of teaching legal ethics as there are teachers, but it sometimes seems so. Here I want to tell you about my own approach, such as it is, when I can summon the energy to implement it. And I also want to tell you about the NYU videotapes, which I find helpful in teaching the course.

For a few years now, I have taught the course in a new way. No final examination. I divide the class into quarters according to the first letter of the student's last name. Call these sections A-D. Each section is responsible for writing five or six papers during the semester. Each section has different papers. All of the papers are based on the problems in the casebook or others I'm developing. They have a 700-word maximum. I read the papers in advance of class discussion. There are great advantages to this method. At least one quarter of the class has been forced to think hard about the problem and to commit to a solution. That significantly enhances class discussion, as well as the level of interest. Further, since I know which student took which position, I can call on particular people in an effort to enliven the debate and sharpen the issues.

Make no mistake. This means more work for the instructor. If you have a hundred students and six papers each, you will read 600 papers (although each is only two pages long) during the semester. At one point, I not only read the papers, I commented on each one in the margins and graded each one on a scale of 1-10. (By now you're probably saying this guy is a complete nut.) It was a lot more work, but, frankly, it was worth it for the improved class discussion and for the opportunity to respond to the students' work. Furthermore, the students knew I would be responding to their work and that seems to have encouraged them to pay more attention. To help them understand how to write their papers, I did a model answer for one of the earlier papers. The papers were graded mostly on accuracy and cogency, but I also let the students know that I expected them to hand in a product they would be pleased to deliver to their first boss, which meant they had to proofread it for typos, grammatical lapses, and repetition. (While vice dean, I have continued this practice but have been unable to comment on and hand back papers. However, I offer to meet with any student who, after class discussion of the issue, wants to go over his or her paper.)

Although the work is substantial, if you stagger the assignments, it is not overwhelming. I recommend five papers per student (which means less than every other week on average), and a sixth final paper, which is the same for the entire class. I distribute the question for the last paper on the next to the last day of class, to be returned on the last day. That paper is graded without comment since it will not be discussed in class. Because it can incorporate themes from throughout the course, and is a bit more complicated, the page length is longer, three pages instead of two. And it counts double in the final grade

I have not yet experimented with web-based discussion boards as a place where students post their papers for all students (and me) to read. I may try that. But if I do, I think it is necessary that no student be able to read another student's posted paper until all papers are posted.

Now to the NYU videotapes.

As many of you know, for two summers running, we produced first nine and then six dramatic vignettes on videotape. By "we" I mean NYU School of Law, which owns the tapes. The first tape is called "Adventures in Legal Ethics." If you think that sounds unimaginative, consider that the second tape is called "Further Adventures in Legal Ethics." We have also produced a composite tape, which consists of thirteen of the fifteen vignettes from the first two tapes. Two were eliminated from this third, composite tape.

The money to produce the tapes, using professional actors (some of whom had switched from being lawyers), came from NYU School of Law on my earnest representation that we would be able to sell enough tapes to law schools, CLEs, and law firms to recoup our investment. (Uh, oh.) Well, we did, and we even earned a nice profit, which we used to produce a third tape in 1996.

The third tape is called "Dinner At Sharswood's Café." In it, four thirtysomething lawyers meet for dinner at their law school reunion. Each has a story to tell about his or her practice and each story raises a professional responsibility issue broadly defined. While they dine, a waitress appears now and again to take and deliver their orders. She is the comic relief throughout the tape and then, at the end, she allows how she has overheard the entire conversation and characterizes each lawyer's behavior from her lay perspective. The text of "Dinner at Sharswood's Café is also in the Appendix. Also included in the Appendix are discussion about how to use the tapes in teaching and my general thoughts on the resolution of the issues the tapes raise. None of the vignettes on the tapes is included in the fifth edition with the exception of Karen Horowitz/J. Blair Thomas, which can be found in Chapter 5(A).

Three years ago we produced the final and most ambitious videotape, which lasts 40 minutes with about 10 places to stop for discussion. It can be used early in the term to generate interest in legal ethics issues without solving them, although you can refer back to particular quandaries as they emerge in the course of the semester. You can also use this tape at the end of the term to review doctrine. The tape is called "Amanda Kumar's Case."

More than 150 law schools have purchased one or more of the tapes, as have many law firms and a couple of state bar groups. If you want more information about the videotapes, please e-mail Shirley Gray at grays@juris.law.nyu.edu.

I try to teach the course through the vehicle of stories, whether they are the stories of the cases, stories I describe in class, stories from the press, stories in the various problems contained in the casebook, or stories on the videotapes. I go from the concrete to the general. Many of us have had the following experience: An issue we might discuss in class will generate no heat in class but intense debate before practicing lawyers. Lawyers understand immediately the consequences of a particular rule to their professional life, their income, their practice, their clients, in short to their work in all its manifestations. Law students do not because they have not yet been lawyers. One rule is as good as another rule. The differences are only theoretical. This is not true, of course, and the attitude, while entirely understandable, is something we have to disturb.

Stories are a way to disturb complacency. Wherever they come from, stories are concrete and if ably presented can encourage identification with their characters. I say "if ably presented" because, of course, it is not possible to assign *Anna Karenina* or even (all of) *Measure for Measure*. While I try to present stories that are not mere stick figure hypotheticals, there is only so much detail one can provide in the time allowed.

Beyond that, making the story real requires the energy of the instructor: to embellish, to cajole, to personalize. So I find myself sometimes running around the classroom talking too loud, waving my arms, coming up to students, expressing exaggerated shock, amazement, and confusion. I want them in the story.

A story is something that threatens no one. It didn't happen to anyone in class. Yet it is a common experience to which everyone in the class can respond. A story is about "real" events that happened to "real" people and took, or threatened to take, a "real" toll. A story is as close as it is possible for us to get to the environment of practice in our classes. But to make this story plausible and immediate to the class requires our active agency, our narrative skills, a confrontational but playful persona.

THE SIXTH EDITION

The sixth edition has essentially the same structure as the fifth and many of the same cases. But it also has some new principal cases and some new areas of coverage. Throughout, I have tried to make the book lively, with engaging writing and topical references. A casebook should not be the author's research files between covers. It should have a "voice" that is accessible and recognizable.

I have also tried to populate the book with summaries of the facts of many cases or news items. This is a pedagogical judgment. Not only do we teach the law governing lawyers, but we also teach the profession itself. I sometimes think of the profession as a tribe that we study, like anthropologists. To understand this particular and sometimes peculiar society, we have to understand its culture. The classroom environment places severe constraints on the extent to which we can do that, but we can do it a little bit in order to afford students some understanding of the dense professional context within which the issues and the rules arise. For this reason, too, I add cross-citations throughout the book. I don't mean to say that the material is a "seamless web," but I do believe that the various themes of the course echo across it. The cross-references are the traces of that echo.

Here are some of the attributes of the "new improved" sixth edition. I mention highlights only. There are literally hundreds of changes to clarify concepts, introduce new ones, update old ones, and signal open issues. Many of these are identified in the pages on individual chapters.

1.   Most of the problems have been revised and pre-tested. There are new problems, also pre-tested.

2.   Sections of the Restatement of Law Governing Lawyers as adopted have been cited and summarized where appropriate throughout the book.

3.   As of November 2001, the ABA has worked its way through Rule 1.10 of the Ethics 2000 Commission's proposed revisions to the Model Rules of Professional Conduct. Those changes that have been tentatively adopted at the August 2000 ABA convention are identified here. All other changes proposed by the Commission, but not yet addressed by the House of Delegates, are identified where pedagogically useful. The ABA will address the balance of the E2K proposals at its meetings in February and August 2002. At page 6 of the casebook, students are introduced to the work of the E2K Commission and directed to its web site.

4.   Chapter 2 (Defining the Client-Lawyer Relationship) retains the same principal cases as in the fifth edition, but there are other changes. Added to the material on government attorney-client privilege is the D.C. Circuit's opinion refusing to recognize one in the context of a criminal investigation. A brief new note identifies the policy reasons advanced in favor of confidentiality rules.

5.   Chapter 3 (Protecting the Client-Lawyer Relationship Against Outside Interference): I have added a new section on "testers," drawing on the *Gidatex* decision recognizing these testers as an exception to the no-contact rule. I have also cited to the Oregon Supreme Court's decision in *Gatti*, which disciplines a lawyer for violating that state's no-contact rule and, in dicta, says it will apply that rule, plus prohibitions against misrepresentations in the state statute, against testers and all prosecutors, state and federal. At publication time, efforts were underway to amend the Oregon rules to exclude application of the *Gatti* decision to prosecutors. The state bar had proposed one revision which the Supreme Court rejected. The state bar was in the process of proposing a different revision. Meanwhile, the legislature had repealed the language of the statute upon which the *Gatti* court separately relied. The new problem ("The Sting") means to dramatize the application of the no-contact rule in the case of criminal prosecution.

6.   Chapter 4 (Financing Legal Services (And Dividing the Money)): I have substituted *Matter of Fordham* for *Bushman* as a better case to illustrate the application of fee limitations in the ethics rules. I tried to compare the fees in *Fordham* with the fees in *Brobeck* measured in constant dollars. "What Are You Worth?" has been edited to make it a harder problem and to compare medicine. There is a new section on the impropriety

6

of inflating legal bills. That issue is also addressed briefly in Chapter 13D. An article by Deborah Rhode has been substituted for the David Luban excerpt on the question of whether pro bono should be mandatory. The material on nonrefundable fees has been augmented.

7.   Chapter 5 (Concurrent Conflicts of Interest): I have done some editing on the introductory material laying out the varieties of conflicts. The goal is to provide a general introduction, not a fully comprehensive treatment, as students approach what may be the most difficult material in the course. In the material on client-lawyer conflicts, I have included the problem "May the Lawyer Be Our Client?" to give students an opportunity to identify a lawyer-client conflict that is not so obvious as a business deal or other financial arrangement. Part 5B contains a new section on *Holloway* error, especially pertinent in light of the Supreme Court's impending decision in *Mickens*. The material in Chapter 5B3 on the common interest privilege has been strengthened and updated. This is a difficult subject, not least of all because the courts are not entirely clear, but an important one. I continue to address it in an extended note. I also continue to use *Simpson v. James* as a predicate for discussion of malpractice based on conflicts. I find this works very well. The note material following has been enhanced.

8.   Chapter 6 (Successive Conflicts of Interest): The principal cases here are the same and the notes have the same titles, but most of them have been updated and enhanced in various ways.

9.   Chapter 7 (Ethics in Advocacy): The introductory material on the adversary system is unchanged except that I dropped the material on Sofaer from Chapter 7B ("Are Lawyers Morally Accountable for their Clients?"). I have added, as a problem, an excerpt from <u>Anatomy of a Murder</u>, called "The Lecture." It is the scene in which the lawyer visits his client in jail and lays out the elements of possible defense to homicide before asking the client to tell him any facts. Also included in this section is Robert Bennett's letter to Judge Wright withdrawing an affidavit of Monica Lewinsky that he had submitted at President Clinton's deposition in *Jones v. Clinton*. This is a manifestation of the application of the remedial obligations contained in Rule 3.3. Chapter 7B has been partly revised. The section on literal truth draws heavily on the *Jones v. Clinton* litigation and the ensuing grand jury investigation. Two new problems – "The Eyewitness (I) and (II)" – mean to tease out the proper restrictions on jury summations. The new decision (*Mullaney v. Aude*) imposing monetary sanctions against the lawyer who used sexist language at a deposition appears in the section on hardball tactics (7G). I have chosen a new case to illustrate the obligation to reveal adverse legal authority (*Matter of Thonert*).

10.   Chapter 8 (Real Evidence): This chapter has been entirely revised and shortened to address what was the heart of the former Chapter 8, namely a lawyer's responsibility when coming into possession of real evidence, whether because the client gives it to the lawyer or otherwise. In addition to *People v. Meredith*, which I retain, I have added the

famous old case, *In re Ryder*, because on rereading it I find it so apt and not likely to be intuitively obvious to students. The material on spoliation of evidence has been enhanced.

11.   Chapter 9 (Lawyers for Entities): This chapter has retained the same principal cases and the same note material, but the notes have been updated and edited throughout.

12.   Chapter 10 (Negotiation and Transactional Matters): I have added the *Rubin* case because the lawyer's role in negotiating the underlying financial transaction is prominent and because the en banc court's decision (with a dissent) can be compared with the decision of other courts on similar facts. The note material following has all been enhanced and ABA Opinion 366 has been further edited.

13.   Chapter 11 (Judges): The material here is largely the same, though updated. A new problem identifies allegations of conflict in the Supreme Court in *Bush v. Gore* and asks students to address them.

14.   Chapter 12 (Control of Quality: Reducing the Likelihood of Professional Failure): The new problem, "The Racist Bar Applicant," draws on the headlined Illinois case. The material on transient lawyers has been significantly enhanced. The *Birbrower* case is of course included at some length. I have an extended note on decisions in other jurisdictions and a new problem on lawyer multijurisdictional practice – "Practicing Nationally From St. Louis." An interview with Professor Laurel Terry provides comparative insight on the European practice.

15.   Chapter 13 (Control of Quality: Remedies for Professional Failure): Because *Baker v. Dorfman*'s facts are so unusual, I have used them to include a note on fraud (resumé padding) as a basis for lawyer liability to clients. I have taken a new case to illustrate the risk of discipline when lawyers begin intimate relationships with their clients (*Matter of Tsoutsouris*). Otherwise, the principal cases remain the same but the note material has all been enhanced.

16.   Chapter 14 (Control of Quality: Lay Participation in the Law Business (And Law Firm Ancillary Services)): I have added material on multidisciplinary practice and also on cooperative business arrangements. The new problem asks students to identify the ways in which lawyers and other professionals might be able to work together consistent with the current limitations ("How Can We Get Together?").

17.   Chapter 15 (Free Speech Rights of Lawyers): This material is mostly the same with editing to bring the note material up to date.

18.   Chapter 16 (Marketing Legal Services): There have been no major developments in this area, and so the only change you will see in this chapter is editing to bring the note material up to date.

WHAT WILL YOU ASSIGN?

Your assignment will depend upon whether you are teaching a two-credit or a three-credit course. After many years of teaching a two-credit course, I switched to three-credits and am glad I did. Following are coverage suggestions. Much here is discretionary and can vary from semester to semester. A fair amount of material can be assigned for home reading without direct discussion in class. For example, at the start of Chapter 5 is an introduction to conflicts of interest. Essentially, it attempts to lay out the map for what follows in that chapter and the next one. It need not be discussed directly. At the start of Chapter 7 are selections from five authors who criticize, defend, or describe the adversary system and the role of lawyers in it. These selections can also be assigned as background reading for the material that follows. Similarly, a subject like the advocate-witness rule can be assigned without discussion. It is short and the points it makes can be referenced briefly in discussion of the other conflicts material or not at all.

I strongly urge you to assign the Preface to Students. It provides an abbreviated explanation of the reasons for the course. I tell students that this is the most important course they will take in law school -- the most important to them -- because it is about them. That is the point the Preface attempts to make. It is brief and demands no class discussion.

I hope you will also assign Chapter 1, which can be mostly for home reading, although I would introduce its themes in class. One theme is the several sources of ethics rules. The chapter lays out a brief road map for the varieties of materials the student will soon encounter. This will be the first sustained introduction most students will have to the provisions of the Model Code or Model Rules or to bar association ethics opinions. Many will have no idea about the ways in which their "self-regulated" profession is actually regulated, including the role of bar associations and the respective authorities of courts and legislatures.

A second theme of Chapter 1 is a critical but not unsympathetic introduction to the concept of professionalism as the purported antidote for the perceived commercialization of the law business. Is professionalism a real idea? Or is it a brilliant public relations gambit? Is it both of these? Is it about behaving decently or is it mostly about money? I don't think we can fully know what if any long-term role the idea of professionalism will play in the evolution of lawyers' work and its regulation. Certainly, professionalism is not about to disappear as an animating idea, although whether it takes on more definite qualities, whether it even should and how, is an open question. These points are touched on here and (like the rest of the chapter) percolate throughout much of the book, critically but not unsympathetically. They appear especially in the material on "hardball" litigation tactics, law firm marketing, lawyer-owned ancillary businesses, and lay participation in the law business. This and other material use the professionalism ideal to test the motives and justifications of lawyers in their resolution of particular issues.

Chapter 1 also introduces students to the Restatement and the Ethics 2000 Commission.

Things get more fluid now. No sequence is obligatory. One strong, but still not an essential, connection is between Chapter 2 (Defining the Client-Lawyer Relationship) -- and especially Chapter 2B (Elements of the Client-Lawyer Relationship) -- on one hand, and the material on conflicts of interest (Chapters 5 and 6), on the other. It's useful to have an introduction to, for example, confidentiality and loyalty, before one encounters conflicts. Chapter 2A is also worthwhile to assign up front. It is the first introduction to the sometime sticky question of whether a purported client is indeed a client, or is at least entitled to some of the benefits of "clienthood" and, if so, which ones. That theme reappears many times throughout the book.

Chapter 3 -- on protecting the professional relationship -- is intriguing but certainly in the discretionary category. Part A1 deals with the "no-contact" rule in civil cases, part A2 in criminal cases. You can cover neither, either or both. Overlapping but not congruent policies apply and in the criminal context we also have the separation of powers, federalism, and law enforcement interests that have caused so much stir in recent years. Part B is a brief introduction to ways in which the professional relationship is protected beyond the "no-contact" rule.

My sense is that debate over the cost of legal services will only escalate, leading me to encourage you to think of some selections from Chapter 4, perhaps parts A, B and C. Part A can invite discussion of the debate over the size of fees claimed by lawyers who have settled class action tobacco cases. In Part B, you'll find the Massachusetts high court's recent opinion in the *Fordham* case, disciplining a lawyer for too high a fee in a drunk driving case. The conclusion is certainly debatable. I compare the seemingly disparate results in *Brobeck* and *Fordham*. Part C has material on contingent fees and "loser pays" rules that should spark good class discussion. Other portions of Chapter 4 can be assigned from year to year. The material on mandatory pro bono, Chapter 4F, often makes for good classroom discussion.

I am partial to the entirety of both conflict chapters (5 and 6). Conflicts is the one kind of problem that virtually all students will face (their own conflicts or those of a colleague or opponent). Less important, from the point of view of the likelihood that students will encounter the issues, are materials on conflicts in criminal cases and the advocate-witness rule. But you might wish to teach these occasionally. Defense lawyer conflicts present especially intriguing problems, among them the risk that the government will use them to deny a defendant his or her choice of counsel. This subject is on the front burner with the *Mickens* case in the Supreme Court. Chapter 5B2 has a problem on prosecutorial conflicts (page 254), posing prosecutors who are conscientiously opposed to enforcing certain criminal laws (*e.g.*, the death penalty). As before, Chapter 5B3 has a malpractice case in which conflicts served as a basis for establishing liability. Students should understand that discipline is not the sole risk.

Chapter 6 addresses the important issues of successive conflicts (both in private practice and after and before government service. It is only 50 pages. I encourage you to assign all of it. The five problems in Chapter 6 work very well. Some of the note material can simply be assigned for home reading.

The materials on ethics in advocacy (Chapters 7 and 8) are a rich source for classroom discussion. As I wrote above, Chapter 7A can be assigned for reading. Depending upon coverage of Rule 11 in civil procedure, you may want to subordinate Chapter 7E. Let me suggest that you pay serious consideration to assigning Chapters 7C and most of D. Chapter 8, which deals with destruction or concealment of physical evidence, is inherently interesting but discretionary.

I believe that Chapter 9, whose subject is lawyers for entities, is important enough to assign routinely. It also raises the retaliatory discharge question. The debate on that is not yet over, although the issue is certainly discretionary. It can be done in an hour and a half or two hours and is well worth the effort. The lead case here, *Tekni-Plex, Inc. v. Meyner and Landis*, addresses conflict issues that arise in the context of a corporate acquisition. I continue to include the *Murphy & Demory* bench opinion because it's a bench opinion, has interesting and dramatic facts, involves a prominent firm and shows how corporate conflicts and disloyalty can lead to civil damages.

Chapter 10 on negotiation is, in my view, a preferred elective. It is not essential. On the other hand, many students will be spending a great deal of their professional time in negotiation. The *Rubin* case reveals the exposure of negotiating lawyers to civil liability for security and common law fraud. ABA Opinion 92-366 tries to explain, not always clearly, when a "noisy withdrawal" is allowed or required, within the broader context of a transactional lawyer's duty to avoid assisting client fraud. This will be the sole examination of the concept of the "noisy withdrawal."

The chapter on judges, Chapter 11, is certainly elective, but consider assigning it from time to time, especially in a 3-credit class. Some of the issues are engrossing. Judges are like lawyers but they're not lawyers. Because they wield public power, the rules governing their conduct are different. Appearance standards do apply forcefully here. In addition, the constant issue of judicial bias, often in the news, helps us tease out what we mean by impartiality and what the sanctions should be for inappropriate comments.

Students are naturally interested in Chapter 12A because they will soon have to apply to the bar for admission. I try to include part of it each semester, although I am not always successful. The introductory material now contains, courtesy of Judge Posner, a "law and economics" analysis of bar admission restrictions. That analysis plays into Part B, whose focus is transient lawyers. This material ties in nicely with Chapter 12F on unauthorized practice of law. We are talking about economics here, or should I say "money," and I think students should see both the supply and demand sides of the equation. The *Birbrower* case and UPL by lawyers (Chapter 12B) is now hot and fascinating. I commend it.

The material on malpractice and liability to third parties in Chapter 13A, B, and C is always hard to contain. So much is happening. I urge its coverage, especially Chapter 13A, which defines the bases for liability. Part B, less important, deals with proof of malpractice. The causation issue in criminal cases makes for good discussion but is certainly elective. The case here (*Peeler v. Hughes & Luce*) is a good one. Part C's focus is lawyer liability to third parties, an area of constant growth (alas). The lead case (*Petrillo*) is a bit dense, but a real testing case with a dissent and a discussion of the Restatement's position. I have tried to set it up in an introductory paragraph to make it clearer.

Chapter 13D's subject is discipline. You can assign the first three parts for home reading. They are short. Chapter 13D4 is well worth classroom attention. Its subject is the acts that can result in discipline. Whether you want to assign Chapter 13E, which covers constitutional protection in criminal cases, depends very much on your interest in the area and the likelihood that students will have covered the same issues elsewhere.

Chapter 14 is a favorite of mine. It talks about rules limiting the ability of lay persons to participate in the "law industry," either through entities that are not-for-profit or those that are profitmaking. This is truly about the supply side of the equation and I think will be a constant theme in the years to come as well as a significant influence on the structure of the bar. This will especially be so as American law firms continue to compete with foreign law firms that operate under different, more permissive rules on lay-lawyer arrangements. Take a look at the chapter. It is certainly not essential, but it is a different kind of chapter and well worth considering every so often. The MDP debate – and the new idea of cooperative business arrangements – will continue to keep these issues prominent.

The free speech rights of lawyers is the subject of Chapter 15. It is also a different kind of chapter and also well worth considering. Issues here can generate good debate. I wish the *Gentile v. State Bar* case could have been shorter. I did my best to edit it down, but in the end felt that there was only so much chopping one could do. One hopes that someday the Supreme Court will write a new opinion on the subject and that it will be more coherent. Nevertheless, the story the case tells is compelling and Justice Kennedy's language invites response.

My sense is that different instructors have different views about the importance of law firm marketing. I suppose I'm somewhere in the middle. I try to cover some of Chapter 16 each year. Chapter 16C, which tries to digest the Supreme Court's methodology here, can be assigned for home reading. The lessons it conveys inform the balance of the chapter. You can assign Chapter 16A, and B1, and B2 and feel you've done a good job. Time permitting, I would also try to read *In re Primus* in Chapter 16E. But if you assigned *Button* in Chapter 14A, you will already have covered some of the *Primus* themes.

You will recognize many of the problems in this sixth edition. They appeared in the fifth edition. Some are modestly changed. Some changes are insignificant. Some of the earlier problems have been deleted and some new ones appear.

The book contains many more problems than you should ever expect to cover. My own preference is to emphasize conversation over coverage. I'd rather have a deep discussion about one problem than more casual discussions about two or three. We all must decide which problems work best for us. As I move through the material, I will try to identify some of my favorites and how I use them.

Naturally, you expect a teacher's manual to tell you the author's "solution" to the questions and other problems contained in the casebook. And of course I will try to do that. But some of these questions and other problems are . . . well, real hard. They may not have a single right answer. I always forget when I set about writing the questions that I'll be expected to know the answers. But it comes with the territory, doesn't it? (That happens on exams, too. Just kidding.)

You may disagree with my answers, marginally or absolutely. You may want to begin a class discussion by saying something like this: "Now the author of this casebook, believe it or not, thinks that lawyer Jones actually has an obligation to go to the prosecutor and spill the beans. Can you imagine that? Why is he wrong?" If you want to begin your class that way, that's quite all right with me. It also comes with the territory. Anyway, what I don't know can't hurt me, right?

I have tried to prepare a detailed index that will enable a user of the book to find all materials on a theme relatively quickly. This can be helpful not only in connection with classwork, but also for those who wish to use the book as a preliminary research tool. The book's frequent references to further reading also has research value.

It has been nearly 20 years since I started work on the first edition of this book, around the time my older daughter was born. The manuscript was delivered in 1984, just a few days before my younger daughter was born. Between editions, I collect cases and other materials on a weekly basis for editions to come. I opened my file on the book's seventh edition the day I delivered the manuscript for the sixth. Inevitably, then, in spending so much time on a single subject, one begins to see it as a unit, with multiple overlapping themes, with interconnectedness. I guess I could write a book called "Zen and the Art of Ethics Casebook Maintenance."

Our analytic tradition and the nature of the casebook genre require that the work be divided into parts, subparts, and even lesser units. And yet, the deeper patterns continue to emerge, even insist on due recognition. They're irrepressible. Ultimately, of course, those deeper patterns are the stuff of academic books and law journal articles. Still, I have tried to preserve them in the casebook through frequent cross-references. Echoes have educational and literary value. Echoes also lead us into the future, as we follow the sound. A cross-reference is a kind of echo. The ones here will, I hope, help students to detect, and you to convey, the broad themes of the course even as you and they parse its details.

Stephen Gillers
November 2001

CHAPTER I

Where Do "Ethics" Rules Come From?

This is an important chapter though it need not be discussed at any length in class. It is important because it tells students, who are accustomed to researching cases, statutes, and perhaps administrative agency regulations, that the subject they are studying depends on other sources of rules as well. So this chapter introduces students to the judicial authority in the adoption of legal ethics rules (**page 1**); the extent to which the legislature has authority (**page 2**); the Code and the Model Rules (**page 3**); the work of the Ethics 2000 Commission (**page 6**); the status of ethics rules as legal authority (**page 7**); the problems when rules conflict in multijurisdictional representations (**page 7**); the Restatement and other authorities (**page 9**); and influence from secondary sources (**page 10**). Students are also introduced to "professionalism" (**page 11**) and are offered sources for further reading (**page 15**).

Authorities and themes in this brief chapter will reemerge in the pages that follow so early introduction has an advantage. I often spend the first hour talking about the "structure" of legal ethics rules and their enforcement. One of my early points is that the term "legal ethics," while fine as a shorthand, really does not fully capture the myriad of rules governing the behavior of lawyers and judges or convey the risks if they are violated. It's the word "ethics" that can suggest the subject isn't about "real law," but of course it is.

PART I

THE CLIENT-LAWYER RELATIONSHIP

CHAPTER II

DEFINING THE CLIENT-LAWYER RELATIONSHIP

Much of this chapter is prologue to other sections of the book. The chapter is also the first of three to examine details the client-lawyer relationship. Chapter 3 addresses how law protects that relationship from interference by outside forces. The subject of Chapter 4 is financing legal services, including traditional fee arrangements, fee-shifting statutes, and mandatory pro bono.

This chapter begins with an issue that repeats throughout the book. So much of what we teach in our courses concerns a lawyer's responsibility to his or her clients. Whether a professional relationship exists, for what purpose, its scope, and its duration are all critical issues. These issues arise when discussing confidentiality and loyalty, conflicts of interest, entity representation, and malpractice, among other subjects. I have therefore chosen to raise the question early and return to it often. Students will be surprised that they can have professional duties to persons they have never met and of whose particular existence they may even be ignorant.

Chapter 2, in section 2A, begins with Lord Brougham's observation about the nature of an advocate's duty to a client **(page 21)** and then immediately follows **(page 23)** with Judge Sprecher's tantalizing assertion in *Westinghouse Electric* that the "client is no longer simply the person who walks into a law office." The balance of the introductory material focuses on the ways in which professional relationships can be established, the absence of a need for payment of a fee, the importance of the putative client's reasonable expectations, the fact that even if a professional relationship exists it will usually have a limited scope, an introduction to the possibilities of multiple representations and joint-defense agreements, and brief discussion of client identity in a class action.

This introductory material can be assigned for home reading. In my view, it should be. It makes important points, it's brief, and it's clear. Since the theme recurs, it's worth introducing early.

B. ELEMENTS OF THE CLIENT-LAWYER RELATIONSHIP (page 27)

The centerpiece of this chapter are the several elements of the professional relationship: competence, confidentiality, agency, fiduciary status, the duties of loyalty and diligence, and the duty to inform. To one degree or another, one or more of these elements will reappear in the material on advocacy, conflicts of interest, malpractice, entity representation, and negotiation.

1. **Competence (page 27).** These few paragraphs, and the quote from Elihu Root, mean to impress on the student that competence is, perhaps, the most important quality a lawyer can bring to the professional relationship. Okay, we can debate which is most important, but surely it is among the top two or three. The issue of competence resurfaces in the material on malpractice, discipline, and effective assistance. (Chapter 13A, D, and E respectively.)

2. **Confidentiality (page 28).** The material here will introduce the student to the basic rules, including the differences between the evidentiary privilege and the ethical proscription. The Fifth Circuit's decision in *Brennan's, Inc.* (**page 249**) draws this distinction nicely. The distinction resurfaces in the material on successive conflicts of interest (Chapter 6). **Page 30** highlights distinctions between the Code, Rules and Restatement in the definition of protected information. I've added a brief note on the two primary reasons for confidentiality rules (**page 31**): empirically, to encourage clients to speak candidly so lawyers can effectively represent them; and normatively, to respect the autonomy of the client by giving him or her a private space within which to seek legal counsel.

Legislative history from drafts of the Model Rules (**page 32**) reveals something of the debate over scope of the confidentiality duty and the nature of the final compromise. It is worth looking at how states chose to diverge from the ABA's vision of the proper scope of confidentiality. Several more prominent variations are listed at **page 33**. If you are using, as your rules supplement, *Regulation of Lawyers: Statutes and Standards* (S. Gillers & R. Simon, eds.), the material following Rule 1.6 contains additional state variations. A note at **pages 33-34** itemizes the Restatement's confidentiality exceptions.

As they head into the next principal case, students should understand the difference between the information protected by the privilege and the information protected by professional conduct rules – what is the scope of each category, and what is the consequence of being in each category. Students should also appreciate some of the salient variations among jurisdictions and different arguments even though there may be no reason to memorize these.

Perez v. Kirk & Carrigan (**page 34**): This is an unusual case but one that properly upholds a claim of breach of fiduciary duty for alleged revelation of confidential information. The lawyers gave the client's statement to the prosecutor, an act that was detrimental to the client but potentially helpful to Coca-Cola. Things to note are that the court credits Perez's view that Kirk & Carrigan were his lawyers. The court also rejects the argument that the claim should fail because the presence of a third person negates the privilege. This isn't a case about privilege but fiduciary duty (which includes confidentiality) and the firm had an obligation not to reveal the information, privileged or not. Finally, the court recognizes damages for mental anguish as legitimate. Students should understand this as a conflict situation. What should the firm have done after Perez made his statement? Probably, the firm should have dropped out of the matter. Could it also have told its other client, Coca-Cola? There's some debate about this. It pits the duty of loyalty against the duty of confidentiality in a multiple client situation. I don't think the firm could have told Coca-Cola. There was no warning to Perez and no indication that Perez was sufficiently sophisticated in dealing with lawyers to understand that, as a joint client, even if that's what he was, his statements to counsel could be shared with his employer, let alone the prosecutor. From a preventive perspective, the firm representing Coca-Cola should probably not have been talking to Perez at all and certainly not without a warning. See Rule 4.3.

I checked to see what happened to Perez in his criminal case. See **page 37**. I also tried to find out what happened in his civil case but could not.

Students are reminded **(page 37)** that the confidentiality duty applies as well to information gained from potential clients.

Cases in which lawyers have been disciplined for revealing client secrets to the client's detriment, however benign the lawyer's motive, include (in addition to *Thiery* at **page 37**) *In re Pool*, 517 N.E.2d 444 (Mass. 1988) (reinstatement after suspension); *In re Rhame*, 416 N.E.2d 823 (Ind. 1981); and *Pressly* and *Holley* **(page 29)**. In *O'Hagan* **(page 29)**, use of confidential information led to criminal conviction.

"My Client Is HIV Positive" (page 38)

The prior reading establishes that this information is ethically protected and privileged. If no exception applies, it cannot be revealed, except to advance the client's interests or with his permission. It cannot detract from the lawyer's duty to make the best case possible for pretrial release. This means the lawyer cannot tell the court about her client's condition, nor can she tell the woman with whom her client lives. Is there anything she can or should do? Should she encourage her client to seek treatment or tell his lover? Confidentiality rules don't prohibit those efforts, but is that really the lawyer's job? Her job is to help her client avoid conviction and otherwise protect his freedom in the criminal matter. Her job is not to make him a more responsible person. Still, is she simply supposed to ignore the information she has and say nothing? For all she knows, her client is unaware of available treatments or the practices that increase the risk of transmission of HIV. Can she talk to him about these things? Should she? Can or should she encourage him to go to a treatment center? Certainly, the answers are yes.

The last paragraph assumes that no exception to confidentiality applies, but does one? It would be difficult to invoke Rule 1.6(b)(1). There is probably no future crime or "imminent" injury. For the first of these reasons, the Code provision also does not apply. Some jurisdictions may have rules that permit revelation -- *e.g.*, Florida **(page 33)**. The Restatement may as well **(page 33)**. So, too, the E2K version of Rule 1.6 **(page 68)**. Do students think the lawyer should be allowed to warn? After all, all that will happen to the client is that he may lose his lover, but what may happen to the lover and her child?

This problem also permits a preliminary exploration of the "who is a client" problem. The lawyer was contacted by Anna, her former client, who is paying the fee. Is she a client here? No, under Rule 1.8(f). What if she were still representing Anna in the probate matter? It would make no difference. She's not a client on the criminal matter. However, wouldn't the lawyer be wise to explain that to her?

There is a lurking issue here that it is probably premature to identify but a student might. If the lawyer is currently representing Anna on her probate problem, and conceivably even if the probate matter is over, the lawyer's knowledge of Ken's HIV status and the possible effect it might have on Anna's health could be seen as pertinent to her work for Anna. In other words, information a lawyer could not reveal to Anna may be information she would be expected to give her to do a competent job. This dilemma is addressed directly in "In a Box," at **page 84**.

"I Know There's a Gun" (page 38)

Someone actually asked me a variation of this question. I'm still not sure what the answer is. The lawyer is in an excruciating position, isn't she? The odds are pretty good that a future arrested person -- tomorrow, next month, next year -- will find the gun behind the seat. If one does, the consequences could be terrible. Yet revelation of its existence would implicate the client in an armed robbery. Espinoza's knowledge of the gun's location is privileged and ethically protected. She can't tell unless an exception applies. Conceivably, depending upon the state, the penal law might make the client's continued silence a future crime under the circumstances. I say conceivably. If so, then it is possible that that crime would fall within the particular jurisdiction's future crimes exception to the duty of confidentiality, even if we assume that the information is privileged. (See the *Purcell* case at **page 64**.) Assume the conceivable is true and the lawyer is empowered, but not required, to reveal the "future crime." Should she? If she does, the client may be indicted for the armed robbery. She may even be required to testify to her conversation with the client. A court may conclude that his confession to her about the existence of the gun was not privileged. That eventuality won't be very good for her practice, will it? (But again see *Purcell*, which suggests that the lawyer may be able to reveal information without a client thereby losing the privilege if there was one.)

If the goal is really to encourage clients to tell lawyers all, then Espinoza should say nothing even if she can say something. But while she's doing the research, she might also ascertain whether her own silence would be a crime under state law. Unlikely.

If Espinoza concludes that she cannot tell, what should she do? Students might assume the answer is nothing. She has no choice. But she does have choices. She can ask the client to let her try to strike a deal with the prosecutor whereby she provides information about the gun in exchange for a promise of no prosecution or in exchange for not using the evidence. She can tell the client that if she does not do this and that the gun is later used to kill or injure police officers, the client will be in an even worse position. She could encourage the client not to take that chance.

If the client's silence is a future crime, some states may mandate revelation. The Restatement **(page 33)** would permit revelation even if it is not a crime. So would E2K **(page 68)**. What do students think is the right rule? If revelation should be permitted or required here, does it follow that the prior problem should be answered the same way (where the loss to the client from revelation is less)?

Entity Clients (page 39)

This is the students' introduction to the relationship between lawyers and fictional creations of the state. Issues raised here will reappear in the material on the no-contact rule (Chapter 3), and in the chapter (9) on entity representation, as well as elsewhere. One question that will arise in these materials is whether the holding in *Upjohn Co. v. United States* casts the net of corporate secrecy too broadly. This issue surfaces in "Slip and Fall" **(page 53)** and reappears in *Niesig v. Team I* **(page 111)**, whose subject is contact with an adverse company's agents and former agents. See also "Slip and Fall Redux" **(page 122)**.

I excerpt *Upjohn Co. v. United States* **(page 40)**, remind students that states can have a different rule **(page 43)**, then set out *Samaritan Foundation v. Goodfarb* **(page 43)** as one example of a thoughtful decision that takes a different view of things. As did the Illinois high court in a decision *Goodfarb* cites, Arizona's Supreme Court rejects a broad "subject matter" test, the test the Supreme Court apparently adopted in *Upjohn*. But *Goodfarb* also rejects the "control group" test embraced by Illinois. *Goodfarb* adopts a "functional" analysis, which would make the privilege dependent upon the function of the employee who is reporting to counsel. An employee who merely witnesses an event and tells counsel will not have made a privileged communication unless the employee has approached counsel to get legal advice. If it is the corporation that initiates the communication, the communication must concern "the employee's own conduct within the scope of his or her employment and [be] made to assist the lawyer in assessing or responding to the legal consequences of that conduct for the corporate client." The

Arizona Court believes that *Upjohn* can even be read this narrowly (it can) while recognizing that a broader reading is also possible. On the facts before it, the court concludes that the operating room employees were interviewed in their role as witnesses and not to give them legal advice.

Notice that the hospital attempted to define the employees as clients in their own right, not merely agents of the corporate client, in order to privilege anything the employees might have told counsel. The court rejects this argument and sees it as an acknowledgment that the communication would not be privileged if the employees' only status was as agents of the corporate client. This argument is important because it highlights a theme here, and in Chapter 3A, of overbroad corporate secrecy. If *Upjohn* is read broadly and, as some have argued, if in addition all corporate employees are agents of the client for purposes of the no-contact rule discussed in Chapter 3A, then the ability of the opponents of corporate entities to get information will be seriously eroded.

As you will see on **page 49**, the Arizona legislature, perhaps impelled by lawyers in the state, "overruled" *Goodfarb* and substituted a broad subject-matter test. This shows students where real power lies. I chose nonetheless to retain *Goodfarb* in this edition because the facts are helpful in understanding the competing interests and because the analysis is careful.

The Restatement's position appears at **page 50** and is seemingly as broad as the most devoted adorer of the privilege could realistically hope for. But see **page 116** for the Restatement's restrictive view of the scope of the no-contact rule.

What's the Right Policy? (page 50)

These seven questions mean to give the students a platform from which to discuss the competing policy considerations. Let me highlight a few of them.

Question 3 makes the point that *Upjohn* encourages companies to hire lawyers to conduct internal investigations. So long as the work can be connected to a legal service, rather easy after cases like *Allen* and *Rowe* **(page 51)**, whatever the lawyers find will be protected. A few courts, as in *Payton* **(page 51)**, seem to balk at that use of lawyers. Nice work for lawyers, though.

Using Question 4, you can telegraph the no-contact issue here. Justice Rehnquist assumed that government investigators could speak to the same employees as did Upjohn's counsel. **(Page 42)**. But more than a fair argument could be made against that conclusion under the no-contact rules cited in the text. Perhaps the situation is different because the government has special privileges. See **page 122**. Could the government send investigators to speak with the Upjohn employees or would it have to subpoena them before a grand jury? If the former, would Upjohn's lawyers have a right to be present? That would rather frustrate the government's purpose, wouldn't it? This is a good problem to flag now because it arises again in Chapter 3, because it is timely, and because it contains important lessons about federalism and governance of the profession (state rule, federal case).

Question 5 wonders about the empirical accuracy of the majority's assertion that the privilege was necessary here to encourage communication. If that's true, it's because the court expects that employees will not be as forthcoming with counsel if they know their comments must (or, if work product, might) be provided to the government at its request. But if that assumption is correct, if employees would be shy under those circumstances, then what reason is there to believe that they will be forthcoming with IRS agents who ask them the same questions Upjohn's counsel did? Justice Rehnquist really doesn't believe that federal agents will be able to have the same conversation with Upjohn employees as Upjohn's lawyers had, does he? The opportunities to get equivalent information are even further diluted if we assume, as will often be true, that the employees will be represented by counsel at their interviews. That counsel will likely be provided by Upjohn, paid for by Upjohn, and may, subject to the conflict rules, simultaneously be representing Upjohn. So is this the real world the Court is talking about, or what?

Paragraph 6 (**page 52**) makes the point that the privilege is absolute. Despite the occasional suggestion that on appropriate facts courts are free to disregard the attorney-client privilege (see **page 65**), they rarely (if ever) do. So the price of an expansive privilege in the entity context is complete denial of the communication. And if the information is not available elsewhere, the opposing party simply will not get it. One alternative, suggested by the intermediate appellate court in *Goodfarb*, is to recognize a privilege for communications to or from corporate employees but to make it a qualified attorney-client privilege, just as the work product privilege is qualified. The Supreme Court of Arizona chose not to take this route.

The last question (**page 52**) asks whether, as a policy matter, it is wise to give corporations attorney-client privileges in the first instance. Gradations are possible. Small family-owned entities can be treated differently from General Motors. But the larger question is this: As a matter of social policy, should the loss of information about the conduct and operation of powerful institutions within our society outweigh what we <u>assume</u> will be the improved legal advice that those institutions will receive if they enjoy the privilege? Is this assumption even correct?

"Slip and Fall" (page 53)

This question, which reappears in connection with the no-contact issue at page 122, asks students to identify whether each of certain conversations are privileged under the various entity privilege rules they've studied. (We're ignoring workproduct protection and also whether the conversation might be privileged on the theory that the company lawyer also formed a professional relationship with the interviewee.)

The first thing to recognize is that since Todd is operating as an agent of lawyer Parr, his conversations with others are privileged if hers would be. So that's the question: Would hers be? It seems to me that all tests would privilege Todd's talk with Burkow; the Restatement, *Goodfarb* and *Upjohn* would privilege Todd's talk with Morse, whose conduct may have caused the accident. But the control group test would not protect that conversation under the entity's privilege. The Restatement would protect the conversation with Sandstrom, as would *Upjohn*, if read broadly (see **page 47**), but the other tests would not. Probably only the Restatement would protect the conversation with McCormick (see **page 50**), at least if the text means what it says, which is an odd result. No test would protect the conversation with Kuhl. The most debatable questions are whether there should be protection for the conversations with Sandstrom and McCormick. *Goodfarb*, making a distinction between employee-witnesses and employees whose conduct creates liability or who initiate the conversation, would protect neither.

Is There a Government Attorney-Client Privilege? (page 53)

This question is asked in light of the Eighth Circuit's 2-1 decision (**page 53**) refusing to find one when (what would otherwise be) privileged information is subpoenaed by a federal a grand jury (in this case Whitewater Independent Counsel Kenneth Starr subpoenaed notes White House counsel took at meetings with First Lady Hillary Rodham Clinton), and the D.C. Circuit's (2-1) later agreement (**page 55**). I suggest at the end of the note that the rulings, a loss for President Clinton, actually strengthen the presidency in its powers over other branches of the federal government and over state governments. (Wouldn't it follow that if federal subpoenas can reach federal officials' communications with government counsel, they can reach those communications by state officials and their counsel?) Except for the occasional (and now ended) Independent Counsel, it is the Attorney General and the Justice Department, both of which are within the Executive Branch and are controlled by the President, that issue federal grand jury subpoenas. The D.C. Circuit opinion is even stronger because the communications were between the president and his own counsel. Judge Tatel, who seems to me to have a point, worries that the effect of the opinion will be to cause future presidents to seek legal advice on highly sensitive matters from private counsel (**page 55**).

Exceptions to the Privilege or the Ethical Duty (page 56)

The note material at **pages 56-68** is important. It corrects the popular misconception among practicing lawyers that confidentiality rules are virtually absolute. The note lists several of the important exceptions to both the privilege and the ethical duty. (We earlier covered the exceptions for future crimes or other harm.) You might simply assign these pages for reading without class discussion, but I suggest you consider highlighting these prominent or interesting aspects of the exceptions:

(1) The Rules expand the Code's self-defense exception while narrowing the circumstances under which a lawyer may reveal client confidences to protect others. Is this defensible, or is it simply a case of "lawyers first, lawyers first?" The Rules, like the case law, allow a lawyer to reveal client confidences to head off an accusation. Lawyers must have good reason to believe that revelation is necessary and may reveal only to the extent reasonably required. Self-defense exceptions exist for both the ethical duty and the privilege **(page 58)**. This exception comes up again in Chapter 9 **(page 571)** in the discussion of whether employed lawyers should have retaliatory discharge claims. Assuming the jurisdiction otherwise recognizes such claims, shouldn't the employed lawyer be able to use Rule 1.6(b)(2) to enable him or her to reveal confidential information to the extent necessary to establish the claim? That is, if a lawyer can do as much when suing for a fee, why not for other claims?

(2) The exception **(page 58)** to enable the lawyer to collect fees (no matter how small) is even more vulnerable to the "lawyers first" criticism, especially given the ABA's refusal to permit a lawyer to reveal client confidences in the face of a client's concluded or prospective fraud (including criminal fraud) on another, no matter how large.

(3) A client can constructively waive the privilege or confidentiality by making confidential communications relevant to a proceeding **(pages 58-59)**. Partial revelation, even to a government agency, will achieve the same result. **(Page 59.)** You might want to contrast these rules with the Second Circuit's protective response in *In re Von Bulow*. Because the revelations there were not in the litigation context, the waiver was limited to the information actually revealed. The U.S. Sentencing Guidelines for Organizations give credit for entity targets that cooperate with law enforcement. Will cooperation in order to win points under the Guidelines also waive the privilege for the information provided and any other information on the same subject? The cases at **pages 59-60** would suggest that an entity will have to expect waiver. The MIT case at **page 59** is particularly instructive. The school argued that it had no choice but to share the allegedly privileged information with DOD. Consequently, it said, waiver should not be inferred. But the court said that the school did have a choice when it decided to contract with DOD knowing the disclosure requirements. Inadvertent waiver is discussed at **page 61.**

(4) The crime-fraud exception to the privilege (**page 61**) is broader than the exception to the confidentiality obligation in those jurisdictions that have adopted the Model Code or Model Rules. The Code and Rules are, respectively, limited to all crimes or (in effect) violent crimes. Neither would apply to non-criminal frauds. Students should understand why a lawyer's knowledge of a prospective crime or fraud is not protected. The policies supporting privilege simply do not apply when the client is not seeking representation about a concluded act or advice about how to achieve a future one legally. We do not recognize the legitimacy of legal advice about future crimes or frauds. What is a fraud? Cases on **pages 61-62** show a variety of answers. *Milroy* would require intentional misrepresentation, but other cases, including *American Tobacco* and *Philip Morris*, are less demanding. The interesting problem here is the procedural one. How do we unravel the issue when an allegation of future crime or fraud is made to defeat the privilege? The problem is most intriguing when the crime-fraud cited as a reason to defeat the privilege is the same crime-fraud alleged in the complaint or indictment. The material at **pages 62-63** sets out one complex procedure utilizing shifting burdens and sources of proof.

(5) The *Purcell* case **(pages 63-64)** makes a nice point. Legal Aid lawyer Purcell revealed what he thought was his client's intent to commit a violent crime (arson) but then refused to provide the same information when subpoenaed, citing privilege. The court agreed. By invoking the exception to the confidentiality obligation, Purcell did not thereby waive the privilege. The court feared that a contrary result would discourage lawyers from using permissible authority to protect persons against future harm.

(6) The battle over protection for identity and fees **(page 64)** has generally favored those who oppose protection. On the need for some exception to the non-protection of client identity, consider the following: The District Attorney announces an investigation of the state legislature after police discover a slush fund. A month later, the District Attorney subpoenas the dozen most prominent criminal defense lawyers in the state before the grand jury and asks for the names of all state legislators who have consulted each defense attorney on any matter in the last month.

(7) Every so often a court will intimate that there may be a public policy exception to the privilege **(pages 65-67)**. The best known effort to defeat privilege on public policy grounds was, at least in recent years, Kenneth Starr's subpoena to Vincent Foster's former counsel. Starr argued that he needed the communication for his law enforcement purpose and that, Foster being dead, there was no other way to get it **(page 66)**. A 6-3 Supreme Court majority rejected the argument. The D.C. Circuit had accepted it in a 2-1 decision. This was also the circuit that declined to recognize a government attorney-client privilege for conversations between Clinton and Deputy White House Counsel. If, as Justice Rehnquist said in *Upjohn*, it is important for clients to know that communications are confidential (and that the "control-group test" threatens that knowledge), then how can there be a public policy exception to the privilege?

Finally, the note reminds students that in order for there to be an exception to a confidentiality rule or privilege, the rule must apply and it won't if there is no professional relationship **(page 67)**. The fact that a lawyer is part of a relationship does not make it a professional one, in the sense we are discussing.

Ethics 2000 **(page 68)**: The ABA has tentatively approved the E2K proposal to expand the exception to confidentiality for certain future acts. If death or substantial physical harm are reasonably certain, a lawyer may reveal client confidences even if the harm will not be committed by the client, even if it is not criminal, and even if it is not imminent. Note that under the current exception all three criteria are required. A new exception would allow a lawyer to reveal client confidences so the lawyer could himself or herself "secure legal advice about the lawyer's compliance with these Rules." E2K proposals to expand a lawyer's freedom to reveal client confidences when the client's misconduct is a future fraud, or a completed fraud that has yet to have harmful consequences, were rejected at the ABA Annual Meeting in August 2000. "Noisy withdrawals" are still possible, however.

3. Agency (page 69). Having taught Agency twice, I've expanded this section a bit over the years, including a note on the lawyer's confidentiality duty as an agent **(page 75)**. Students should appreciate the agency predicate of the attorney-client relationship. Fiduciary and similar obligations developed in the agency context are pertinent to the professional one between lawyer and client. So are rules imputing statements and liability for action or inaction. Many rules we study are specific applications of agency law to the client-lawyer relationship.

In *Taylor v. Illinois* **(page 69)**, a lawyer failed to observe a state procedural rule requiring notice of a criminal defendant's witnesses. As a result, the client was not allowed to call a witness. The Court upheld the constitutionality of the exclusion notwithstanding that the client may not have participated in or been aware of the lawyer's misconduct. The dissent argues that even though a client may be bound by a lawyer's tactical errors, he should not be bound by the lawyer's intentional misconduct because misconduct is never a legitimate option for a lawyer. Misconduct can be deterred by punishing the lawyer directly. A parallel issue arises in the context of federal habeas review of state convictions. See **page 74**. See also page 897. Should Taylor be able to sue for malpractice? Most cases would require him to prove actual innocence or to have his conviction overturned in order to succeed **(page 800)**.

Visiting the procedural and discovery defaults of lawyers on clients is a rule whose application was learned nationwide in the O.J. Simpson trial. Recall that Judge Ito sanctioned the defense for discovery lapses. One of his opinions imposing a sanction cited *Taylor v. Illinois*.

Cotto v. United States **(page 71)** shows just how consequential a lawyer's default can be in a civil case. The young plaintiff's claim was tossed out because the lawyer had failed to prosecute. The court goes out of its way to raise the possibility of a claim against the lawyer.

The note material at **pages 72-75** does several things. It shows that a lawyer's statement can be the vicarious admission of a client both in negotiation and litigation. The *McKeon* case (**page 73**) is factually interesting because the statement there occurred in court. The note also distinguishes between vicarious admissions and judicial admissions -- statements a lawyer makes in court that will relieve an opponent from having to prove the truth of the statement -- which are, in effect, binding. The question of a lawyer's authority often arises where the lawyer purports to settle a matter and the client then disavows the settlement as in excess of authority. The cases at **pages 72-73** discuss actual, implied, inherent and ap-parent authority to settle.

4. Fiduciary (page 75). The lawyer's fiduciary status, violation of which can serve as a basis for liability, is described in *Milbank* (see also the note at page 778), *Cooperman*, and *Pagano*. *Pagano* arose in the context of a fee agreement. The court distinguishes between agreements reached during the professional relationship and those reached before or after it. At the end of the material, I emphasize that using a client's confidential information to the client's disadvantage will also violate fiduciary duty **(page 77)**.

The three cases noted at **pages 76-77** illustrate the operation of the lawyer's fiduciary duty in diverse circumstances. In *Benson*, an insolvent lawyer borrowed money from his client. In *Smith*, a lawyer was disciplined when he sought to exploit a <u>former</u> client's trust by eliciting incriminating information for the police in an effort to reduce his own legal exposure. And in *Lerner*, a lawyer who was a member of a co-op board and its legal committee violated his fiduciary duty by splitting a legal fee with a law firm to which he had referred the co-op. The fiduciary status is also pertinent to analysis of post-retainer fee agreements (page 164). See also *Severson, Werson, Berke & Melchior v. Bolinger*, 1 Cal. Rptr. 531 (Ct. App. 1991): A law firm, having quoted certain rates, cannot increase those rates during the representation without telling the client. The written agreement with the client is strictly construed against the firm. The court stresses that lawyers have always had "a professional responsibility to make sure client's understand their billing procedures and rates."

5. Loyalty and Diligence (page 78). Loyalty will of course undergird the conflict rules discussed in Chapters 5 and 6. Diligence means the lawyer does the promised work with dispatch. Lack of diligence is one of the most prominent reasons for client complaints. If the lawyer is slow, but the lawyer's slowness does not prejudice the client as a matter of law, should the lawyer be subject to discipline? Surely, the answer must be yes, although what usually happens is that the client complains, the lawyer hops to it, and the disciplinary authority loses interest. Should a lawyer who is not diligent be liable in malpractice for the client's anguish even though the client's legal rights are not compromised? I know of no case that so holds, but why not? What better way to ensure diligence? The pain can sometimes be quite real. Think about a person eager to see the end of her divorce action. Or a client who has incurred financial obligations to relatives following an accident and wants to repay the loans as soon as possible.

Or the terminally ill client who fears that he will die before his will is executed. Perhaps the reluctance to permit malpractice actions for lack of diligence causing only emotional distress reflects a fear of litigiousness, the difficulty of proof, and hesitation in permitting lay juries to decide how quickly lawyers should do particular work. Further discussion of emotional distress as a kind of damage recoverable in malpractice appears at page 810. But none of the cases discussed there awards damages for emotional distress attendant on a lack of diligence standing alone. Something else has happened to the client to cause pain. See also *In re Shaughnessy* on **page 83**.

6. The Duty to Inform and Advise (page 79). This is the final strand that, together with prior material, is sometimes said to comprise a right of informed consent, whatever that means exactly. One might say that a lawyer has a duty to inform a client whenever the client has final authority to make a decision and the information bears on the decision. See Rule 1.2(a) and comment; Rule 1.4(b). Two problems with this view are that the matters within the client's domain seem to be rather narrow and the comment to Rule 1.2 (as well as case law) is vague about the boundaries. Earlier drafts of the rule were more generous toward the client. Rule 1.3 of the 1980 draft, for example, said that a lawyer "shall accept a client's decisions concerning the objectives of the representation and the means by which they are to be pursued. . . ." (Emphasis added.)

Even where an ultimate decision clearly rests in the lawyer's province, the client ought to have the right to be consulted -- after all, it's her "case." Accordingly, Rule 1.4(a) requires that a lawyer "keep a client reasonably informed about the status of a matter and promptly comply with reasonable requests for information." (What would be an unreasonable request for information?) Compare this requirement of "reasonableness" with the broader duty contemplated by Rule 1.5 of the 1980 draft (and rejected). That provision required a lawyer "periodically" to advise "the client of the progress and status of [a] matter"; to "explain the significant legal and practical aspects of the matter and foreseeable effects of alternative courses of action; and . . . promptly [to] comply with reasonable requests for information about the matter." Was resort to the language of "reasonableness" an improvement?

The Restatement is more client-oriented. See §20. It would also allow the client to negotiate for greater authority than the ethics codes afford. In theory, that can be true even under the Rules or Code but neither is as explicit as the Restatement in this regard. See generally Restatements §§ 20-23. The Rules' Terminology, with its definition of "consult," a word whose root appears in several key Rules, is also pertinent. **(page 84)**.

The recommendations of the E2K Commission set out at **page 84**, would substantially expand the duty to inform. These were tentatively approved at the ABA meeting in August 2000.

Nichols v. Keller **(page 79)** is a case in which a lawyer was denied summary judgment after a former client, who had hired the lawyer for a worker's compensation claim sued because

31

the lawyer had not informed the client that he might have a civil claim as well. This case can be used to explain how clients might look at problems factually while lawyers might look at them in terms of the kinds of legal services they may require. The duty to inform requires the lawyer to explain the information in words the client can understand. Failure to delineate the scope of the matter (or as we see in Chapter 2D, its end) can create liability. Here, the client reasonably believed that the lawyer he consulted would advise him on all available remedies. The lawyer apparently saw himself as a worker's compensation specialist. As between the two, the duty to clarify should fall on the lawyer.

The article by Robert Caine (**page 81**) should effectively bring home the importance of communication. Caine is himself a lawyer who wrote this article in the form of a letter to the *New York Law Journal*. There is nothing to make a lawyer as aware of the dilemmas of the client than to be one. Given the frequency with which nonlawyer clients complain about non-communication, Caine's letter is invaluable.

The material on **page 82** identifies the duty to convey settlement offers. Compare California Rule 3-510, which says that a member (*i.e.*, of the State Bar) "shall promptly communicate to the member's client . . . all terms and conditions of any offer made to the client in a criminal matter; and . . . all amounts, terms, and conditions of any written offer of settlement made to the client in all other matters." The prior California Rule 5-105 required communication of "any written offer of settlement made by or on behalf of an opposing party."

"In a Box" (page 85)

This question pits the duty to inform against the duty of confidentiality. Two clients of one firm are willing to consent to let a different firm represent one of them (Endicott) in connection with their planned joint venture. However, Chin, a partner in the first firm, knows that Endicott is the subject of an ongoing criminal investigation. Endicott will not allow Chin to give this information to the other firm client, Marsh. Endicott is prepared to consent and its consent would be valid. But what about Marsh? The firm can't tell Marsh information about Endicott that would seem to be material to the joint venture. It can't even tell Marsh, in order to get consent, that it has information about Endicott that it can't tell her and, as discussed below, won't be allowed to independently "discover." Even that disclosure would alert Marsh to a problem, which Endicott won't allow.

Why can't the firm simply say that whoever represents Marsh will not have the information? So what difference will it make whether someone else does it or the firm does it?

This question is patterned after L.A. County Opinion 463 (1990). On similar facts, the Committee concluded that the firm could not represent Marsh if it were not permitted to reveal

Endicott's situation. But, again, if Marsh is not going to find out in any event, what difference does it make? The answer is that we do not use a "proximate cause analysis" to determine the contours of the lawyer's duty to inform. A lawyer knowing of material information bearing on a client's matter but who cannot reveal that information cannot be the lawyer for the client on that matter. But perhaps considerations of causation are behind our prohibition after all. Not only is the lawyer unable to reveal the confidential information, he or she is unable to "discover" it. A truly independent lawyer might do the thorough search that would turn up the information. The firm cannot do that search. Sometimes, to be sure, situations will arise in which no lawyer could possibly discover the confidential information. In one of those situations, the firm could honestly say that there would be "no harm done" to Marsh if it represented Marsh. But who will decide whether the facts of the case truly present that circumstance? The lawyer is an interested party. Isn't it better to have an absolute prohibition?

On the same facts, could the firm represent Endicott and let Marsh get separate counsel on the matter? Then, it would not be withholding information from a client on a matter in which it represented that client. Should it matter that the firm represents Marsh on other matters? I don't think so. Firms often have client information that other clients would like to know but the firm cannot reveal. In order to get Marsh's consent to represent Endicott, the firm would not have to reveal Endicott's problem. Marsh would, or can be made to, understand that in representing Endicott, information about it pertinent to the deal would be Endicott's confidential information just as information Marsh gives to whomever she hires would be confidential between her and her lawyer. So I do believe that the firm can get valid consent from Marsh to represent Endicott. It follows that the firm can choose to represent neither, and can continue to represent both in unrelated matters, without telling Marsh what it knows about Endicott. Marsh has no right to this information. Interestingly, at this early stage of the course (assuming you do Chapter 2 early), students intuitively think the opposite. Many think that if the firm has information Marsh would want to know about Endicott but cannot reveal, the firm cannot represent Marsh on anything. Some students assume that by virtue of having a client on any matter there is an obligation to give the client information the client would want to know even if it is unrelated to that matter. It is also worth pointing out that the conflict that we have identified would be firm-wide. That is, whatever Martin can't do, Sally can't do. Students have not yet studied conflicts, of course, but this one should be intuitively understandable and signaling it now will prepare them for work later.

C. AUTONOMY OF ATTORNEYS AND CLIENTS (page 85)

The material here and in Section D (Termination of the Professional Relationship) is discretionary. It is, however, interesting and worth an occasional excursion. The material in Section D can be assigned for home reading. It is brief. It is important when we come to the conflict material because the particular conflict rule that applies will depend on whether or not

33

there is a current client-lawyer relationship. So students should have some idea how these might end.

The introductory material (**pages 85-87**) broadly asks how much of a client's free choice he or she surrenders on retaining a lawyer. This goes to the meaning - at least one meaning - of what it means to be a professional. At one extreme is the image of the lawyer as the "mouthpiece," who is little more than dummy to the ventriloquist client. At the other extreme is the lawyer who assumes total control over the client's "matter" and says, in effect: "Go away, I'll call you when I need you." The introductory note refers to informed consent in medicine and asks whether it is a useful guide for defining the client's authority in law. The medical standard (see **page 98**) is one that lawyers helped establish as a limitation on the professional freedom, or in the view of some, arrogance, of doctors. In any event, isn't it precisely because lawyers will usually be making important decisions for their clients -- decisions clients lack the learning to make on their own -- that we impose the fiduciary and other duties described earlier in the chapter?

Students should recognize that there will always be ambiguity (in fact, a lot) and that in the ambiguous range lawyers will generally not be second-guessed. But they should also recognize that the ambiguity can be partly resolved by agreement. A client can insist on a greater role in the conduct of his or her matter than the lawyer might otherwise afford. Should lawyers explore that issue with the prospective client? See Restatement §§ 20-23. Douglas Rosenthal (**page 86**) reported that lawyers who invite clients to be active in their matters get better results. Is that because client involvement improves results or because lawyers who encourage it are better lawyers? Interesting question. Students may be inclined to favor significant client participation. But they should also understand the practical limitations. Obviously, during a trial, but also in office work, many small and large decisions, some needing special knowledge, have to be made. It would not be feasible for lawyers to consult clients on many of these.

1. The Lawyer's Autonomy. *Jones v. Barnes* (**page 87**) may have put the issue of informed consent on the map. When the holding in *Jones* is added to agency authority rules and to *Strickland*'s test for establishing prejudicial ineffective assistance (**page 885**), we can see the extent to which a client is at the mercy of his lawyer's skill and conscientiousness. When the client is an indigent criminal defendant who must generally accept the lawyer whom the court appoints or the legal aid society has assigned, the client's fate is even more clearly out of his or her control. Think of it from the point of view of a client. The court is saying: "Here is your lawyer. She can do whatever she wants in defending you except plead you guilty or make you testify or (perhaps) decline to appeal a guilty verdict if you want to do so. If you don't like the way your lawyer is representing you and you are convicted, you can try to meet the *Strickland* burden and demonstrate constitu-tional incompetence. If you can't, you might be able to raise the issues your lawyer ignored, despite your request that she assert them, in a collateral attack on your conviction, but don't count on it."

Sounds glum, but what's wrong with it? Do clients who retain lawyers have much greater autonomy? Could the system work if the client called the tune, note by note? It would seem that our comfort with this arrangement in criminal cases against poor defendants depends on the competence of court-appointed lawyers, which on a national basis can euphemistically be described as mixed. Further discussion of these issues can be picked up in Chapter 13E.

The note material after *Jones* **(pages 91-93)** reveals that the New York Court of Appeals will not *require* intermediate appellate courts to accept pro se briefs, although it recommends acceptance. The note also questions the scope of the authority Justice Brennan would allow counsel. And it lists the several instances in the Code and Rules in which lawyers are given discretion to act or refuse to act.

Students should understand that *Jones v. Barnes* interprets the Sixth Amend-ment, which is not necessarily the test (indeed should not be the test) for ethical conduct. That issue arises again in *Nix v. Whiteside* at **page 431**. See especially Justice Blackmun's concurrence.

Clemmons v. Delo **(page 92)** is a case remarkably like *Jones v. Barnes*. The Circuit, rejecting a claim of procedural default, allowed a habeas petitioner to raise a Brady point in federal court even though his court-appointed lawyer had not raised that point in state court. The prisoner had asked the lawyer to make the Brady argument and, when the lawyer did not for reasons similar to those in *Jones*, he submitted a pro se brief to the state supreme court, which rejected it. Although *Jones* and *Clemmons* both arise in a collateral attack on a conviction, *Jones* did not resolve whether the defendant could raise the issue his counsel rejected in a subsequent habeas petition. *Jones* only asked whether counsel's failure to include the defendant's claims amounted to a violation of the Sixth Amendment. *Clemmons*, by contrast, addresses the issue avoided in *Jones*: Should the procedural default be excused so that the defendant's claim could be addressed in federal court?

"Ms. Niceperson" (page 93)

This problem asks how miserable a wretch a lawyer *must* be if it furthers the client's interests. (I've refined it since the last edition.) Okay, okay, I'm tipping my hand. Let me rephrase it neutrally: Must (or may) a lawyer take advantage of the family misfortune and ignorance of another lawyer if it will enable her client to win? A majority or your class will say yes, the lawyer must do so. (Bet?)

The question is self-explanatory. The other lawyer, out of town with a sick parent, calls to get an extension of time to restore a case to the calendar. Ms. Niceperson knows that the time is jurisdictional and that if the motion is filed after it expires, the court will not be able to grant relief. Can she take advantage of the other lawyer's situation? Must she? It will mean that the other lawyer will be guilty of malpractice. Can Ms. Niceperson go so far as to sign a stipulation that she knows will be ineffective?

My view is that Ms. Niceperson, at the least, has discretion not to take advantage of the other lawyer and in fact I say she must not. Her client should not be able to override her and indeed she need not tell him. This is not a situation in which the opponent has left a claim or defense out of a pleading and the opposing lawyer thinks it must be an oversight. Maybe, maybe not. Here, though, we know for certain that the opponent is just making a mistake, perhaps because his problem with his sick parent has consumed his attention and has taken him away from the books that would reveal the error. This error is not tactical.

Not everyone will agree with me. But some will. I draw some comfort from an ABA opinion (86-1518). Two lawyers, A and B, have negotiated a contract. Lawyer A prepares the first draft but omits a clause favorable to his client, to which Lawyer B had already agreed. The Opinion says that B can alert A without telling the client (though the opinion declines to say what B would have to do if the client learned of the omission and directed B not to tell). Also pertinent is Opinion 92-368, which directs lawyers who receive confidential documents in error (e.g., the misdirected fax) not to read them.

Anyway, this question is important because it forces us to ask how far the duty of loyalty to clients extends and how much autonomy lawyers have to do "the right thing."

If some students do come around and say that Ms. Niceperson does not have to, perhaps may not, exploit the other lawyer's misfortune and ignorance, try this variation: The other lawyer has no sick parent, is in his office, has mistakenly assumed that a written stipulation will extend the time to move, but it will not because the rule is jurisdictional. The court will have no choice. Now may Ms. Niceperson exploit the lawyer's ignorance? Must she? Must she not? In other words, does the "sick parent" dimension change our analysis? It certainly makes it easier to let Ms. Niceperson be a nice person. For my nickel, I would still say that Ms. Niceperson may explain the mistake to her opponent. I would even go so far as to say that she must, but I am probably in the minority. Certainly, I would not let her sign a stipulation knowing it was worthless. Anyway, you can see how this can be an interesting problem.

2. The Client's Autonomy (page 94). The only thing surprising about *Olfe* is the action of the trial court, proving once again the reluctance of judges to second-guess lawyers, even where the lawyers failed to make a "first guess" or wholly ignored the instructions of the person for whom they were working. There is the additional dimension here that the defendant misled the plaintiff into believing that the second mortgage was a first mortgage, but the court's opinion does not rest on that fact. Now what if Olfe had not thought to insist on a first mortgage but told her lawyer that she was "willing to take back a note if I'm protected because I need the money." Could the lawyer have accepted a second mortgage and said nothing to Olfe? (My answer: No.)

What if Olfe simply told the lawyer that she was willing to provide "some financing"? Would Gordon have had a duty to explain that the only mortgage he could get was a second mortgage and to describe its risks? (Yes.) Did Olfe win only because she was specific? (I hope not.)

These are good questions with which to test the scope of the lawyer's and client's authority (and the lawyer's duty to inform) in civil matters. The more vague Olfe was, perhaps the greater Gordon's freedom. Or is that wrong? Should we say that Gordon had an obligation to confer with his client about the financing in any event? That's my view. It is Olfe, not Gordon, who will have to live with whatever security Gordon obtains. See Rule 1.4(b) and comment and **page 95**. E2K and the Restatement support me.

The note material **(pages 95-98)** asks why Barnes lost while Olfe won. Why indeed? If anything, wasn't Barnes' interest more significant than Olfe's interest? Freedom as opposed to money. One possible answer is that Barnes was seeking to vacate his conviction while Olfe was suing in malpractice. So the legal tests differed. Should Barnes now bring a malpractice action? The likelihood of success is near to nil. See **page 800**. A second difference is that Barnes was directing his lawyer on means, not ends, although that distinction breaks down if you push it. The ends were freedom and security, respectively. The legal arguments and the mortgage were means, not ends, to achieve these.

Petrovich **(page 96)** brings home the point that freedom brings responsibility. The defendant who did not want the jury charged on lesser included offenses made a decision that belonged to him and he had to live with the result. On the other hand, clients who are denied their autonomy may have claims against counsel, as the cases at **pages 96-98** show. The *Shahade* case **(page 97)** shows just how hard it is to distinguish between ends and means.

I conclude with some discussion of the medical analogy **(page 98)** referenced earlier.

A lawyer, familiar with the unsettled state of the law over whether a military pension is community property in a dissolution of marriage case concludes that it is not community property and does not claim an interest in the husband's pension on behalf of the wife, his client. Later, the courts reach a contrary result. The client sues the lawyer, claiming he was under a duty to advise her of the unsettled state of the law and let her decide whether or not to assert the claim. What result? *Davis v. Damrell* **(page 98)** held for the lawyer. The court wrote:

> While we recognize that an attorney owes a basic obligation to provide sound advice in furtherance of a client's best interests . . . such obligation does not include a duty to advise on all possible alternatives no matter how remote or tenuous. To impose such an extraordinary duty would effectively undermine the attorney-client relationship and vitiate the salutary purpose of the error-in-judgment rule. . . . Under [that] rule, if an attorney acting in good faith exercises honest and informed discretion in providing professional advice, the failure to

anticipate correctly the resolution of an unsettled legal principle does not constitute culpable conduct.

Is this right? Didn't the client have a right to know of the unsettled state of the law? How unsettled must the law be before the lawyer has an obligation to inform the client of a decision he or she is making with regard to the best way to proceed? The Nebraska Supreme Court rejects this reasoning in the *Wood* case at **page 97**. "Where there are reasonable alternatives, the attorney should inform the client that the issues is uncertain, unsettled, or debatable, and allow the client to make the decision." But aren't many issues "uncertain?" Must lawyers inform clients of all nonfrivolous arguments for positions contrary to the one they are prepared to take? (These cases can also be discussed in connection with malpractice. See **page 799** for a problem based on *Smith v. Lewis*, an earlier California case.

In *Zimmerlee v. Williams*, 728 P.2d 49 (1986), the defendant shot her former boyfriend while he was breaking into her home. Her lawyer had not told her, before she entered her guilty plea, of defenses based in statutes relating to the shooting of a burglar or of a trespasser about to commit a felony. The lawyer had rejected these defenses as inapplicable. The court held that the client could withdraw her plea. Although a "tactical decision whether to assert a defense" may be proper, the defendant has a right to know about all "viable defenses" before pleading guilty. Does that mean that the lawyer would not have had to tell the client anything if the case had gone to trial? Or that, after learning of the defenses and declining to plead guilty, the client would have to defer to the lawyer's "tactical" decision to ignore them? How does this square with *Jones v. Barnes*, where counsel rejected legal theories on appeal? The differences would seem to be that the strategy is factual as well as legal *and* that the information bore on whether to plead guilty. Would a lawyer have to clear it with a client before deciding not to assert an entrapment defense because, the lawyer has concluded, the jury would not be receptive to it?

Actually, these questions deserve a little more reflection. The *Zimmerlee* court's decision seems absolutely right. Before the defendant chooses to plead guilty, she ought to have some idea of what the defenses are. But if that's true, then why shouldn't the decision whether or not to assert a defense at trial, especially one that would negate guilt, be up to the defendant as well? We would hope that the lawyer and the defendant could come to an agreement about the best strategy. But if not, who decides? If this feels a little different from giving the defendant the right to know about the defenses before pleading guilty it is. In *Zimmerlee*, the court held only that the defendant had a right to information before making a decision that belonged to her. Once at trial, does the defendant have a right to choose the defense strategy? It is a broader right, to be sure. So maybe that's the distinction. On the other hand, it seems illogical to say that the defendant has a right to know the possible defenses before pleading guilty but that if she then chooses not to plead guilty, the lawyer decides whether or not to pursue those defenses at trial. Yet I bet that the general sentiment at the bar would be that the lawyer decides. I think that if the decision to pursue a particular defense has almost no chance of success, perhaps the decision should belong to the lawyer. Certainly that would be so if the decision is frivolous. But if the defense has merit, the decision whether or not to assert it would seem to be not all that much different from a decision whether or not to accept a plea bargain. Obviously, there are grey areas where the defense is not frivolous, but weak, and where asserting it could have negative strategic implications.

At **page 98**, the note on clients with diminished capacity draws on Justice Pollock's opinion for the New Jersey Supreme Court in *Matter of M.R.* In the end, a lawyer for an incompetent must act as an advocate of the client's objective, where possible. The attorney may not choose instead to pursue what he or she believes to be the client's best interests. However, where the client's objectives and the attorney's perception of his or her best interests conflict, the attorney may tell the court of the possible need for a guardian ad litem.

"I'd Rather Die" (page 101)

This problem and the next one both posit clients who are making choices that the run of us might believe inadvisable, perhaps even the product of emotional disturbance or turmoil. How should the lawyer respond in that situation? One answer, of course, is to wait a while, but what if the client maintains his position? Here, the client insists on dropping appeals and proceeding to execution. This dilemma, though still rare, does arise. The client tells Emily that if she won't go along with his plan, he'll fire her, thereby terminating the agency relationship and ensuring that no appeals can be pursued. What should the lawyer do in this situation?

Obviously, there is no easy answer and students divide. Some would have the lawyer act to save the client's life notwithstanding. If the lawyer is fired, the lawyer will still attempt to appear for the client and pursue the appeal. Leave it to the courts to ignore the lawyer if they will, but the lawyer will not abandon the client despite the client's wishes.

Others might recognize that the client's choice, though difficult to accept, is not entirely irrational. They will defer to it however reluctantly. What if the lawyer asserts that the client has become incompetent? Then, wouldn't the lawyer have to consider moving to stay execution on that ground?

P.D. (pedagogical tip): With this question, the next one, and many others, I find class works well if I pose the dilemma in the role of the lawyer who's asking the question (or if I put the student in that role and become the client). So, *e.g.*, I'll be Emily and I'll say to a student, "Sam, I came to see you because I have this problem and everyone said you'd know what to do. I do death penalty work and I have a client who . . . . " If Sam tells me to defer to my client's wishes, I'll stress how strong the new argument is. If Sam says to ignore my client's wishes, I'll stress the hellish life he's living. You take it from there.

"Accept the Offer" (page 102)

      Here the divorce client, a wife, instructs a lawyer to accept an offer substantially less than the least the lawyer knows from experience he can get with a single counteroffer: a quarter of a million dollars on the property division, and about $50,000 yearly on support. The lawyer believes the client is operating out of guilt and perhaps she is. The lawyer's long experience convinces him that the client will desperately regret her decision.

      Now this is certainly a decision the client has the right to make. Perhaps the lawyer can stall and hope she changes her mind. Stalling would certainly be legitimate if the client is under stress. But here the speaker anticipates that it might be six months before Chloe relents.

      One thing the speaker can do is refuse to represent her. Rule 1.16(b)(3) would allow the lawyer to withdraw, with consent of the tribunal, if an objective lawyer would consider the client's decision "repugnant or imprudent." Perhaps the very threat to withdraw will change the client's mind. Perhaps not. At the very least, the lawyer can have the client sign a notarized document acknowledging that she is accepting the offer over the lawyer's fierce objection, and that the lawyer has counseled her that she could receive substantially more at trial or in a later settlement. Should the lawyer also have the client seek professional advice on her competency to decide? That would be a bit extreme unless the facts warrant it.

      Other points worth making:

•The lawyer has to worry about malpractice (especially given the amounts at issue) if the client later regrets her decision and complains that the lawyer should have recognized her depressed state and should have refused to help her hurt herself.

•The lawyer doesn't know if the client is aware of the difficulties she may have living on the settlement she wants to accept. Perhaps she has never had to budget her expenses. Either he can review the numbers with her (after having her make a budget) or he can send her to a financial adviser. He can certainly insist that she prepare a budget. Perhaps competence requires it.

•It may be possible to negotiate for the right to revisit the financial settlement after a defined period of time. Perhaps the client and the other side will agree to that. Perhaps there can be a "trial period," during which Chloe may become more realistic.

• Note that Russell is a banker, and presumably makes a good income. Chloe hasn't worked outside the home for more than twelve years. Previously she taught third grade. So the problem suggests that the income disparity (or the capacity to earn income) is substantial.

D. TERMINATING THE RELATIONSHIP

1. Termination by the Client (page 103). This is fairly straightforward. Subject to the interests of others, a client can terminate for virtually any reason. The client may, of course, continue to be liable to the lawyer for work done, depending in some jurisdictions on the reason for the termination. The client's right to terminate is circumscribed by antidiscrimination laws and by the evolving tort of retaliatory discharge, discussed in Chapter 9. These qualifications are signaled at **page 103**. Judge Martin's opinion in *Mass v. McClenahan* may be the only one in which a *retained* lawyer was held to state a claim under antidiscrimination laws.

2. Termination by the Lawyer (page 104). This is not quite as easy. The lawyer does not enjoy the client's freedom. I ask whether the Model Rules tolerate too much freedom in a lawyer to terminate. They certainly go beyond the Code in this regard. This might be a good place to test the profession's definition of professionalism. The material asks how lawyers can claim to put the interests of the public and their clients ahead of their own interests and, at the same time, authorize withdrawal under the circumstances identified in Rule 1.16(b) and (b)(5).

Worth highlighting are *Auguston, Faro*, and *Bell* **(page 104)**, where lawyers who withdrew, with permission of the court, were denied a fee for their work when the client, with new counsel, later recovered. Despite court permission to withdraw, the withdrawal was improper because the lawyers' reason was the client's rejection of a settlement offer, which was within the client's authority to do.

3. Termination by Drift (page 106). Most representations end not because the lawyer or client choose to end them but because the work is completed. No one says anything. But sometimes there can be an ambiguity over whether the work is completed or whether, even if it is, the relationship is over.

In *Lama Holding* **(page 106)**, the client thought the law firm was going to continue to inform it about changes in tax laws. The law firm did not. Based on earlier, now superseded, advice, the client sold certain assets that resulted in a substantially higher tax bill than had the sale been structured in another way. That stated a claim, even though the law firm believed that its work had concluded and its duty to the client to tell it of tax law changes had ended. Conflict rules also vary depending upon whether the client is current or former. This is a good place to flag that issue.

CHAPTER III

PROTECTING THE CLIENT-LAWYER RELATIONSHIP AGAINST OUTSIDE INTERFERENCE

This chapter identifies rules that protect the professional relationship against outside interference, generally by an adversary. Most prominent is the no-contact rule in each of the civil and criminal contexts. This rule is easy when the client is a civil litigant, but becomes exponentially harder when the client is an entity and the contact is with its agent or former agent; or when the client is a focus of a criminal investigation or a defendant in a criminal matter. Most difficult, perhaps, is the situation in which the entity client is under investigation by civil or criminal enforcement agencies.

This chapter is optional, although parts of it do get close to core issues and echo some of the material in the prior chapter, especially the material on confidentiality. If you would like to cover the operation of lawyer regulatory issues in the criminal context, then *Hammad*, the Thornburgh memorandum, the Reno rules, and the McDade Amendment in Part (A)(2) are all for you. Or you might choose simply to focus on the no-contact rule in civil context, covering *Niesig* **(page 111)**, and the note material following. This material reintroduces the issue of entity secrecy and rules that encourage or interfere with it. "Slip And Fall Redux" **(page 122)** echoes "Slip And Fall" **(page 53)** and asks whether, each of the individuals the investigator interviewed (and the investigator himself) can be contacted by plain-tiff's counsel without Tracy's lawyer's permission.

This chapter raises the following knotty issues among others. (1) social policy considerations regarding entity secrecy in the civil context; (2) the extent to which government lawyers engaged in civil and criminal law enforcement are bound by ethical rules that purport to afford targets of investigation greater protection than does substantive law, including the Constitution; (3) federalism and separation of powers issues - i.e., who answers question (2), the courts, the executive or the legislature; and if the courts do, can state courts impose their rules on federal lawyers admitted in their states but exercising federal power?

The introduction **(page 107)** reminds students that, while the focus of much of the chapter is the no-contact rule, other rules also aim at protecting the client-lawyer relationship.

A. COMMUNICATING WITH ANOTHER LAWYER'S CLIENTS (page 108)

The introductory material on **pages 108-110** does two things. First, it delineates exactly what the no-contact rule prohibits and what it does not. Especially noteworthy is the fact that a lawyer can violate this rule, as others, through the actions of another, including an investigator or client. Second, the discussion identifies six reasons advanced to support the no-contact rule **(page 110)** and asks how much weight we should give the countervailing interests in inexpensive access to information, compliance with Rule 11-type obligations, and law enforcement. With regard to the policies supporting the rule, consider the following. The interest in preventing lawyers from getting damaging admissions from an opposing client sounds right, but when applied to an opposing client's agents, whose admissions are only vicarious, it significantly broadens the circle of secrecy. (A separate question is why let the evidence rule determine the sphere of the ethics rule rather than the other way around? See below.) The interest in preventing opposing counsel from getting a concession, even a settlement, can be met with rules that make the concession or settlement unenforceable. The other interests listed on **page 110** are fairly strong when dealing with an individual client. As for entity opponents, the applicable policy depends on whom you talk to: a member of the entity control group who knows nothing about the underlying event but directs the litigation; or someone lower down who happens to have factual information but no say in the litigation. This distinction is worth making. But all of this says nothing about the relative strength of these interests as against the competing interests in informal access to information and law enforcement, a balance we shall have to make as the material progresses.

Points to stress on this introductory material are: (1) the requirement that the lawyer have actual knowledge that the opposing party is represented by counsel on the matter **(page 108)**; (2) the seemingly paternalistic but correct decisions that deny the opposing client the right to waive the protection of the rule **(page 109)**; (3) and the fact that the rule is not meant to prevent the client from getting a second opinion **(page 108)**. Also, for comparative treatment, look at the New York version of the rule DR 7-104(B), which creates an exception when the lawyer effects the contact through the lawyer's own clients so long as the opposing lawyer is given reasonable advance notice.

1. Civil Matters (page 110). The introductory paragraph quickly disposes of the application of the no-contact rule in the context of individual clients. It moves to the more daunting task of assessing its application when the opposing client is an entity. The student is reminded of Justice Rehnquists' assumption, in *Upjohn*, that government counsel were free to question the same Upjohn employees as Upjohn's counsel questioned.

Niesig v. Team I **(page 111)** has by now, perhaps, become the leading state case on application of the no-contact rule in the entity context. It has been favorably cited a number of times. It summarily rejects the argument that the rule applies to former agents. As for current ones, it creates rather elaborate categories for determining who is and who is not within the no-contact zone. Notice that Judge Kaye distinguishes the federal cases by distinguishing the federal vicarious admission rule from the narrower New York rule. The concurring judge (opinion omitted) would create a single category of off-limits employee -- members of the control group. Interest in truth -- and therefore greater access -- is his apparent motivation. Some pointed questions about the reasoning in *Niesig* and problems in the area generally appear in the note following the case (**pages 115-117**). They are:

(1) Why is it that unions, public interests groups, and a law enforcement person (the state attorney general) all urged reversal? What is the common interest of this disparate group? Exactly who is on which side and what are we fighting over? Informal and inexpensive access, it seems.

(2) Although Judge Kaye takes former employees out of the rule, she then creates categories that can logically apply to former employees too. For example, an opposing lawyer cannot contact an employee "whose acts or omissions in the matter under inquiry are . . . imputed to the corporation for purposes of its liability." But can the opposing lawyer then do so the day after that employee retires? Think about the truck driver who dumped the hazardous waste.

(3) One way to disaggregate the evidence and ethics rules is to permit contact but forbid vicarious admission (**page 118**) as discussed further below. The Restatement has opted for the opposite solution – favoring access despite the vicarious admission rule, excepting only three or four small categories of agents. (**Page 116.**) New Jersey seems to have accepted this test. Of course, as stated at **page 116**, Rule 3.4(f) lets entity counsel ask entity agents not to talk to the opposing lawyer. Why isn't this protection enough?

(4) Courts seem now to agree with *Niesig* that the rule does not generally cover former employees. So does ABA Opinion 91-359.

(5) Where the lawyer is permitted to speak to an agent or former agent of an entity opponent, what kind of warning should she have to give? See Rule 4.3 and the final paragraph of *Niesig*. Obviously, the more explicit the lawyer, or her agent, the less information is she likely to receive. So long as no one lies, and Rule 4.3 is literally followed, why require more? It is, after all, in the cause of truth.

(6) Whom does the rule protect? We are inclined to say that it protects the entity, but is this really true? If the employee, current or former, has her own lawyer, she can talk to whomever she wishes without the consent or presence of entity counsel. The only category of information opposing counsel could not then properly receive is information the agent learned as part of the entity's legal team or perhaps information whose transmittal would violate a fiduciary duty. See Part B of this chapter. How can it possibly be that the entity loses nearly all its veto power once

the employee gets her own counsel? One partial answer may be that if a current agent talks to the opposing lawyer with her own counsel her statements could no longer be deemed vicarious admissions of the entity (assuming they otherwise would be).

When the Government Is the Adversary (pages 117-119). Did the New York Attorney General know what he was getting himself in for when he urged reversal in *Niesig*? After all, the state is an entity. Did the AG really want to make it easier for lawyers opposing the state to speak to its agents? On the other hand, the state is also, and often, in the enforcement business and may wish to speak to the agents of targets of its investigation. The policy reason against applying the no-contact rule with the same force when the opponent is the government as we do when the opponent is a private corporation is plain. The governed have a right to speak to government. How can we recognize that right without compromising the government's legitimate interests as an adversary? The comment to Rule 4.2 recognizes the problem but isn't really helpful. Some authorities that have attempted to solve this problem are summarized at **page 118**. Take a look at the creative solution in *B.H. v. Johnson* (**page 119**). The court refused to be hemmed in by the vicarious admission rule. It allowed the interview with the government employees but ruled that if they were not parties for purposes of the no-contact rule, then neither would they be parties within the meaning of the vicarious admissions rule. Two other courts have allowed opposing counsel to talk to non-managerial persons in a government agency that was adverse to counsel's client, but required warnings. See the *Carter-Herman*, *Brown*, and *Rivera v. Rowland* cases at **page 118-119**.

Is this an equally wise solution where the opposing party is a private entity? It ensures cheap access to information while protecting the adversary entity against the legal consequences (*i.e.*, admissibility) of that information. The NYU Law Review Note cited on **page 122** makes this suggestion. See also *Instituform of North America, Inc. v. Midwest Pipeliners, Inc.*, 780 F. Supp. 479 (S.D. Ohio 1991), refusing to disqualify a lawyer who had an ex parte conversation with the opposing entity's employees but holding that the statements would not be admissible against the entity under the vicarious admission rule. The court also said that testimony about conversations with employees whose statements were admissible other than vicariously would be received, as would visual observations. This case represents the court's response to a completed act. Should it be the *a priori* solution?

New to this edition is a note on "testers." (**Page 119**.) The note draws on the *Gidatex* decision that finds that the use of testers is not a violation of the rule where the lawyer employing them suspected that another party was guilty of violation of intellectual property rights. Testers are also used in connection with discrimination cases. The Oregon Supreme Court's opinion in *Gatti* is cited at **page 121**. That case did not involve a tester, as such, but rather a lawyer who misidentified himself in an effort to get information for a civil claim. Consumer groups and the federal prosecutor in Oregon asked for exemption from the rule but lost and a battle is now raging in Oregon over application of the rule in criminal investigations. Federal prosecutors have to worry about the implications of McDade, which would, if valid, obligate them to abide by Oregon ethics rules, at least if they are admitted in Oregon. See **page 130**. You might be interested to know that in connection with the antiterrorism legislation Congress passed in October 2001, both Oregon Senators succeeded in getting an amendment in the Senate version of the bill that would substantially override McDade. However, the House version of the bill omitted this amendment and the law does not include it. The ABA opposed the amendment.

The E2K Commission (**page 121**) would, among other things, allow a lawyer to advise a client regarding communications the client was "legally entitled to make." Unlike the New York version of DR 7-104, there is no obligation to alert the opposing lawyer.

"Slip and Fall Redux" (page 122)

This problem asks whether Cora Lundquist, plaintiff's lawyer, can privately contact any of the individuals with whom the defense investigator, Mike Todd, spoke, and also Todd himself. If, for any, the interview notes are privileged and contact is also forbidden, information will only be available in formal discovery. Students are asked what the rule would permit on the facts posed. Burkow and Morse can probably make vicarious admissions and Burkow may be in the control group or working with counsel on the matter. (Todd is certainly working with counsel.) Further, their conduct may be imputed to the entity for liability purposes. Kuhl, the customer, is certainly excluded from the scope of the rule. That leaves Sandstrom and McCormick, respectively the employee at a nearby counter and the employee shopping on his day off. Sandstrom may be able to make vicarious admissions depending on the jurisdiction's evidence rules. McCormick could not. He saw nothing within the scope of his employment. So the Rules could place Burkow, Morse, and Sandstrom beyond contact, but not McCormick and Kuhl. The Restatement, which is broad enough to privilege the conversations between Sandstrom or (even) McCormick and Todd, "makes up" for this broad secrecy by letting Lundquist interview them. *Niesig* would, too, because the New York evidence rules would not make their statements vicariously admissible. The Restatement would even seem to allow interviews with Todd and possibly Burkow, depending on his authority. Morse would be off base. Counsel could not seek to get confidential information. §§ 100, 102.

2. Criminal Matters (page 122). Whether and to what extent no-contact rules apply to prosecutors and law enforcement persons working with them has been the subject of great controversy. **Pages 122-124** review earlier cases and emphasizes judicial concern in cases involving interviews with indigent defendants who are in custody. While in-custody interviews are disturbing, do they violate a rule? Technically, no lawyer has yet been appointed but only because the prosecutor has not done the final act -- file a complaint -- that would trigger appointment of free counsel. In any event, the no-contact rule, unlike *Miranda v. Arizona*, does not depend on an assumption about the pressures of custodial interrogation. It applies whether the interviewee is in custody or not and in civil as well as criminal cases. Presumably, the custodial interviewees in these cases received their *Miranda* warnings. Prosecutors argue that defense lawyers are attempting to use the no-contact rules to expand *Miranda* and ban custodial interrogation in these cir-cumstances altogether. Are they right?

Matter of Simels **(page 128)**, reversed discipline against a criminal defense lawyer who interviewed a represented person even though that person would soon be, though was not yet, named in an indictment with the lawyer's client. To reach this result, the Circuit had to engage in a hypertechnical definition of the word "party" as used in DR 7-104(A)(1), a definition at odds with a fair reading of (at least) Rule 4.2 and its Comment. For one thing, no one has ever thought that Rule 4.2 applies only in litigation. Yet in negotiation, there are no "parties" in the technical sense. It is clear to this reader, at least, that *Simels* was driven by dis-like of *Hammad*, which for reasons of its own the Circuit did not want to reverse. *Simels* was written by a district judge, David Traeger, sitting by designation. Judge Traeger had been the U.S. Attorney in the Eastern District of New York and no friend of *Hammad*. Rule 4.2 has since been amended to change "party" to "per-son," but not in the New York version.

United States v. Hammad **(page 124)**. The fascinating history and consequences of this case -- the Court's multiple opinions -- is described in the note material at **pages 127-133**. What's left after the third revision? It seems that in the end, the government's inconsequential error was to use a sham grand jury subpoena. While the court applies the no-contact rule to prosecutors, and does so at a point in the investigation earlier than when Sixth Amendment rights attach, the court also invokes the "authorized by law" exception to the no-contact rule to permit government to "employ legitimate investigative techniques," a phrase that includes the use of informants. But giving the informant here the sham subpoena made him an "alter ego of the prosecutor" and violated the rule. How about the fact that the informant was wired? Why didn't *that* make him an alter ego of the prosecutor? Although an earlier *Hammad* opinion characterized the prosecutor's conduct as "egregious," the final opinion drops that word and tells us that the law was "previously unsettled in this area." Suppression was therefore inappropriate. (Suppression was also found inappropriate even when the conduct was seen as "egregious.")

While *Hammad* for a time looked like it would become an historical curiosity and the focal point for internecine professional battles, as discussed at **pages 131-132**, a state supreme court and the Ninth Circuit have recently endorsed it and given it new respectability.

Hammad sparked an intense war of words. Those in Attorney General Thornburgh's infamous memorandum produced the most heat **(page 129)**. The AG may have overreacted to the ABA's response -- especially when he started using the definition of treason to describe his opponents -- but in truth, the policy considerations here are potentially enormous. Consider two factual circumstances in which the *Hammad* rule could have significant consequence to law enforcement: investigation of organized crime or continuing criminal enterprises; investigation of corporate crime. This last context is created when *Hammad* meets *Niesig* **(page 132)**. In any event, notice how far we've moved from the plight of the indigent in-custody defendant.

Law enforcement is alarmed, quite rightly in my view, that the no-contact rule will be used by targets of investigation to preempt legitimate law enforcement. If a suspect has retained a lawyer on the subject of an investigation and so informs the prosecutor, is he or she then shielded in some way from investigation for completed conduct? If the suspect is an "it," does the notice of counsel mean the prosecutor cannot speak to those of its employees who fall within one of the *Niesig* categories or whose statements would be vicarious admissions against the entity?

The post-*Hammad* history takes us through the Thornburgh memorandum, the reaction to it, the Reno Rules, and the Eighth Circuit's opinion finding that the Department had no authority to write its own no-contact rule. **(Pages 129-131.)** The McDade amendment is described.

As mentioned earlier, the Senate passed an amendment to the antiterrorism bill in October 2001 that would have substantially repealed McDade, but the provision did not appear in the House bill or in the law finally adopted. However, a free standing bill that would accomplish much the same result is before the Senate.

The note material concludes with two cases, one from the Ninth Circuit and one from the Minnesota Supreme Court, that endorse *Hammad* as valid law **(pages 131-133)**.

Among questions to pose in class are the following: *First*, who should decide what the rule should be? On one view, the executive's law enforcement authority would give that power to the attorney general and local counterparts so long as their conduct is not *illegal*. Another view would have it that the legislature decides, or at least that it has the authority to decide if it chooses to do so. In this view, the executive makes the decision under its law enforcement authority if there is legislative silence, but the lawmakers can overrule or preempt that decision. This is, of course, what Congress did with the McDade Amendment, and the authority to do so has not been challenged. Whether state courts would tolerate the same legislative activity at the state level is another question, one that would turn on state constitutional interpretation. On yet another view, courts have the inherent right to control the behavior of lawyers who practice before them. So we have a separation of powers issue. If courts decide, which courts decide? This is a federalism issue. Who controls the conduct of a federal prosecutor who is admitted to both the federal and state courts? See Wisconsin Opinion E-91-6 (all Wisconsin lawyers must comply with the state's rules, rejecting Thornburgh memo).

The *Hammad* issue raises further questions. Perhaps the most important is: What is the right rule on the merits? Especially in a criminal case, a rule giving prosecutors greater leeway than defense lawyers to avoid the strictures of the no-contact rule "unlevels" the playing field.

The Second Circuit's *Simels* opinion (**page 128**) will keep the playing field from becoming too tilted, but even *Simels*, because it turns on a formality, won't put prosecutors and defense lawyers at the same starting line when the person each would like to interview is, unambiguously, a "party" because prosecutors can try to invoke the "authorized by law" exception. Defense lawyers can't.

We have been assuming that the lawyers whose conduct is at issue are prosecutors. But what about a government lawyer who litigates discrimination cases? Isn't that as important as crime fighting? Is it also within the "authorized by law" exception? Notably, the Reno Rules extended to DOJ lawyers who engage in civil law enforcement.

"The Sting" (page 134)

This problem gives you an opportunity to discuss some of the questions identified above. First, we have to accept (although we can question) the operation of the McDade amendment imposing on federal prosecutors a state's no-contact rule. Would the rule forbid the contact here? Workman would be using Blakely to elicit incriminating information against Wall. So that facially would seem to violate the rule since Workman knows that Wall has a lawyer on the matter. Wall is a "person" within the meaning of the rule and protected against direct or indirect contact unless an exception applies. Does one? *Hammad* would seem to recognize an "authorized by law" exception for law enforcement so long as Workman does not carry a sham subpoena. But what about wearing a wire? That seemed to be okay with the *Hammad* court. Perhaps this can be justified on the ground that a subpoena is court process where the court has special sensitivity, although the distinction does seem a bit artificial. Also note that the focus of the conversation will be both past bribes and ongoing efforts to conceal the crime. Those ongoing efforts may themselves be criminal, in which case we have not merely a past crime but a current and prospective crime. No one has suggested that the rule can prevent government lawyers from investigating ongoing and prospective crimes, so here at least Workman would seem to be on safe ground. But insofar as Workman uses Blakely to elicit confessions from Wall about past criminal conduct, she may run into trouble. Again we have an artificial distinction because incriminating statements about ongoing crimes (cover-up of bribery) will inevitably include statements about the concluded bribery itself. So how does Workman thread this needle? It would seem virtually impossible to separate the two subjects.

Even after McDade, Workman has an argument that she is free to use Blakely in this way, even if her sole purpose is to gather evidence to prosecute Wall for past crimes. The argument goes this way: McDade obligated federal prosecutors to observe the ethics rules of their state of admission. The no-contact rule has an "authorized by law" exception. *Hammad*, whatever else it did, seems to hold that the conduct would have been allowed but for the sham subpoena and notwithstanding that the prosecutor's effort was to gather evidence of past criminality. In other words, *Hammad* could be read to say that this effort was "authorized by law" within the meaning of the rule. That would allow prosecutors to use undercover agents and informants to elicit incriminating evidence from suspects the prosecutors know are represented on a concluded alleged criminal act. If *Hammad* allows that, then what are we fighting about? There is little else left and McDade will make no difference. But maybe *Hammad* does not allow that. There is a reading of *Hammad* that would view the prosecutor's effort as one to gather evidence of ongoing (not concluded) criminality, specifically a cover-up, through obstruction of justice, of the fact of the underlying crime.

B. IMPROPER ACQUISITION OF CONFIDENTIAL
INFORMATION (page 134)

In the last few years we have seen several cases raising the issue of the propriety of lawyers seeking to "invade" the opponent's case by learning information the opponent considers confidential and which may in fact be protected by the attorney-client privilege **(page 134)**. The difference between the material in this section and the material in the prior section is that the lawyer is seeking to acquire information other than (or not only) from the other lawyer's client or the client's agent or employee. It's a form of espionage. One example concerns the conduct of Sullivan & Cromwell in *Beiny* **(page 134)**. There, the firm allegedly abused procedural rules to get information to which it was not entitled. In *MMR/Wallace*, Judge Burns disqualified a law firm that had attempted to gain information about the opponent's strategy from a former member of its team. Disqualification and other remedies have also followed when lawyers tried to learn their opponents' secrets from expert witnesses **(pages 134-135)**.

Several permutations are worth spotlighting. First, at **pages 134-135**, I summarize and discuss the New York Court of Appeals decision in *Lipin v. Bender*. The Court affirmed dismissal of a case after the plaintiff took defense documents from the defense table during the argument of her motion. After learning of this, the plaintiff's lawyer failed to correct the matter. The court excoriated both the plaintiff and her lawyer, who was later disciplined. A second development is what I call "The Case of the Misdirected Fax." What do you do when your opponent faxes you a document intended for someone else? The discussion on **pages 136-139** shows that the authorities are divided on the question, but the ABA opts for not taking advantage of the error and authority seems to be leaning that way. (I concur.) We also have the New York Court of Appeals decision in *Madden v. Creative Services, Inc.* **(pages 140-141)**. The court refused to recognize a claim for mental distress where the defendants had hired private investigators who infiltrated the office of the plaintiff's counsel and intercepted privileged information. The investigators were caught (and prosecuted) before they could get away with the information. The court, responding to a certified question from the Second Circuit, concluded that any claim against a third party for invasion of the professional privilege "should at least require some element of harm to plaintiffs that arises directly from a breach of the privilege." Supposedly, actual use of the information to the clients' disadvantage would constitute such harm.

The issue arises in the criminal context where the defense alleges that the prosecutor has placed an informant in its camp. What should the defense have to show? Justice White's dissent from a denial of certiorari **(page 139)** identifies the various approaches. In essence, the question is whether the defendant should have to show prejudice? If the remedy were simply disqualification, the courts *might* be more inclined to presume prejudice. But the defendants here generally seek dismissal of the charge, a more extreme remedy. Maybe the better solution is to disqualify the prosecutors who authorized or had access to the protected information. That should inhibit the conduct. On particularly disturbing facts, the South Carolina Supreme Court in *Quattlebaum* both reversed a conviction and disqualified the prosecutor's office. **(Page 140**.)

"Something You Should Know" (page 141)

ABA Opinion 94-382 concludes that the lawyer in a situation like this may receive the documents if not otherwise illegal to do so but should not review them except as needed to determine how to proceed. She should then contact the adverse party's lawyer and follow his instruction or "in the case of a dispute, refrai[n] from using the materials until a definitive resolution of the proper disposition of the material is obtained from a court." The opinion reviews caselaw and also state ethics opinions that would permit the lawyer to use the information even if confidential. In some ways this can be seen as a "testing" problem. Is the lawyer's duty only to avoid illegal conduct? Or is there a "higher" duty? Of course, receipt of the documents *could be* illegal or actionable -- if for example they're stolen or provided in violation of the intermediary's fiduciary duty -- so the lawyer who uses them without inquiry runs a significant risk.

CHAPTER IV

FINANCING LEGAL SERVICES

This is the final chapter in the introduction to the client-lawyer relationship. Lawyers cost money. Someone has to pay. It may be the lawyer herself, should she choose (or be required) to work for free, or it may be the client, or a third person, or an IOLA program, or the state, or the opponent in a fee-shifting case, or some combination of these. The point to be made is that in some sense the client-lawyer relationship is an economic relationship. This may raise conflict and confidentiality issues, among others. These issues will be addressed hereafter. In this chapter, however, we focus mainly on the varieties of possible economic arrangements and rules that forbid or constrain them. The introductory matter (**pages 143-145**) summarizes these points after a couple of well-chosen quotes. Take note of the continuing litigation over the constitutionality of IOLTA plans. The Fifth Circuit's reversal of the lower court's decision upholding the Texas plan is surely to be revisited en banc and in a petition to the Supreme Court (**page 145**). The Ninth Circuit's consideration of the issue is now before that court en banc.

A. THE ROLE OF THE MARKETPLACE (page 146)

The *Brobeck* case (**page 146**) should be interesting to students because it reveals (a) how complicated a retainer agreement can be, (b) how much money can be charged for a rather narrow service if the client is desperate, (c) that contingent fees are not limited to personal injury cases, (d) what a lawyer can get a million (1975) dollars for if he or she has a reputation in a particular area, and (e) the court's standard of review in passing on the challenge to Lasky's fee. The case also permits instructive comparison with *Fordham* (**page 154**).

How can we explain the court's hands-off attitude in *Telex*? Does it turn on the fact that Telex negotiated the fee arrangement through counsel? Was the court evaluating Lasky's work product, his reputation, or his result? Probably all three, plus his immediate availability. Note most prominently the court's test for an unconscionable fee. Both Rule 1.4 and DR 2-106 purport to limit the size of legal fees. That is, the market is not the sole determinant. But what is the limit? The Ninth Circuit definition of unconscionability, taken from the California courts, is a contract that "no man in his senses and not under a delusion would make on the one hand, and as no honest and fair man would accept on the other" (**page 149**). Is that a limit? Is it a limit more restrictive than the test for unconscionability of commercial contracts? Should it be more restrictive? Even if it should, of course, that would not necessarily mean that Brobeck's fee here would be unconscionable.

The note at **pages 149-150** questions the Circuit's standard for unconscionability. It offers the example of a top flight criminal defense lawyer who accept the representation of a person who, it turns out after a few hours of work, was misidentified as the subject of an investigation. Can the lawyer keep what would otherwise be a reasonable $50,000 retainer for someone of his prominence? The answer should be yes if, as the Circuit wrote, the reasonableness of the fee agreement is determined at the time it is made. But see **pages 174-175**. This issue resurfaces in "What Are You Worth?" at **page 162**, a hypothetical that can be great fun to debate.

Hourly or Value Billing? (page 150)

I inject the phenomenon of "value billing" here and elsewhere. Contingent fees are of course the best example of value billing. "You win, I win. You lose, I lose." The issue of value billing also arises under fee-shifting statutes and will be addressed there, too. In fact, I quote from a dissent of Justice Rehnquist's in *City of Riverside v. Rivera* (**page 189**). The dissent is an appeal to value billing in a fee-shifting case. I remind students of this dissent later, in discussing fee-shifting, and in particular in discussing the majority opinion in *City of Burlington v. Dague* (page 190). This note also signals the view of some that hourly billing promotes inefficiency and is a potential source of conflict (**page 151**). See also Professor Ross's work cited in the footnote on **page 151**.

B. UNETHICAL FEES (page 154)

We move now from the marketplace as a limitation on legal fees, with some modest judicial oversight, to the ethics rules as a limitation. Our forum also changes, from civil litigation to discipline. *Fordham* at **page 154** is not an easy decision to defend. The client was not as sophisticated as Telex, to be sure. He was fully informed. No one doubts that Fordham had worked the time, nor did anyone challenge the size of his hourly rate. It's just that $50,000 was too high for the service, no matter what! The upshot is that this contract is out of bounds as a matter of law. The next client to come along in the same situation, eager to agree to the same deal, will be told to go away. The court won't allow it. So the market price for the service has a ceiling set by government. Price controls? See what students think and then press those who disagree with the result using the facts of "What Are You Worth?" below. At **pages 161-162**, I compute Lasky's fee in 1989 dollars, which is when Fordham reached his fee agreement. I have to make an assumption – that Lasky spent 250 hours on the certiorari petition, or about 6 weeks of work. I think this is probably high since Lasky had the Tenth Circuit opinion to work from and a cert petition is not a very long document. In 1989 dollars, Lasky's hourly fee comes out to about $9,000 hourly. Even if we just use Lasky's $25,000 retainer, which he was guaranteed, he earned the same hourly rate as Fordham. So how can we explain the difference? Is it simply because Fordham's client was an individual, although one who certainly knew the arrangement, whereas Lasky's was a large company negotiating through counsel?

"What Are You Worth?" (page 162)

I hope you get to do this problem now and again. The $500 million fee nets out to $166,666 an hour, and it's also 250 times what Scheck would once have charged. (I think I've done the math right.) But so what? The case was not charged on an hourly basis. Big time lawyers who win class actions can get contingent percentages of huge recoveries, so why can't Scheck charge a high absolute fee. It's only two percent of Porgby's wealth, which he'll earn back pretty fast if he's acquitted, which he was. No one's forcing Porgby to hire Scheck. Still, Rule 1.5(a) must mean something. It can't mean that the market is the sole determinant. Otherwise, where the client is knowledgeable and informed, we'd just say that "reasonable" is whatever the market allows. But if that's so, why was Fordham disciplined? If the market controlled, Fordham should have won. Using the test in *Brobeck*, applied to this question, can we say that "no man in his sense and not under a delusion. . . ." yada yada yada. Porgby is a smart guy. He's not under delusion. Stress, yes. Delusion, no. Stress can't be enough.

Notice that when Scheck took the case it was anticipated that the work would take as much as 4000 hours, but it took 3000 hours. Previous users of this problem will notice that I have changed the numbers to give Scheck a better case. But it's still dramatic. Students who side with Scheck have to figure out how to answer Porgby's lawyer's comparison with doctors **(page 163)**. Would we tolerate a brain surgeon charging a billionaire $5 million for an operation that would otherwise cost $200,000? My experience is that even students who support Scheck (and even when Scheck's fee was higher) balk here. Why?

The notes following *Fordham* discuss inherent judicial power to modify fee arrangements **(page 163)**, the greater scrutiny applied to post-retainer fees **(page 164)**, and the wisdom of the requirement that legal fee agreements be in writing **(page 164)**. The last issue is of particular interest because early drafts of the Rules did require written agreements absent special circumstances, but this provision was dropped in the final version. The deletions seem especially self-serving to the bar and not in the interest of those clients who are less sophisticated in dealing with lawyers. In addition to California, other jurisdictions that generally require a written fee agreement, even in non-contingency cases, are the District of Columbia, New Jersey, and Pennsylvania. Virginia requires that fees be "adequately explained to the client" and that the basis or rate of the fee "be furnished on request of the lawyer's client."

I have added a brief note on the improper practice of inflating bills (**page 165**) because there seemed to be a disturbing number of cases imposing discipline for this practice. The issue reappears in Chapter 13D4(a).

The E2K Commission (**page 165**) proposed that a writing be required for legal fees with some exceptions. But the ABA tentatively rejected this requirement in August 2000.

Nonrefundable Fees (page 160)

This brings us to the subject of nonrefundable fees and the New York Court of Appeals' decision in *Matter of Cooperman* (**page 167**). Let me put my cards on the table. I think *Cooperman* is wrong. I quickly add that I can be as cynical about lawyer fees as the next academic. My problem with *Cooperman* is that it paints with too broad a brush. The case could have been decided on its facts (i.e., the law-yer's conduct, the size of the fees, the client's lack of sophistication). There was no need categorically to ban nonrefundable fees and imprudent to do so. Decisions of other courts have been more realistic. (**Pages 171-173.**)

Let's be clear on what we are talking about. The court does not forbid (though it does not define) so-called general retainers. General retainers have always been nonrefundable. In the past, they secured the lawyer's availability and excluded his or her availability to the opponent. Not only couldn't the client get the money back, but the retainer purchased nothing but availability. Actual services were separately billed. A lawyer might argue that promising availability has real value. It guarantees the client that the lawyer will be there. It keeps the lawyer (and others in the same firm) from representing the opponent or accepting other conflicting matters. It may keep the lawyer from accepting wholly unrelated matters, in order to ensure free time. Aren't these legitimate arguments at least to the extent that they are advanced in support of a reasonable nonrefundable general retainer? *Cooperman* seems to say yes. In other words, their availability is a promise lawyers can sell.

Cooperman also permits, but does not define, minimum fees. However, the lower court's decision suggests this definition: A minimum fee is the fee that the client will have to pay for the defined task, if completed, even if the lawyer's hourly rate multiplied by the hours required to complete the task yields a number lower than the minimum fee.

What *Cooperman* does not allow is a "special nonrefundable retainer fee." It purports to define this fee in its second sentence as: "Essentially, such arrangements are marked by the payment of a nonrefundable fee for specific services, in advance and irrespective of whether any professional services are actually rendered." That's all the definition you are going to get.

What this may all mean is that the lawyer who charges a general retainer cannot agree with the client to make any of it available against time or he or she will suffer the consequence. The consequence will be an obligation to refund the portion of the fee that is paid against time but unused. This can work out to a higher fee for the client. The cost of good intentions? Bottom line: You can sell availability and you can sell time but not for the same dollar.

I have tried through a hypothetical set out at **page 166** and continued, following *Cooperman* at **page 170**, to crystallize these issues. The hypothetical imagines a top notch antitrust lawyer whom a client wishes to hire just to be on call with regard to a particular matter. It asks the reader to explain what it is the lawyer would be selling, other than time, and how consistent with *Cooperman* she may do that.

Essentially, what *Cooperman* fails to recognize is that just as a lawyer who charges a general (or even a special) retainer provides value (independent of work), so does a lawyer who *also* makes a portion of that retainer, or even all of it, applicable against time. There is no reason to permit nonrefundability for the former and not the latter. But by doing just that, *Cooperman* requires lawyers and clients, *as a matter of ethics*, to disaggregate the two categories even when it might be in the economic interests of both not to do so and even though both are sophisticated in the purchase and sale of legal services.

The question in each case should be whether, under the circumstances, the fee is reasonable. A lawyer who charges a nonrefundable retainer against time also sells the guarantee of availability, the promise to forego other matters if they will interfere with the required time, and the reality that in accepting the particular matter, the lawyer (and by imputation all of his or her colleagues) will be conflicted out of a range of other matters at least while the retainer is outstanding and perhaps indefinitely after it is over.

The New Jersey Supreme Court has refused to follow *Cooperman* where the facts showed that an informed client and lawyer reached a "package" deal that gave the client a lower fee and the promise of availability and gave the lawyer the promise of work. (**Page 171.**) *Cohen* did not enforce the contract as signed but neither did it uphold the client's claim that it had a right to ignore its promise cost free. In addition to *Cohen*, see *Ryan* (**page 172**), which enforced a fee of a million dollars though the client fired the lawyer weeks into an annual arrangement. The law firm had relied on the package deal and the package deal gave the client certain advantages that buying time "retail" would not have allowed. There was no claim that the lawyers were discharged for cause. *Sather* (**page 172**) also exudes economic realism.

C. CONTINGENT FEES AND STATUTORY LIMITS (page 173)

The introductory material (**pages 173-175**) identifies the multiple ways in which contingent fees can be structured and the factors that influence the size of the contingency. Lawyers are obviously better able to evaluate these factors than most clients, possibly explaining greater judicial control in the field. Florida is among the most protective of contingent fee clients, requiring that their lawyers give them a "bill of rights."

Contingent fees have been the subject of much challenge and criticism of late. The material here will reflect that, including much new material. Defendants who are often sued by lawyers working on contingent fees have mounted repeated efforts to contain the size of those fees. Those efforts may be about to pay off. In any event, the debate is intense and should work well in the classroom.

In *Green v. Nevers* (**page 174**), where the court refused to enforce a one-third contingent fee where the client was not sophisticated and the matter settled quickly through no special effort of the lawyer. The Maryland Appellate Court has declared that the reasonableness of a contingent fee can be assessed as of the time it was reached but, in addition, a fee reasonable when reached can turn out to be unreasonable when the results are in (**page 175**). This position disagrees with the *Brobeck* court's view that reasonableness is determined solely as of the time the agreement is reached, a position that the note material following *Brobeck* suggests is wrong.

Statutory fee ceilings (page 175). Court rules generally limit contingent fees in certain kinds of matters, traditionally personal injury matters. Of late, these rules have been extended to malpractice cases against health professionals, especially doctors (**page 150**), coupled with other rules intended to limit malpractice awards. Doctors believe that the contingency fee structure encourages high malpractice awards. How do they do that? Presumably by making the lawyer fight for every dollar, presumably because he or she gets a percentage of every dollar. We discuss these assumptions below. Here, it is good to note that courts have rejected challenges to contingent fee caps, including rather clever challenges based on the claim that "sliding scale" caps would promote conflicts of interests between lawyers and clients. See *Roa*. (**Page 176**.) Waiver of these caps is not allowed. How does that square with deference to the marketplace? Why shouldn't informed and willing plaintiffs be able to waive the protection of the statute? Compare *Gagnon v. Shoblom*, cited at **page 177**.

Prohibitions on contingent fees in criminal and matrimonial cases (page 177). The Code did not so clearly as the Rules forbid contingent fees in matrimonial cases. I have heard arguments from matrimonial lawyers -- mainly those who represent wives -- that the prohibition on contingent fees does in fact impinge on a wife's ability to get competent counsel. This is especially true, the argument runs, when the wife has no money of her own and can only offer the fee the court may award from the husband's assets during and at the end of the litigation. Since those fees are unpredictable in amount, take time in coming, and are often smaller than the wife's lawyer believes appropriate, the prospect of a court-awarded fee will often be insufficient to entice counsel of choice. A contingency fee, however, which is not within the court's control (except at the extremes) will be sufficient to attract counsel of choice, or so the argument runs.

The argument concludes by emphasizing that the public's interest in denying the wife the right to offer counsel a contingency fee is minimal. This is a good issue to raise in class.

Because contingent fee agreements must be in writing, while non-contingent agreements generally need not be in writing, and because contingent fee agreements are ordinarily forbidden in matrimonial and criminal matters, it is important to be able to identify whether an agreement is or is not contingent. This may seem easy. But look at the *Alexander* opinion at **page 178**. And what about an agreement under which the lawyer charges an hourly rate plus an additional amount to reflect the reasonable value of the legal services, a sum that will partly depend upon the results obtained. Rule 1.5(a)(4) permits this. Just such an oral agreement came before the Pennsylvania Superior Court in *Eckell v. Wilson*, 597 A.2d 696 (1991). After reviewing precedent, the court concluded that the agreement did not call for a contingent fee. All it did was provide for a method of fixing a fee. The attorneys were to be paid regardless of the outcome (the hourly rate). The court said that a contingent fee agreement carries the risk that an attorney will not be paid (presumably at all) if unsuccessful and there was no such risk here. Does that mean that a fee that is only *partly* contingent is not a contingent fee within the meaning of the prohibition? What if the fee were an hourly rate plus five percent of any property recovered in equitable distribution above $100,000? Would this be acceptable on the theory that it was nothing more than a recognition of the reasonable value of a lawyer's service? It would seem to undermine the reasons to reject contingent fees in matrimonial matters.

Other courts have addressed the issue whether inclusion of a "results obtained" factor in a fee agreement converts the agreement into a contingent fee. Agreeing with Pennsylvania is *In re Marriage of Malec*, 562 N.E.2d 1010 (Ill. App. 1990). Disagreeing is *State ex rel. Oklahoma Bar Association v. Fagin*, 848 P.2d 11 (Okla. 1992).

The note material at **page 178** suggests that the ban on contingent fees in criminal matters is appropriate so that lawyers are free to recommend plea bargains without loss of fee. But *is* the ban appropriate? Compare *Maxwell v. Superior Court* (**page 246**), which permitted a criminal defendant to pay a lawyer with the media rights to his story. Why not let the informed client decide whether or not to hire a lawyer in a criminal case on contingency? And what about the lawyer who accepts a criminal matter for a flat fee knowing that he won't get paid unless his client is acquitted and able to earn the money? In effect, this is a contingent fee, though it is not one in form.

Should Contingent Fees Be Outlawed or Further Regulater? (page 179). This question is posed, and Walter Olson's arguments presented, in lieu of a hypothetical. As anyone who reads the editorial columns of the *Wall Street Journal* knows, "contingent fee lawyers" are the bane of humanity, or at least of business and commerce. Olson's book makes a strong argument against contingent fees. They encourage frivolous litigation. They encourage overly aggressive tactics. They give the lawyer a conflict of interest. They turn the lawyer into the client. They encourage the lawyer to make decisions disadvantageous to the client. They are behind much offensive legal advertising. They encourage dishonesty. They diminish professionalism. They cause chicken pox. (Only kidding.) Other countries don't allow them. Why do we?

How do Olson and others believe poor plaintiffs will be able to hire counsel if they can't sell an interest in their recovery? Sure, the lawyers can charge an hourly rate, but they know they will only get paid if they win, and therefore they will increase their hourly rate to account for that risk. So aren't we back at square one, with a contingent fee? Perhaps (were contingent fees banned) lawyers should be forbidden to enhance their hourly rate based on the risk of nonrecovery. See **page 190** for the application of this principle in fee-shifting cases. That way lawyers would only take very strong cases. Is that Olson's objective?

Given the perception that "value added" fees make more sense than hourly billing, laden as hourly fees are with the potential for conflicts and featherbedding, why not embrace contingent fees as the ultimate example of value billing? It is only if the client gets value that the lawyer gets paid. Doesn't Justice Rehnquist's emphasis on value in his *City of Riverside* dissent (**page 151**) support the view that contingent fees make a great deal of sense? Justice Rehnquist himself, nevertheless, joined the majority, which rejected a contingency factor in *City of Burlington v. Dague* (**page 190**).

At **pages 180-181** is a very short summary of the Brickman-O'Connell-Horowitz proposal, as filtered through a California proposition that almost passed, for limiting contingent fees so they only fully apply to the sums the lawyer "earns" and not to the sums that the adverse party is ready to pay pretty quickly. (See the next paragraph.) The effect of this proposal on motivations and strategies of the participants is too complicated to identify here, assuming they can be fully anticipated at all. The proposal makes some sense in any individual case. The danger is that it would deplete the availability or the incentives of counsel generally to the disadvantage of clients as a group. I've had a good time talking about the proposal in class, mostly because it's hard for students who oppose it, as most do, to explain precisely why it's wrong. Obviously, it can't be wrong because it yields lower fees. They have to search for a "structural" justification for their opposition, some unacceptable effect on the "balance of power" in contingent fee litigation generally.

The theoretical justification for the proposal is that it promotes early settlements or, if no settlement occurs, it generates a fairer fee to the client. Why? If the case does not settle, the lawyer gets a full contingent fee only on the "value added," *i.e.*, the amount she recovered above the early offer. But the proposal should also increase the number of early settlements, surely a value. Many matters can settle early, especially if most of the money is going to the plaintiff. Where that is so, the lawyer runs little or no risk and should not be able to defeat the opportunity for early settlement by demanding so large a portion of it that it becomes unattractive to the plaintiff. The proposals mean to create a "window of time," however brief, during which the parties can settle with nearly all of the payment going to the plaintiff. The defendant can be more generous because it saves legal fees too. In other words, transaction costs during this window should be, and properly can be, as low as possible.

Following is an article from the *Wall Street Journal* by an English lawyer. The article questions the American love affair with "loser pays" rules and the growing hostility in the United States to contingent fees. The author makes some excellent points about the danger of simply transposing part of a legal system to a different regime. For one thing, persons other than the legally indigent have access to free or low-cost counsel in England, either through Legal Aid or unions **(pages 181-184)**.

D. MINIMUM FEE SCHEDULES (page 184)

Minimum fee schedules **(pages 184-188)** fell into disfavor long before the *Goldfarb* opinion **(page 185)** in 1975. Probably they are far removed from the consciousnesses of most lawyers today, let alone students. Through them, the bar literally sought to capitalize on its claim of professionalism. How do we reconcile the "new found religion" of professionalism as dedication to the interests of others with the effort, not so long ago, to use it as a reason to price fix? Or am I being too harsh? A defender may say that while fee schedules may have kept prices higher than they would otherwise have been, nevertheless they also kept lawyers more professional than they might otherwise be by enabling them to focus on the interests of the client without worry about competition and cost-cutting.

The disappearance of minimum fee schedules should be seen in conjunction with the cases permitting lawyers to market their services. Together, these events permit lawyers to compete and to make their competition highly visible. Without marketing, the end of minimum fee schedules would not have amounted to much because most clients would not do the kind of price shopping necessary for consumer choice. Maybe that's unfortunate, come to think of it. If a prospective client has to talk to five or six lawyers in order to learn their fees, at least the client will also learn something about the lawyers as people. If, on the other hand, the client can learn about fees simply by opening the newspaper, the danger is that he or she will choose counsel based solely on price. Interesting.

The note material following *Goldfarb* **(page 188)** talks about the application of the antitrust laws to the conduct of the bar, with cross-references to other places in the casebook that the issue arises.

E. COURT-AWARDED FEES (page 188)

1. Determination of Amount (page 188). The law surrounding court-awarded fees has become a mini-industry. It would be impossible, and unprofitable, to plumb its depths in a course on professional responsibility. Nevertheless, the fact of fee-shifting statutes and the manner in which courts go about applying them are important to the larger issue of "financing" legal services. Furthermore, as *Dague* **(page 190)** and *Rivera* **(page 151)** reveal, the Supreme Court, as well as lower courts, is divided over the best and fairest method for determining fees authorized by fee-shifting statutes.

Perhaps the most counterintuitive issue in *Rivera*, if not the most controversial, is the Court's willingness to allow the fee to exceed the size of the recovery. In *Rivera* the excess is enormous. The clients recovered $13,000 and the lawyers recovered $245,000. The full Court, including the dissent, rejected the "contingent-fee model" promoted by the Solicitor General, under which counsel would receive a percentage of the client's recovery. But why is that wrong? Why should we promote litigation that could not sustain itself in the marketplace? One answer, of course, is that fee-shifting is meant to ensure that certain plaintiffs will be able to assert certain claims that would otherwise be unable to attract counsel using market rates. There is something especially worthy about the claim, and its vindication, that has caused the legislature to remove it from ordinary market considerations. Another and perhaps more persuasive answer is our assumption -- but is it correct? -- that a couple of victories like the one in *Rivera* will prevent numerous other instances of civil rights violations. In other words, we are paying the lawyer for the deterrent effect of the work.

Rivera is a long case to assign and can be a difficult case to teach. The fourth edition substituted *Dague* for *Rivera*, although *Dague* is perhaps even harder to teach (I summarize its salient points at **pages 195-196**), because *Dague* is a subsequent case and resolves the issue of whether a lawyer's fee may be enhanced because of the risk of nonrecovery.

In City of *Burlington v. Dague* **(page 190)**, the Supreme Court held that a lawyer who qualifies for a fee under a fee-shifting statute may not receive an enhancement over the "lodestar" to reflect the risk of receiving no payment. The lawyer would receive no payment if his or her client was not successful. Although the legal question is rather straightforward, the different approaches (Scalia for the majority, Blackmun and Stevens in dissent, O'Connor in a separate dissent) are not all that easy to untangle. At **page 195** I list eight reasons for the majority's conclusion. Students should be able to explain each of these reasons and perhaps critique them. For my money, the most persuasive is number seven. Lawyers who achieve modest results, as in *City of Riverside v. Rivera*, still qualify for fees based on their hourly rate, which can yield a payment many times the amount of the recovery. That's good for lawyers. Don't lawyers want it both ways when they ask for a contingency factor as well? Isn't this asking the court to make the lodestar the floor but not the ceiling? Stated another way, perhaps if lawyers are going to be entitled to a contingency enhancement, they should also have to suffer a contingency reduction when a recovery, although entitling them to something, is puny. Under this model, value billing would be a basis for raising or lowering the lodestar. The answer to this proposal is that we make the lodestar the floor in order encourage lawyers to spend the time to bring these cases in the first place, on the assumption that they have underlying social value above and beyond the successful recovery, whatever the size. Even a small recovery, coupled with a generous lodestar, can serve to deter future wrongdoing in the particular area of social concern. While this response has some merit, does it mean that the lodestar must actually be the floor? Why can't the floor be adjusted for value billing (based on the benefit to the plain-tiff) but not less than is necessary to incentivize future lawyers to bring such cases?

The note on **page 197** describes how the courts differently respond in common fund cases, where lawyers obtain an aggregate amount for a class and the court must also set the fee. Then, courts show greater flexibility. They are willing to award risk multipliers and use contingent fees.

"Those Fees Are Outrageous" (page 198)

Many students support the plurality opinion in *City of Riverside*. So I challenge it directly. (That old trick.) In an age when local governments are in dire need of funds, does it make any sense to give two young lawyers a quarter of a million dollars for winning $13,000 on a federal claim? Even crediting the objectives of the statute, wouldn't we encourage other lawyers to bring these actions if they got only a half or a third as much? There are a lot of hungry lawyers out there. Why didn't the Court evaluate how much of a fee was required in order to encourage other lawyers to take these cases? Does anyone believe that it would have come up with the same number? The City of Riverside could have spent the savings for the homeless, the hungry, pre-school programs, prenatal testing, teachers' salaries, police protection. Shouldn't these interests be considered. How dare a federal judge take a quarter of a million dollars of scarce city money and give it to two inexperienced lawyers for the most modest of victories!

2. Settlement Conditioned on Fee Waiver (page 198). The holding in *Evans v. Jeff D.* **(page 198)** was much debated several years ago and, according to my anecdotal evidence, of consequence in public interest law cases still. An instructor can choose to omit *Evans* of course, especially given its length. On the other hand, the case is quite rich and can generate good classroom discussion. With that pedagogical perspective, I have set out six groups of questions specifically focused on the *Evans* reasoning **(pages 210-213)**. Not all of them must be covered.

One issue in *Evans* is the conflict of interest between lawyer and client. The lawyer has a real interest in the fee promised by the fee-shifting statute but the client has the apparent authority to waive that fee. Consequently, the defense can divide the lawyer and his or her client by making an attractive offer to the plaintiff contingent on fee-waiver. This is true whether or not the plaintiff's case is a class action. Of course, plaintiff's counsel can protect himself or herself by looking to plaintiff for the fee, possibly to come out of the recovery plaintiff accepts, but often this is unrealistic either because plaintiff's counsel is at a public interest law office that will not take money from plaintiff's recovery or because plaintiff's recovery is small or not a cash recovery at all.

In Justice Stevens' view, there is no ethical conflict because plaintiff's lawyer had no "*ethical* obligation to seek a statutory fee award. His ethical duty was to serve his clients loyally and competently" How does this dismissal of the ethical dilemma comport with the recognition in the Code and Rules that conflict between the interests of lawyer and client may caution against, or even prohibit, acceptance of a matter? See Chapter 5A. That is, if the easy answer is that the lawyer, no matter how strong his or her interests, has an obligation to the client's interest over the lawyer's personal interest, then there is no need to worry about any lawyer-client conflicts because the lawyer will always do the right thing. Can Justice Stevens be criticized for not realizing that in some matters conflicting interests make the risk of disloyalty too great to tolerate, notwithstanding the lawyer's "ethical duty . . . to serve his clients loyally and competently"?

Evans is not directly concerned with a different kind of risk that arises in cases with fee-shifting statutes. That is the risk of a "sweetheart" deal between plaintiff's lawyer and the defendant. The defense might seek to buy off the lawyer by offering a generous fee as part of a settlement package in return for persuading the client to take less than the client should reasonably receive. *Prandini v. National Tea Co.*, 557 F.2d 1015 (3d Cir. 1977). Inspired by avoidance of that risk, *Ramirez* and *Coleman* **(page 212)** do forbid simultaneous negotiation of merits and fee under state law. Compare the prohibition against aggregate settlements of claims. See Rule 1.8(g). The danger there is that one of two claimants will be favored to the disadvantage of the other. That danger could also apply when one of the two claimants is a lawyer seeking a fee under a fee-shifting statute.

Justice Stevens seems to identify an exception to the ruling: If a lawyer reasonably believed that the defendant had no realistic defense and that the defendant's offer to settle contingent on a fee waiver was part of a "vindictive effort to deter attorneys," what could the lawyer do if the client wanted to accept the settlement anyway? Wouldn't the lawyer's obligation be to defer to the client just as in *Evans*? What could the judge do? Who would raise the issue?

Question 2 **(page 210)** recognizes that the Supreme Court's opinion does not foreclose adoption of an ethical rule that would forbid simultaneous negotiation of counsel fees and settlement, does it? A proposed California solution (rejected by its high court) prohibited conditional offers. Notice the exception for a lump sum offer. How would a plaintiff's lawyer properly proceed if he or she received a lump sum offer?

Question 2 also contains the language of an unenacted provision intended to "overrule" *Evans*. But one must also ask how this provision would actually work in practice.

Lawyers in private practice who are prepared to take cases under fee-shifting statutes only because of the prospect of a fee and not because the case would otherwise be "worth it" might attempt to respond to *Evans* by asking the client to waive his or her authority to waive the fee. Or the client could be asked to assign the fee to the lawyer. Question 3 **(page 211)** asks whether this would be unethical, possibly on the ground that it gives the lawyer "a proprietary interest in the cause of action or subject matter of litigation" within the meaning of Rule 1.8(j). But how would it differ from a contingent fee? Such an assignment or waiver would limit the client's right to decide whether or not to settle, which contingent fees do not do. Often the lawyers right to approve the fee will amount to veto power on the merits. California Opinion 1994-136, cited in Question 3, would allow a lawyer to ask the client to agree at the outset not to waive or negotiate counsel fees until settlement on the merits is concluded.

No member of the Court would have forbidden simultaneous negotiation of the fee and the merits, but Justice Brennan would give the trial judge the duty to review the final package, even in non-class actions. The majority protests the volume of work that would generate. **(Page 203, note 30**.) What would the trial judge do under Justice Brennan's analysis? If the package were presented and agreeable to everybody, can you imagine a trial judge rejecting it? If the terms were agreeable to plaintiffs, could their counsel object because she was disappointed? If the judge lowered the fee, would counsel have the right to withdraw his or her assent to the settlement? If the trial judge *raised* the fees portion, would a defendant have that right? The answer to both questions in Justice Brennan's view apparently is yes. See Question 5 **(page 211)**.

Finally, Question 6 **(page 212)** asks why the entire Court rejected the resolution of the New York City Bar Association, which, before *Evans*, prohibited simultaneous negotiation of fees and merits in public interest cases. There is, of course, the danger that defendants will be unwilling to settle because they will not know what the full package will cost them. The lump sum solution in California removes that danger. The New York City Bar Association envisioned that the defense lawyer could ask the plaintiff's lawyer to reveal his or her hourly rate and the number of hours spent on the matter. Perhaps the plaintiff's lawyer could be asked to reveal what he or she would seek in counsel fees, so long as there was no negotiation. Why wouldn't this have been an appropriate solution? States are still free to adopt it as an ethical matter, as did the two courts cited here.

F. MANDATORY PRO BONO PLANS (page 213)

When a lawyer works for free the lawyer (or her firm) pays for the lawyer's time. When the lawyer does that because she chooses to do that, all well and good. But can a lawyer be ordered to perform free service as a condition of her license? Even if the answer is yes, as the 1980 Kutak Draft **(page 213)** assumed, should a lawyer be so ordered? If so, what should the mandatory pro bono plan look like? Specifically: How much time should the lawyer have to give? Should all lawyers be obligated, including lawyers who work for government, judges, law professors, lawyers who don't practice law, lawyers who have retired? How should the plan be policed? Should a lawyer be able to "buy" his or her way out of it with a cash grant to the local legal services office? Should a lawyer (a partner) be able to designate another lawyer (e.g., an associate) to satisfy the partner's obligation? Should a firm of a hundred lawyers be able to satisfy the collective obligation of its partners and associates on a firm-wide basis -- *e.g.*, by hiring a lawyer who does pro bono work only? (If so, isn't this buying your way out of it?) And perhaps the hardest question of all: How shall we define the category of "work" that satisfies the pro bono obligation? Working for poor people directly? Working on test-case litigation? Working on a bar association committee? Arguing a Supreme Court case for a civil liberties group?

Before we get to the detail, however, the threshold question is whether mandatory pro bono is a good idea. Deborah Rhode makes a case for mandatory pro bono, both in the profession and the law school, at **page 215**.

The Florida Supreme Court has instituted (and refused to reconsider) a voluntary pro bono plan which requires lawyers to report their pro bono activities **(pages 214-215)**. Two state supreme court judges were prepared to make the obligation mandatory and two others were not willing to create a voluntary plan accompanied by a reporting obligation.

Take a look at the Lubet & Stewart article summarized at **page 218**. It argues that the state can require pro bono work (or payments) because the state gives lawyers "assets" that enhance the value of their services, namely loyalty and confidentiality duties (including privileges). There's something to that. Didn't we recognize, after *Upjohn*, the increased value of hiring lawyers to conduct internal corporate investigations? See **page 50**. So maybe now it's payback time.

G. WHO GETS THE MONEY? (page 219)

This chapter concludes with a discussion about the division of legal fees.

Division within a firm **(page 220)** is virtually entirely unregulated. The owners of the firm decide who gets what. One factor is a lawyer's ability to get clients. If the firm is really a firm (see below), a lawyer can ethically be compen-sated (and handsomely) simply for getting business without ever having to do one day of legal work. At **page 221** I signal the debate over provisions in partnership agreements that deny departing partners funds to which they might otherwise be entitled if they enter into a competing practice. The New York Court of Appeals has invalidated such a provision but the California Supreme Court has allowed them if reasonable. As with *Cooperman* (**page 167**), we have a contest between a categorical rule and a rule of reason. In *Hackett v. Milbank, Tweed, Hadley & McCloy*, the partnership agreement had an arbitration clause. The departure provision, drafted after *Cohen*, tied post-departure compensation not to the departing partner's work but to his or her post-departure income. The partner would lose a dollar in post-departure pay-out for every dollar he or she earned over $100,000. The lower courts, relying on *Cohen*, invalidated this provision, but the New York Court of Appeals remanded the dispute to arbitration. The arbitrator found that the provision did not violate *Cohen*, but then the lower courts vacated the arbitrator's award on the ground that it was against public policy. The New York Court of Appeals reversed. If you are interested in this area of law, you should look at Robert Hillman's book entitled *Lawyer Mobility* (1994).

At **pages 222-223**, I reference several cases that place limits on what a lawyer in a law firm may do covertly to seek to move his or her practice and when the lawyer must alert his or her colleagues.

Detailed rules govern fee divisions by unaffiliated lawyers. (**Pages 223-224**.) The Code prohibited compensation if a lawyer did not work on a matter, notwithstanding that the lawyer was the source of the matter. The Rules changed that, subject to certain requirements. But why should it make a difference whether two lawyers are affiliated? What are we worried about? Brokering cases? If the answer is yes, why *should* we worry? And if we should worry, then why allow an unaffiliated lawyer *ever* to get compensation for work he or she does not do? One answer might be that we just can't stop it. Another answer might be that denial of compensation discriminates in favor of partners and against unaffiliated lawyers for no good reason. So long as the referring lawyer is willing to accept responsibility for any liability arising out of the recipient lawyer's malpractice, aren't the two in a kind of *de facto* firm?

PART II

CONFLICTS OF INTEREST

CHAPTER V

CONCURRENT CONFLICTS OF INTEREST

This is the first of two chapters on conflicts of interest. This chapter deals with concurrent conflicts. The next deals with successive conflicts. Of course, conflicts of interest appears as an issue throughout the book, including in the material on legal fees, lawyers for entities, and malpractice. It's probably safe to say that each of us spends a significant amount of time on conflicts of interest, although few if any of us cover every corner of it every year. It is also fair to say that most of our students, to the extent they confront a significant issue of professional responsibility at all, will have to deal with a potential or actual conflict, either of their own, a colleague's, or an opponent's. Not only is the conflict material important for this immediate reason, but it is also important because the scope of the conflict rules will to some extent delimit the career paths of lawyers, the lure of specialization, the size and work of law firms, and the willingness of lawyers to spend time in public service.

I consider much of Chapter 5 and perhaps all of Chapter 6 to be central to the course and urge you to assign them. In Chapter 5, do assign, at least for home reading, **pages 229-235**, which provides the student with a road map of the ensuing material. All of this stuff will be explored in some detail hereafter, but a bird's eye view at this point makes good sense. I also believe that Chapter 5A should be assigned, even though some of it can be left to home reading. The material on business interests (Chapter 5A1) is the most important. The material on related lawyers **(page 251)** is less important but interesting. The "Karen Horowitz" problem **(page 256)** is always a joy to teach and is available on video. The few pages on financial interests in client matters **(pages 239-242)** can be read at home, perhaps briefly mentioned in class, but should be assigned because of the ubiquity of the rule.

A Typology of Conflicts (pages 229-235). These pages briefly explain why the subject is important and then list the variety of conflicts a lawyer may encounter. They distinguish between concurrent and successive conflicts and identify the considerations that affect the definition of each. They introduce the student to the idea of imputed or vicarious conflicts and to the "revolving door" issue. Finally, they identify the advocate-witness rule. They are dense pages, yes, but an excellent map to the following material here and in Chapter 6. So long as students understand that they don't have to have perfect knowledge based on these pages alone, this early familiarity with the terrain will makes it easier to traverse later (and provides a handy summary at the end).

A. CLIENT-LAWYER CONFLICTS (page 235)

1. Business Interests (page 235). Students were introduced to the fact that deals between lawyers and their clients are viewed with suspicion if they read the material on post-retainer fee agreements (page 141). This point is now brought home dramatically by the principal case and the note material following. The note separates lawyer-client business deals from a separate, less intuitively apparent, prohibition -- the one against lawyers accepting financial interests adverse to their clients. The story of Gus at **pages 241-243** reveals the dangers when lawyers have interests adverse to their clients and the harsh view courts will take of these actions in discipline.

Matter of Neville **(page 235)** is an intimidating case. It is a useful case to teach because it begins with an analysis of whether a professional relationship existed. It did even though all agree that the client was not the client of the lawyer on the immediate matter. It was enough that he was the client on other matters. Neville was disciplined even though Bly was sophisticated in real estate matters and dictated the economic terms of the transaction. In appears that Neville was mostly a scrivener. However, even though Bly dictated the transaction's economic terms, the documents still required resolution of legal issues and the court concludes that these issues were resolved favorably to Neville.

Note, too, that the court was construing the less demanding provision of the Code, DR 5-104(A), which then applied. Rule 1.8(a) imposes yet stronger obligations on lawyers. In my opinion, Rule 1.8(a), with its reference to "pecuniary interests adverse to a client," makes the rule applicable to lawyer-client fee agreements entered during the professional relationship. The only case I know of that has ruled on this question concluded otherwise **(page 239)** after recognizing "compelling arguments" each way. In my view, if lawyers and clients are going to enter agreements in which their economic interests are adverse, these will most likely be agreements over the terms of retention rather than anything else. Eliminating the protection of Rule 1.8(a) in these circumstances is unwise. In the *Renouf* case, the judge said that the protections were not necessary because the new agreement, a contingent fee agreement, was governed by Rule 1.5(c). Perhaps the opinion can be limited to those situations in which the post-retainer fee agreement is a contingent fee agreement. But even then, Rule 1.5(c) does not provide the same degree of protection that Rule 1.8(a) provides.

The note following *Neville* identifies other deals lawyers may have with clients. *Greene* **(page 239)** relies on fiduciary duty and students should understand that predicate for the rule. Further, in *Greene*, the "deal" was really an interest in the client's trust. *Schlanger* **(page 241)** holds that the client's sophistication is no defense to a failure to observe the rule when entering a contract with him.

Especially instructive is *Berkowitz* (**page 242**), where a lawyer's *partner's* business interest was imputed to the lawyer for purposes of the conflict rules. How hard will this extension be to police in a 500 lawyer firm? Yet, Rule 1.10 would work the same imputation if "knowingly" done (one of the rare instances of a mens rea requirement in conflict rules).

The "Internet Startups" note at **pages 243-245** responds to the appearance of law firm investment in these companies in the 1990s.

2. Media Rights (page 245). *Maxwell* (**page 246**) presents one state's rejection of the general rule that an attorney and client cannot enter agreements under which the client gives the lawyer media rights on the subject of the representation prior to its conclusion. *Maxwell* did not explicitly rest on the Sixth Amendment right to counsel, although it cited Supreme Court cases construing that right. *Wheat* (**page 271**) suggests that any such reliance would not have been persuasive in any event. In *Wheat*, the Supreme Court upheld the trial judge's discretionary refusal to allow the defendant to change counsel. The trial judge apprehended a conflict of interest between the interests of the defendant and other clients of the lawyer. The likelihood of that conflict was not very strong, especially when placed against the likelihood of the conflict in *Maxwell*. At least one California appellate court (**page 246**) has adhered to *Maxwell* after *Wheat*. The text questions the wisdom of the New York State Bar Opinion (**page 247**) allowing a prosecutor in a celebrated homicide case to sell the rights to her life story after the conclusion of the case. Isn't there a public interest in avoiding the inference that the prosecutor handled the case in a way that would enhance its publicity value after it was over? Or is that interest too flimsy to overcome a First Amendment claim? Compare prosecutorial conflicts at **page 284**.

3. Financial Assistance and Proprietary Interests (page 247). A draft of the Rules would have allowed lawyers to advance medical and living expenses with repayment contingent on outcome. Rule 1.8(e), 1981 draft. The change was deleted by the final version. Do such restrictions make it harder for poorer litigants to resist, for example, the ability of well-heeled defendants (*e.g.*, insurance companies) to delay efforts to collect for injuries? Does the prohibition against clients assigning lawyers a proprietary interest in their claims, and the one against assigning literary rights, discriminate against clients who have nothing to offer to retain the lawyer of their choice but an interest in their causes and stories? Rule 1.8(d), (j). Why not let an informed client take whatever conflict risk he or she wants to take? We allow waiver in other situations. See Rule 1.8(f) (lawyer may accept fee from A to represent B despite potential conflict). The Florida Supreme Court has recognized a "humanitarian" exception to the prohibition on financial assistance (**page 247**). That decision was over a strong dissent. Why such reluctance? Do we really think that giving a client a few hundred dollars is going to corrode the lawyer's independence?

What do students think of the Maryland court's policy explanation for what otherwise seems a heartless rule -- *i.e.*, to avoid having lawyers bid for cases by offering living expenses at increasingly higher levels of luxury? What do they think about California's solution **(page 249)**, which would allow lawyers to advance such money after employment? Is it possible to police this limitation? Some states are more tolerant of lawyers who advance living and medical expenses than is Rule 1.8(e). The Seventh Circuit case on **page 249** presents a federalism issue. The Seventh Circuit refused to abide by Illinois' limitation on the advancement of litigation costs in a federal class action.

4. Fee-Payor Interests (page 249). The Rules blanketly allow one person to pay a lawyer to represent another, subject to cautions, yet here too there are real risks of disloyalty, as *Wood v. Georgia* **(page 249)** reveals. Why are we so tolerant of the practice? Of course, a permissive rule increases the likelihood that private lawyers will get private clients. But there are good policy reasons as well. Relatives can retain lawyers for relatives, friends for friends. The dangers come when people in superior economic positions retain lawyers for economic subordinates, as in *Wood*, because the lawyer will not want to antagonize the "boss," who may be the lawyer's client in other contexts. Consider also the frequent circumstance when an organization is under investigation and it retains counsel for its officers and employees who may receive grand jury subpoenas. The organization may retain a single lawyer for everybody or a separate lawyer for each person, but in either event the organization pays the lawyer's fee. We witnessed this phenomenon in the investigations of Drexel Burnham Lambert and other Wall Street firms. See *United States v. Jones*, 900 F.2d 512 (2d Cir. 1991), *cert. denied*, 111 S.Ct. 131 (1991). The employee is in a particularly difficult situation because he or she will often be unable to afford counsel otherwise.

Maternowski has particularly good, if simple, facts. The student has to figure out why the fee payor's interest, coupled with the "no bargaining" policy of counsel, created a conflict of interest. The court seems to say that the two together made out the violation and that either alone would be insufficient. The answer, presumably, is that bargaining might have led to the fee payors themselves, which may be the very reason they chose this counsel. But does that mean that lawyers can never accept money from AB to represent CD when CD has information about AB that she can use to cut a deal with the D.A.? No, the case cannot be taken that far. It was the fact of the lawyers' policy, and the likelihood that they were chosen by the fee payor because of it, that made the difference. But why should that matter? Will the payor's interest in protecting himself make the lawyers any more committed to their policy? One must wonder whether the court is really angry about the policy generally but could not sanction the lawyers under Rule 1.8(f) for the policy alone. It is interesting to separate out the two strands, although the court relied on them conjunctively. Strand One: Can a lawyer take money from AB to represent XY, when XY has

74

information that will incriminate AB? Strand Two: Can a lawyer ever have a "no bargaining policy," even when the client agrees? Will that policy by a guarantee of ineffective assistance in some circumstances? At the very least, the lawyer would have to transmit proposed prosecutorial deals.

5. Related Lawyers and Significant Others (page 251). *Gellman v. Hillel* **(page 251)** is a neat little case to use as a platform for discussing imputation of conflicts within a family, here husband and wife. The wife had defended the doctors whom the husband was now suing. The court is not convinced that the two matters are substantially related, but goes on to conclude that it wouldn't matter even if they were, citing ABA and case authority for the proposition that conflicts will not automatically be imputed within the marriage, not even when the husband's success on the matter will benefit the family, and therefore the wife, financially. Truth to tell, we are taking a gamble here that we might not take in a purely commercial situation. The reason: A tighter rule might seriously impede the freedom of lawyer-relatives to pursue their callings. Statistically, this might most seriously affect women, although not only women. The note material at **pages 252-254** explore other authorities. In one of my classes, students challenged the requirement that a lawyer may, in some circumstances, have to reveal the intimate personal relationship with another lawyer. Doesn't that invade the first lawyer's privacy? What if it is a relationship the first lawyer wishes to keep secret? The *Croken* and *Hernandez* cases at **page 253** and **page 254** show that this issue continues to appear.

6. A Lawyer's Legal Exposure (page 254). This material is self-explanatory. For some reason, there has been a mild increase in the number of cases in which lawyers are disqualified because they are somehow at risk in the underlying action. The Second Circuit looks on waiver as a solution to this problem with some disfavor, perhaps because even a waiver will not prevent the criminal defendant from later claiming that the lawyer's conflict rendered him or her ineffective. The Second Circuit's view can, undoubtedly, be traced to the Supreme Court's holding in *Wheat* **(page 271)**.

7. Gender, Religion, Race (page 256). Although not conventionally viewed as a subject for conflicts analysis, a lawyer's interest in particular work may conflict with the client's interest in "casting" the lawyer's role with attention to advantages that can come from particular attributes. "Karen Horowitz's Dilemma" raises that issue and is buttressed by the note material following, which describes Roger Baldwin's view and the history of the school prayer case in the Supreme Court **(pages 258-260)**.

"Karen Horowitz's Dilemma" (page 256)

This case history has generated exceptionally good class discussion. It raises an unusual conflict problem, at least unusual here because the reason for the firm's decision is frankly stated. Karen Horowitz complains because she is losing an important professional opportunity as a result of her religion. The same complaint can be sparked by any of a number of other reasons -- gender, race, national origin, even sexual orientation. How about appearance? ("We want a good looking lawyer before the jury.") A number of you have talked to me about this hypothetical. A few of you have confirmed my experience. In class, a majority, often a large majority, of students willing to speak up support the firm's decision, if reluctantly. After class, students who were not willing to speak up are incensed at the support.

One teacher from a southern school called to tell me that he could not teach this problem because I call southerners "fundamentalist rednecks". I pointed out that it was not "I" who called them that but J. Blair Thomas. That indeed may be a basis for some discussion. Has Thomas too casually assumed the bias of the prospective jury, leading him too quickly to remove Horowitz from the case? Let us not, however, dump on Thomas as a way to sidestep the larger question this case history contains. Assume alternatively that Thomas has good reason to worry. If so, is the firm's decision defensible? After all, no hurt will befall Horowitz's career. If the client loses, the firm has less to "explain" and, perhaps most important, as Thomas said, haven't lawyers always staffed cases in a way calculated to appeal to local biases, including use of local counsel? If a trial is a kind of drama, it requires good casting, doesn't it?

Following are some suggestions for teaching "Karen Horowitz" that I wrote in connection with the use of this problem on videotape:

While it is tempting to view this problem from a realpolitik perspective, a different view is also possible. Under it, we try to anticipate the consequence of numerous decisions like the one Thomas has made. Won't it happen that lawyers of a particular gender, race, or religion in particular areas of the country will be excluded from certain kinds of matters because of what will be defended as entirely rational "casting" decisions? If the county in which Thomas's firm will try this case will have a jury hostile to a female Jewish trial lawyer, does that mean that (when there is a choice) firms in that county will not hire female Jewish trial lawyers (or female trial lawyers, or Jewish trial lawyers)? Through a "tyranny of small decisions" won't we ultimately direct lawyers of particular gender, race, national origin or religion into certain areas of practice in certain areas of the country?

An answer to this answer is that perhaps we will. Nevertheless, correcting for fundamental bias cannot be the function of staffing decisions of law firms. Those corrections must come from other sources. Further, if law firms have to fear discrimination or like actions as a result of decisions not to put certain lawyers in certain positions, won't we simply push the conduct "underground?" Law firms will avoid hiring lawyers who they would be reluctant to place on certain matters so that they cannot later be challenged for a particular staffing decision.

I now want to look at this problem from a different perspective, not as a matter of what the right decision is or is not, but as a matter of process. The scene suggests that Karen was simply presented with the decision after Blair and the client reached it. Is what we have here then a management failure? One question is why the firm was unable to anticipate the danger at the outset. That will ordinarily be possible although, of course, sometimes it will not be. In any event, whenever the decision was made, should the firm have discussed it with Karen beforehand? This doesn't mean that Karen will have the final say, but only that she is part of the team that reviews the issue. If the issue could have been anticipated from the beginning, perhaps the firm should have been willing to defer to Karen's preference <u>not</u> to work on a case she would not be allowed to follow into the courtroom, even if as the most junior member of the trial team. If the issue could not have been identified until later, then Karen is at least more likely to be understanding (if not happy) if she can join Blair and the client in evaluating the risks and determining the proper course of conduct. In fact, Karen might give Blair and the client insights about the issue that have not occurred to them. Given the significance of the issue, Blair might have invited participation from other lawyers in the firm (e.g., the management committee) in addition to Karen, both as regards this case and generally.

One further pedagogical suggestion: I take a student and say: "Lee, you're an associate at Jones and Smith. A partner calls you and says drop everything and come to court to sit at counsel table in a matter now on trial. It seems the partner thinks that having you at counsel table will enhance things with the jury because. . . ." What you say next depends on whom you've chosen. It could be "because the jury has a Korean American on it" where Lee is a Korean American; or it could be "because the jury has a lot of young men or women on it" where Lee is an attractive young woman or man," and so on. Lee is being used for his or her appearance. If Lee says s/he'll go, I remind Lee that he or she is a trust and estates associate who has nothing to do with this case or even with litigation. What if Lee is a paralegal? A secretary? A nonlawyer hired for the occasion? How far are we willing to go in accepting that selection of a trial team is like casting a movie?

The material at **pages 258-260**, taken from a biography of Roger Baldwin, a founder of the American Civil Liberties Union, is pertinent to the "Karen Horowitz" story. Baldwin had no hesitation in choosing lawyers in part based on their ethnic or racial identification. He explains why. For Baldwin, establishing the civil liberty principle was more important than being an equal opportunity client. The Baldwin material is followed with some interesting history about the selection of a lawyer to argue a school prayer case **(page 260)**.

B. CLIENT-CLIENT CONFLICTS (page 260)

Here you might choose to concentrate only on conflicts in civil matters, although from time to time it is well-worth dipping into the criminal arena. Some teachers will often or occasionally emphasize criminal law issues throughout the course. The conflict issues surrounding defense lawyers is more interesting to teach than the conflict issue surrounding prosecutors, which rarely arises in a visible way. When a defense lawyer is disqualified, the defendant loses counsel of choice, a constitutional right. Whenever studying a conflict problem, I suggest a detailed description of the facts of the case and the nature of the alleged conflict. Exactly what might the lawyer be tempted to do in derogation of a loyalty or confidentiality obligation? For example, in *Cuyler* (**page 261**), the lawyers might have been tempted to short sell Sullivan's defense in order to preserve options for their later defense of Carchidi and DiPasquale. Because conflicts issues are so fact specific, solving them requires close factual analysis. This is true however the issue arises.

1. Criminal Cases (Defense Lawyers) (page 260). In order to win, Sullivan had to prove that "an actual conflict of interest adversely affected his lawyer's performance." He had to show that his lawyer did or did not do something because of the conflict. That's a difficult burden. Or is -- or should -- the burden be lighter? Justice Marshall thinks it should be enough to show that the lawyer had an actual conflict without showing precisely how the conflict affected his performance, a test he views as "unduly harsh" and "incurably speculative." In the majority's view, would the defendant have to prove that he would likely have been acquitted but for the conflict? The note material following *Cuyler* (**page 266**) reveals multiple perspectives on the issues of "effect" and causation. Does the Third Circuit on remand follow the majority view, or Justice Marshall's? It would appear to be the former. *Ortiz* is less clear, but it too probably found an actual effect on conduct. So did *McConico*. But none of these cases required the defendant to show that but for counsel's conduct, he would have been acquitted.

One solution is to give each defendant separate counsel. But that's expensive. It also makes it a bit harder for the defendants to mount a "stonewall" defense. What is the propriety of a stonewall defense? So long as the defendants' interests remain congruent, there would seem to be no ethical objection to a single counsel. See Justice Frankfurter's view at **page 263**.

I have augmented this note material to take into account the imminent decision in the Supreme Court in *Mickens* (**page 270**). *Mickens* asks whether the conflict there is of a kind that requires the defendant to show an effect on performance or whether, as in *Holloway*, reversal is automatic. (Even if the answer is the former, there may have been an effect on performance.) Because of *Mickens*, and because it has intellectual interest, I have included a self-explanatory note on *Holloway* error (**page 269**). Note that the Ninth Circuit has disagreed with the *Mickens* court (**page 270**). Also added to the note material following *Cuyler* is *Lettley*, which gives us a colloquy between defense counsel and the trial judge and also a clear conflict that the judge failed to recognize **(pages 267-268)**.

This material is easy to understand and provides a good introduction to client-client conflicts, although in a criminal context. Students have to think about the lawyering that would be necessary adequately to represent one client and how that work might negatively affect the other client. Students also have to understand proof of actual harm, proof of an effect on conduct, and automatic reversal.

In *Wheat* **(page 271)**, the Court employed a highly deferential standard of review to uphold a trial judge's refusal to allow the defendant to switch attorneys. The trial judge concluded (and the government argued) that the new attorney had a conflict of interest by virtue of his representation of other persons who would not, however, be defendants at the same trial. The probability of an actual conflict was quite remote, as the dissent stresses. Surely, had the case gone to trial, with Wheat's chosen lawyer, and Wheat were convicted, he would have been unable to establish a Sixth Amendment violation as defined in *Cuyler*. What is the reason to deny a defendant, who is prepared to waive any conflict, counsel of choice when it could be said with confidence that presence of that counsel would not lead to a Sixth Amendment violation? Or even if it would? Defendants can waive other constitutional rights. Why not this one? *Wheat* seems to say it is because of the need for public confidence in guilty verdicts. Is that a legitimate justification? Is it legitimate when the threat is as tenuous as in *Wheat*? (Not in my view.) True, the convicted defendant, despite waiver, may nevertheless later assert an ineffectiveness claim. The Court doesn't say that that claim should be entertained but notes "without passing judgment" that lower courts have been receptive to them despite waiver. It is worthwhile, again, to identify in class exactly why it was that Iredale's representation of Bravo and Gomez-Barajas presented a conflict with his representation of Wheat.

The note material at **page 278** reveals prosecutorial willingness (eagerness?) to harvest *Wheat* to persuade courts to reject conflict waivers. Sometimes courts go even farther than *Wheat*. Why couldn't Stites use Brooks in his trial **(page 280)**? What does Judge Noonan mean when he writes that nothing in ethics rules permit Brooks to say one thing for one defendant and the opposite for another? The question should be whether the rule forbids it. Perhaps Judge Noonan means that Brooks' credibility as an effective advocate for Stites was constitutionally impossible given what she said as an advocate for Dark. If Stites, knowing all, still wants Brooks, should we say he can't have her? This is different from *Wheat*. There's nothing Brooks can't do or say on Stites' behalf because of a duty to another client, is there? Dark's case is over.

Stites is not alone in perhaps going even beyond *Wheat* in disqualifying defense counsel. Two recent cases, *Loyal* **(page 279)** and *Lanoue* **(page 281)**, seem to take the *Wheat* authority to new heights (or depths). Perhaps this is because courts simply don't want to reverse convictions once the trial has been held and there is no other error. The inability to appeal a disqualification before trial means the consequences of disqualification are significant. Maybe the appealability rule should be reexamined.

The note at **pages 282-283** concerns the appealability of disqualification orders in criminal cases. The lingering question is whether or not we will require a convicted defendant, who is not allowed an interlocutory appeal of a disqualification order, to prove prejudice after conviction. Note that the Seventh Circuit allows interlocutory appeals of disqualification of prosecutors in order to ensure that the decision will be reviewable.

"All or Nothing" (page 283)

Simon will probably have to withdraw from representing all defendants. At the very least, he will have to withdraw from representing Snyder. The case is based on *Thomas v. Foltz*, 818 F.2d 476 (6th Cir.), *cert. denied*, 108 S. Ct. 198 (1987). In it, Thomas ("Snyder") succumbed to counsel's encouragement to plead guilty along with his two co-defendants. The prosecutor's offer was a package deal. The murders occurred in the course of a burglary by the three men. Thomas denied shooting either of the victims. I think that's important. An independent lawyer might have been able to persuade the prosecutor to be more generous toward Thomas, especially if Thomas was willing to testify against his co-defendants. Thomas was the last to agree to the package deal. The joint counsel testified that he "had to lean on the defendants" much more than usual, but he believed that they had no practical alternative. He had rejected offering to have Thomas testify against the other two because that would have been "grossly unfair" since he was representing all three.

Alternatively, an independent lawyer might have been more willing to pursue aggressively Thomas's interest in going to trial. The actual lawyer was not entirely free to do that because his other two clients wanted to accept the deal.

The *Thomas* court begins with the *Strickland* test but adapts it to the guilty plea context. Although joint representation is not automatically ineffective assistance, here the joint representation caused common counsel "to forego . . . potential plea negotiations" under which Thomas might have testified against the other two. Given the "all or nothing" nature of the plea agreement, counsel "was effectively precluded from engaging in any separate plea negotiations on Thomas' behalf, which may have been detrimental to the interests of [the co-defendants]. Furthermore, in order to obtain the benefit of the plea agreement for [the co-defendants, counsel] found himself in a position where he needed to place pressure on Thomas to also accept the plea agreement."

Having established ineffectiveness, the court inquires whether counsel's conduct had an adverse effect. The issue was whether Thomas' guilty plea was voluntary given the conflict, but there need not "be a showing of prejudice as normally required under *Strickland*; rather if the defendant is able to demonstrate that a conflict of interest had an adverse impact on the voluntariness of his guilty plea, prejudice will be presumed." The court cites *Strickland* and *Cuyler*. The magistrate had concluded that Thomas had pled guilty because of counsel's pressure, which was in turn motivated by a desire to "prevent the plea agreement from collapsing." The circuit court found "this analysis persuasive." The court continued:

> In order to protect the interests of [the co-defendants], it was incumbent on [counsel] to convince Thomas to plead guilty, even though Thomas was reluctant and was not in the same situation as [co-defendants]. As Thomas testified at sentencing, he did not shoot either of the victims. This testimony was corroborated by [co-defendants], who admitted that they alone shot each of the victims. . . . We find that [counsel's] pressure, which was tainted by a conflict of interest, had an adverse impact on Thomas' decision to enter a guilty plea.

One judge dissented.

The question permits an alternative scenario: Thomas refuses to plead guilty, the prosecutor withdraws the deal, and all are convicted at trial of a more serious offense. Can the co-defendants complain? They would have to argue that separate counsel would have attempted to persuade the prosecutor to allow one or the other or both to plead guilty under a different deal. That other deal would probably be a plea to a lesser offense in exchange for testimony. Obviously, common counsel could not do that. The co-defendants were eager to make a deal, they would say, but common counsel could accept only a package deal or none.

Although the problem does not directly raise the issue, it might be worth exploring with the class whether the prosecutor acted properly in offering a package deal, take it or leave it. From the prosecutor's perspective, if the case has to go to trial, he or she might as well try all three. And perhaps she doesn't need Thomas's cooperation. The deal is worth it to the state only if it saves the expense of trial. Is that a sufficient justification? I believe it is. The prosecutor can make an informed decision about how to deploy her resources. If she can get a plea from all three, she saves resources and that may encourage her to be somewhat generous. But if there is no appreciable benefit to the prosecutor, because one of the defendants insists on a trial, she may conclude that justice and the administration of justice are best served by trying all three.

Turning to the particular facts of our problem: Andy Simon has to make a decision. Snyder is the least culpable. He wants to go trial but Dash and Kennedy want to accept the plea bargain. The prosecutor has made an "all or nothing" offer. If she has to try the case for any, she may as well try it for all. Putting aside whether her conduct is appropriate, I think Simon has to get out of some or all of the representations. An independent lawyer might be able to cut a deal for Snyder (perhaps testimony against Dash and Kennedy). In any event, an independent lawyer will have no interest, arising out of loyalty to Dash and Kennedy, in pressuring Snyder to accept the plea. If the lawyer does withdraw from representing Snyder and the case goes to trial against all three, and Snyder does not testify, the lawyer may be able to continue to represent Dash and Kennedy depending upon the theories of the defense. Simon cannot be in a position of taking issue with Snyder's factual defense where Simon previously represented Snyder in this very matter.

2. Criminal Cases (Prosecutors) (page 284). The *Young* Court **(page 284)** was much-divided about the basis for its opinion and whether harmless error rules applied. Our concern is for confidence in prosecutorial decisions, something we can't have if the prosecutor has a second master. Ultimately, the holding in *Young* is that supervisory powers will be exercised to prevent appointment of prosecutors who are counsel for private parties that would benefit from conviction for criminal contempt. Here, the prosecutor's conflict arose because conviction would advantage his private client on the very subject of the prosecution. This case would seem to be easy. Three justices would, however, apply a harmless error analysis. Is that right? Can we ever untangle the motivations and have confidence in the result? Even if the evidence more than adequately supported a conviction, we can't know but that a truly independent prosecutor would have been satisfied with a generous plea bargain.

The note material following *Young* **(page 287)** sets out a number of cases with varying facts. Tennessee lets a husband's lawyer in a divorce case prosecute a wife for contempt, relying on the fact that the sanction was modest and if the husband's lawyer didn't do it, no one would. So there is a judicial interest in vindicating a court's order. Even before *Young*, the California Supreme Court in *Clancy* **(page 289)** invalidated a conviction where the state used a private prosecutor who had an ideological motive and who was being paid on a contingent basis. Even without a contingent basis, the Tennessee Supreme Court in *Culbreath* also invalidates a conviction where the private lawyer was being paid by a private group **(page 289)**. Part-time prosecutors create special problems that are identified in the cases as **pages 289-290**. These arise when they or colleagues in their private practice firms have an interest in the resolution of cases in the part-time prosecutors public office. Failing to keep the two worlds separate can result in reversal of convictions and discipline. Students should have no problem seeing those conflicts.

Young was distinguished in *American National Cellular* **(page 290)** on the ground that the interests of government lawyers in prosecuting contempt of an order obtained by other government lawyers was not, by itself, sufficient to undermine our confidence in the prosecution. Why not? Their careers will be enhanced. The government may get some more money to fund these efforts. What if the lawyers need that money to keep their office open?

"Contributions to Justice" (page 291)

This problem is generally based on *People v. Eubanks*, 927 P.2d 310 (Cal. 1997). That was a prosecution of Eubanks and Wang for theft of trade secrets from Wang's former employer, Borland, allegedly for the benefit of Eubanks' employer, Symantec. The investigation was being conducted by the Santa Cruz County District Attorney. The D.A. lacked the resources to hire experts to help his staff understand the technical parts of the case, which centered on computer technology. Borland offered to pay the expenses of one expert, Klausner. The D.A. hired a second expert, Strawn. Klausner's bill was modest ($1400). But Strawn's bill was higher, ultimately reaching more than $12,000. After the D.A. incurred this debt to Strawn, he authorized a request to Borland to pay it as well, which Borland did. The defendants moved to recuse the entire district attorney's office on the ground that the receipt of these payments created a prejudicial conflict. The court mainly focused on Strawn.

Essentially, the question was this: Under general principles and under a California statute, did Borland's financial assistance create an unacceptable risk of influencing the way in which the D.A. would exercise his prosecutorial discretion. "[T]he courts, the public and individual defendants are entitled to rest assured that the public prosecutor's discretionary choices will be unaffected by private interests, and will be 'born of objective and impartial consideration of each individual case.'"

It influenced the court, though it was not determinative, that the payment was made to relieve a debt already incurred. This was seen to create a heightened sense of obligation. The court also stressed that Borland made the payment in response to a request from the D.A. The court further said that the "size of the contributions here also tends to show recusal would be within the trial court's discretion." Finally, the court noted that the underlying case against the defendants was weak.

The court stressed that under California law "appearance of impropriety" was not an adequate basis for disqualifying the prosecutor's office. Rather, the facts must show that the contributions could actually have affected discretionary decisions. Here they did so because of the "sense of obligation to Borland" that they could inspire.

This reasoning is also apt for analysis of the casebook problem.

"Conscientious Objectors" (page 291)

The issue raised here is perplexing. It arose in New York when the Governor, pursuant to state law, took a homicide case away from the Bronx D.A. on the ground that the D.A. had, through various public statements, let it be known that he would never seek the death penalty (or so the Governor understood them). The victim was a police officer. The D.A. had several months to decide whether to seek the death penalty in the particular case but if he decided not to do so, that would be final. The Governor feared he would decide not to seek the death penalty pursuant to his declared policy and removed the case before the decision was made. The D.A. maintained that his prior statements did not absolutely foreclose seeking the death penalty in any homicide case, pointed out that the capital statute left that discretion to the local district attorney, and argued too that the people of the Bronx, knowing his death penalty views, had overwhelmingly reelected him. The D.A. challenged the Governor's action and lost 4-3 in the New York Court of Appeals (correctly in my view).

But that's a matter of state law, not ethics especially. The more interesting question is whether the D.A.'s policy (which, despite backpedaling, I think the Governor correctly read) is a violation of his duty as a lawyer for "the People of the State of New York." The D.A. is a state official who, though elected locally, represents the People of the State, not the people of the Bronx. The law pretty clearly contemplates that the D.A. will exercise discretion in each case, and not decide in advance that he or she will always choose not to seek the death penalty, which the problem asks you to assume the D.A. did.

To provide a "counter" example, intended to assure that this issue is discussed without regard to the underlying law (or it only), I imagine a D.A. who has categorically refused ever to seek to prosecute a domestic violence case as a felony and a Governor who removes that D.A. from such a case.

In my view, with which many may disagree, in each case the D.A. violates the law by making a categorical decision against a particular prosecution, notwithstanding that the law delegates discretion to the D.A. Discretion means you have to be free to choose A or B. You don't exercise discretion by deciding *a priori* that you'll always choose A. If the D.A. is conscientiously unable to decide, he or she should find some alternate process to do so.

This problem should start students thinking about the extent to which prosecutors, who have a large amount of discretion, can also let their discretion be influenced, and to what degree, by their own consciences, especially when those may be inconsistent with the balance that the law seems to strike.

Let me offer some arguments in support of the prosecutor who declines to seek the death penalty. Resources are tight. Perhaps the prosecutor concludes that a jury in his or her county will not convict or sentence to death. In capital cases particularly, seeking the death penalty is quite expensive. If the prosecutor is actually correct that a randomly selected jury in the county will not return a unanimous death sentence, then conserving those resources makes a whole lot of sense. This argument works best if the prosecutor has a good-faith basis for the belief. Perhaps some unsuccessful capital cases will suffice. I don't think opinion polls are adequate.

3. Civil Cases (page 291). *Fiandaca* **(page 293**) is a factually detailed case but well worth study. First, it arises in a public interest context, which is unusual in conflict situations. Second, it discusses remedy as well as conflict. Third, the court provides a closely reasoned analysis of the application of Rule 1.7 to the facts before it. Notice that it is the state's offer of settlement that injects the irresolvable conflict. What if the state made the offer specifically to force the disqualification of opposing counsel? On remedy, the court declines to upset the verdict simply because counsel was conflicted. Rather, it looks "to the actual adverse effects caused by the [lower] court's error in refusing to disqualify NHLA as class counsel. . . ." This is the same approach appellate courts take in criminal cases -- applying a higher standard for conflict avoidance before trial than when they review allegations of conflict after trial. The court concludes that it is with regard to appropriate remedy, where NHLA was most obviously conflicted because of its representation of a different class, that remand was required.

Notice how the court deals with the proximate cause issue. It cites the district judge's refusal to approve a settlement that would establish a facility for female prisoners at LSS as the basis for its conclusion that, even with separate counsel for the plaintiff class, settlement could not have occurred and a trial would have been inevitable. But somehow the district court's opposition to a facility at LSS did not constitute an independent impediment to that remedy following judgment for plaintiffs at trial. Why would the district court have been more amenable to the LSS solution after trial than before? The Circuit apparently wants new counsel *to be free* to argue in favor of an LSS facility, instead of the relief the trial judge did order, *if* new counsel is so inclined. The NHLA was not free to make this decision. The circuit wrote that the trial judge's ban on the use of LSS "has at least the appearance of having been tainted by NHLA's conflict of interest."

As I said earlier in discussing *Cuyler v. Sullivan*, it is important to emphasize the facts of cases analyzing claims of conflict -- *i.e.*, to tell the "story" of the case. Most any conflict situation should be amenable to description with a sentence something like: "On the one hand, the lawyers had a duty, if they thought it best, to urge or advise [*fill in the blank*], but on the other hand, their obligation to another client (or their own interest) interfered with their freedom to do so by [*fill in the blank*]." The result can either be a need for a consent or an obligation not to accept the matter or to withdraw from it.

Mitchell Simon at Franklin Pierce Law Center supervised the *Fiandaca* case at NHLA. He sent me the following reflection which you can use in class. It is not often that we get this sort of thing and I am happy to include it.

Teaching the *Fiandaca* case for me is a bit like playing the lead in the movie Groundhog Day, in which Bill Murray relives the same day over and over until he gets it right.

I left my teaching position at Franklin Pierce Law Center on November 1,1986 (just about 10 days after the Rule 68 motion was filed) to supervised all litigation for NHLA, including the *Fiandaca* case. Having now returned to academia, I, each year, get to fill in the facts of the case

85

and to show my students how the view from the "field" can be different than that seen later by an appellate court.

Let me briefly give you some missing facts and frame the issue as we saw it. At the time of the filing of the motion, NHLA did not know what the *Garrity* class would think about the proposal. The remedy we sought in the *Garrity* case was total closure of the state institution for persons with developmental disabilities. The federal court, however, did not give us full relief, but reduced the population from almost 1200 to the 200 individuals confined at LSS at the time of *Fiandaca*. The state's offer in *Fiandaca* would have resulted in the move of about ½ those remaining at the institution to homes in the community, something we could not compel the state to do under the remaining court order.

In light of this, the issue for us at that time was not whether the conflict between the groups was a waivable one, but rather whether there was any conflict. If the *Garrity* class chose to accept the new placements, there was no conflict. Only if they rejected the new placements, would there be an issue.

We knew that getting this information from each group could pose a challenge. We could not fully counsel the groups, but nor could we walk away from the cases just prior to trial without knowing more. We were mindful that at all times during the discussions, we needed permission from each group to share relevant information on each group's position with the other group. We also sent a supervisory team to all meetings, told the groups that we could only provide information and not full counseling, and made sure that both groups had outside lawyers present.

Much to our surprise but in a heartfelt move, the *Garrity* group felt that the stigma for any remaining residents of being on "prison grounds" would outweigh the benefit of the new placements for those leaving. That being their choice, we got permission to take this information back to the *Fiandaca* class.

The woman, with Mr. Astles present, concluded that even if they accepted the state's offer, they would not get the building since the *Garrity* class (represented by their private counsel) would intervene to block the settlement. Further, the women felt that, given NH's history of institutional litigation and lack of compliance with prior court orders, they would not get implementation without counsel to file enforcement actions. If they chose to accept the offer, they knew NHLA would have to withdraw from their case and from the *Garrity* case due to an irresolvable conflict. Finally, a number of the plaintiffs had children with some degree of learning disability and talked passionately to the group of not wanting to fight with other needy individuals.

Based on these discussions, the Executive Director of the program wrote the infamous letter of rejection, which the court cited many times. However, the letter was accurate, if not as clear as it needed to be. It was the *Fiandaca* plaintiffs not the plaintiffs' lawyers who rejected the settlement based on the interests of the *Garrity* class and the other considerations described above. This was confirmed in court in a two days hearing by the testimony of each *Fiandaca* class member.

Each time I teach the case, I wonder how the First Circuit could conclude that we were forgetting the plight of the women, with whom we worked for three years to further the rights of a prior client group. We knew that the women, who once convicted of crimes were shipped all over the country and unable to see their kids or talk to their lawyers, had a just and winning case. The dilemma seemed to us to be how to present the options fairly to both groups (especially since the "conflict" was created by the defendants) prior to analyzing any potential conflict. If the settlement was accepted by both or rejected by both, we had, as the Court recognized, no conflict. I hope other teachers and students will offer their thoughts.

The note material following *Fiandaca*, partly expanding on its themes, introduces students to imputed conflicts (**page 297**), the standing issues (**page 299**), the prohibition against acting adversely to a client on an unrelated matter (**page 301**), confidentiality and privilege in joint-defense and multiple representation (**page 306**), class conflicts (**page 311**) and appealability of civil disqualification orders (**page 311**). A word about each:

Imputation of conflicts is an issue in this and the next chapter. *Fiandaca* treats the NHLA as a single lawyer but since no one challenged that treatment, students might miss the imputation. It is not self-evident that one lawyer in a firm is disqualified because a different lawyer in the firm is disqualified. Indeed, Rule 1.10(a) distinguishes among bases for conflicts in determining whether to impute that status. Why not do so here, especially given the paucity of law offices available to represent the indigent? The imputation in this context presumes a fundamental disbelief that one lawyer can act adversely to the client of a lawyer with whom he or she is affiliated and still represent the clients effectively. Or is the assumption merely that the profession cannot ask the client population to believe as much? *Mustang Enterprises* (**page 297**) is an interesting case given the increase in the phenomenon of law firm "affiliations" (by whatever name). It imputes conflicts within affiliated firms that touted their connection. *Miller* and *Reynoso* are exceptions to the imputation rule created for policy reasons when the firm is a public defender's office (**page 298**).

The E2K Commission (**page 299**) would change the imputation rule where the conflict was based on a personal interest of a lawyer and there is no "significant risk of materially limiting the representation" by other firm lawyers.

The note on standing identifies the division of authority on whether a non-client can object to a lawyer's representation on conflict grounds. *Infotechnology* (**page 300**) takes a middle position -- the non-client has to show that the representation will "prejudice the fairness of the proceedings." The First Circuit in *Fiandaca* permitted the state to raise the conflict issue even though it was not ever a client of NHLA. The First Circuit earlier took the position that nonclients can raise conflict issues in its decision in *Kevlik v. Goldstein*, cited at **page 294**. The standing issue intersects the waiver question. If a client is not objecting, although it could, should we infer that it has no objection and has therefore waived the conflict, assuming the conflict is waivable? In *Infotechnology*, the client who would be in a position to object was not a party, but would be a witness. Could the court have disposed of the appeal on the ground that the client's silence equaled consent? Is the issue merely the presumption we draw from silence? *Dawson* (**page 300**) collects the cases and concludes that non-client standing will almost never be allowed.

The note at **pages 301-306** introduces students to the important lesson that the loyalty obligation will generally prevent a law firm from opposing one of its own clients even on wholly unrelated matters. The absence of threat to confidential information is of no moment. Clients can't be required to work with lawyers whose colleagues are their adversaries. It destroys the trust and comfort the relationship demands. This rule limits the availability of counsel. Firms may seek waivers, even before the representation is accepted, that would permit them to oppose current clients on unrelated matters. Sometimes the waivers may run only to opposition to the affiliates of clients. My own anecdotal experience has identified a kind of "private ordering" that has gone on, whereby large corporate clients are sometimes willing to waive conflicts, even prospectively, in order to get the lawyer they want. Although they may then find "their" firm opposing them, or their parent or subsidiary, on an unrelated matter, they view that prospect as untroubling.

In teaching this material, try to get students to explain why it is that Lawyer Jones in the Chicago office of the law firm cannot sue (nor negotiate against) Client XYZ simply because Lawyer Smith in the Atlanta office of the same firm is representing XYZ on a wholly unrelated matter. Confidences are not at risk. You might begin by hypothesizing that the same lawyer at the firm is both representing the client and suing it on an unrelated matter. Then assume different lawyers. The interest is in the client's expectation of loyalty -- that the lawyer and firm it hires will not act adversely to it. At the very least, won't it be hard for that client thereafter to trust its lawyers? Won't it be hard to sit down and plan strategy when the very next day a partner of the lawyer who represents you will be, perhaps, taking your deposition with the goal of destroying your credibility and causing you great financial loss? Students should work through these questions.

Some have suggested (**page 303**) that given the size of some firms and some clients, the nearly per se rule against adverse representation should be changed to a rule of reason in which we ask whether there is really a danger to Lawyer A's loyalty if his partner (B) is representing an adversary on an unrelated matter (or, conversely, if there is a danger to B's loyalty if A is opposed to her client). (If there's a danger to confidences because the matters are related, the per se rule would remain in place.) In this view, a client can bargain for a per se rule at the outset of the representation, but a per se rule should not be the default rule. The question is then: Who should have the burden of asking for a private arrangement to displace the default rule? The lawyer or the client? If the default rule is a rule of reason, in one view, it should be the client who has to ask for something more protective; if it's a per se rule, it should be the law firm that must ask for something more flexible. No one doubts that most concurrent conflicts can be waived, especially by informed, sophisticated clients. My own view is that the burden should be on the lawyer, not the client, since loyalty in this regard is something a client is likely to expect absent warning and the legitimate expectations of the client should be determinative.

The *Research Corporation* case **(page 305)** is useful because it shows how easily a firm may find itself, unwittingly, in a concurrent conflict situation (here arising out of a merger) and how quick the client was to seek to take advantage of it, apparently tactically. The court rejected disqualification but found a violation of the Rule. Is there a violation? Probably, technically, it was, although it does seem rather harsh to say so.

Woodside **(page 304)**, with significant qualifications, permits attorneys for a government entity to sue the government entity under a state statute even while continuing their employment with the entity. This seems absolutely right, doesn't it? It should be seen as part of the same trend that permits employed lawyers to sue for retaliatory discharge. See Chapter 9. Of course, the lawyer suing for retaliatory discharge no longer works for the employer and is not seeking to get his or her job back. So *Woodside* is more "extreme," measured in terms of the degree of deviation from traditional doctrine. One might also say that the legislature, by passing a statute protecting employees, including lawyers, will have purported to overrule the traditional prohibition against suing your own client. But can the legislature do that? Isn't that within the court's inherent power? Conveniently, there is a dissent **(page 266)**.

The longish note at **page 306** describes what happens to the privilege and the duty of confidentiality in joint representation and multiple representation. The doctrine here is a bit complicated and a little confusing. I have tried to clarify it. The note addresses some daunting issues that arise when lawyers have multiple or joint clients on a single matter. These include the contest between the confidentiality duty and the duty to inform, and the authority of any of the clients to waive confidentiality or privilege over the objection of the others. Included in this edition is the Restatement's position on the issue of disclosure **(page 309)** and waiver **(page 310)**.

The brief note on class conflicts **(page 311)** identifies the Supreme Court's *Amchem Products* opinion (1997) but as a practical matter can (together with a mirror note in Chapter 6 on conflicts in successive representation) only give students a glimpse of the scope of the issues.

The final note **(page 311)** reveals that federal civil disqualification rulings (either way) are not appealable as of right before final judgment. The effect is, as a practical matter, that federal trial judges are the judges of last resort in nearly all such cases.

"Will You Represent Us Both?" (page 312)

I present myself to a student as one of the prospective clients pleading with the student to take the case. There is no one else in town. If the student represents only one of the two prospective clients, the other will have no counsel. We run through the possible sequences. At what point may a conflict arise? Can it be waived? How should the lawyer go about eliciting the waiver? What information should she offer?

DR 5-105 and Rule 1.7 provide the standards. The problem is that the two plaintiffs may eventually be adversaries if the job opens and both want it. But although their interests are potentially in opposition down the road, are they so in the current action? To the extent there is a litigation, I would say not if the object of the action is to establish that the denial of the promotion to both of them under current policies was in violation of the statute, and not a judgment that either of them should be given the promotion instead of the candidate who got it. What relief is the complaint going to demand? If both plaintiffs want to demand the job, it would not be possible for one law firm to represent them. But they may, if fully informed, choose to pursue different relief, such as a change in employer policies or a declaration that the promotion of the white employee was invalid.

Similarly, if the center is negotiating for an out-of-court settlement, it could not negotiate for the job for either client because that is what the other client also wants. Since joint representation necessarily means foregoing particular relief, at least for the time being, the plaintiffs ought to be made fully aware of that necessity before the case is assumed. They can accept a limited representation under Rule 1.2(c). One last angle is this: Perhaps the facts will show that the employer's policies discriminate against blacks and not hispanics or vice versa. If that's apparent at the start, of course, then the case of the potential plaintiff who is not a member of the disfavored group ought not be taken. If it becomes apparent while the case is in progress, then the case of that plaintiff must be dropped. If during the pendency of the case, establishment of either plaintiff's entitlement to any relief will require proof inconsistent with the other employee's claim for relief, the firm will have to drop one plaintiff and possibly both. (For example, depending on the facts, it may be that the proof of discrimination against blacks will tend to show that there was no discrimination against hispanics in general or Nunez in particular.) At the outset, however, this prospect is too speculative, I think, to exclude the joint representation of a black and an hispanic, or of both as class representatives.

This problem, concise as it is, works very well if you present it in role. (I sometimes present myself in the role of Sheila, the lawyer, seeking advice.) The student has to recognize, ultimately, that whether there is a disabling conflict, or merely one that consent can cure, will depend on remedy, specifically on whether either client will seek a remedy inconsistent with the goals of the other, and to a lesser extent on whether, even if the remedies are consonant, either will be advancing factual or legal arguments that compromise the position of the other client.

"May We Do Both Cases?" (page 313)

I've tested this in class. It requires a complicated analysis but the very discussion is educational. Again, I suggest presenting yourself in the role of the questioner. Essentially, this question is about "issue" conflicts. Before getting into the facts, some background.

Rule 1.7 comment [9] would permit this conduct, "unless representation of either client would be adversely affected." What does the quoted language mean? Obviously, establishment of a precedent, even in another state or another circuit that is contrary to the rule a second client wishes to establish will "adversely affect" the second client's argument. It won't bind the second court, but is that what the rule requires? Could a lawyer make inconsistent arguments in two intermediate appellate courts in the same state? Comment [9] to Rule 1.7 should be consulted, too. It says that concurrent representation in different trial courts is ordinarily allowed but may be improper in "an appellate court." This is not very helpful.

In its formal opinion 93-377, the ABA concluded that a lawyer should not accept a matter where he or she would have to advocate a position contrary to the position the lawyer or the lawyer's firm is advocating for a different client if "there is a substantial risk that the law firm's representation of one client will create a legal precedent, even if not binding, which is likely materially to undercut the legal position being urged on behalf of the other client." Client consent after full disclosure is permitted. The opinion stresses that its conclusion does not depend on whether the two matters are being litigated in the same jurisdiction. The key question is whether, even if not precedentially binding, resolution of an issue in one matter "is likely to have a significant impact on its determination" in another matter. The opinion concludes that in some circumstances even client consent will not cure the conflict. This will be true if the lawyer or firm will be inclined to "soft-pedal" the issue in one matter or alter its arguments in one matter in order to avoid affecting the resolution of the other matter.

California Opinion 1989-108 would permit a lawyer to argue opposite sides of the same legal issue in unrelated cases pending before *the same trial judge*. The opinion recognizes a risk of harm to the client as well as risk to the lawyer's credibility. But the committee identified considerations that outweighed these concerns. It said that issue conflicts were common; that a ban would create insurmountable problems in small communities and specialized areas of legal practice; that a ban would intrude on a client's right to choice of counsel; and that it would be difficult to detect and avoid issue conflicts in firms. The committee suggested, however, that lawyers inform clients of issue conflicts and give them an opportunity to retain other counsel in those instances where the conflict could harm the client. Finally, the committee said that clients had no reasonable expectation that lawyers would not accept other matters in which they advocated inconsistent legal positions. Philadelphia Opinion 89-27 permits a firm to accept multiple clients even though it will be arguing inconsistent positions on the same issue at trial. But the opinion requires informed client consent and forbids the representation on appeal. It also refuses to permit screening. Maine Opinion 264 (1997) concludes over dissent that under that state's rule a lawyer can argue opposite positions on the same legal issue for different clients in unrelated matters, rejecting the ABA's cautionary limitations. The Opinion points out that unlike the ABA Rules, the Maine Rules do not have the commentary on which the ABA Opinion relied. D.C. Opinion 265 (1996) cites and relies on the ABA Opinion.

In the immediate problem, the student should recognize that even the amicus client is a client. Either case may be decided on non-constitutional grounds and in a way that will have no influence on the other. Even if the first is decided on constitutional grounds, federal courts in the Seventh Circuit don't bind California state courts and vice versa. But, of course, the opinion of either court can be highly influential. How will the Wisconsin clients react if the Circuit cites reasoning in a constitutional victory for the amicus, based on an argument its own firm advanced? Not well. Finally, both cases can go to the Supreme Court and then, surely, the firm cannot appear for both sets of clients. So at the very least, someone has to be told that the representation will be limited to lower courts. Another problem that my class pointed out was that the lawyer with the amicus may hesitate to make powerful arguments on the constitutional point, fearing that if the state court adopts them, they'll hurt the paying Wisconsin clients; or fearing at the least that the adversaries in the Wisconsin case will discover his good theories and appropriate them. The opposite is also theoretically if not practically true. Finally, neither client will be able to enjoy the expertise of the firm's lawyer for the other client in connection with their work. For although, for example, the California lawyer could work for the Wisconsin client arguing the opposite constitutional position in federal court in the Seventh Circuit, as a practical matter that seems remote.

Malpractice Based on Conflicts (page 313). You have to make a pedagogical decision here. I include a case in which lawyers were found liable in malpractice in part because of a conflict of interest. I did this because the risk of malpractice liability for conflicts ought to be made clear and because I found a short case that so perfectly segues into note material that should be covered in this part of Chapter 5. Some of you will cover the malpractice material at length and may choose to assign **pages 313-325** later. Some of you may not plan to spend much time on malpractice in a particular year and will find access to this material now advantageous. Even if you plan to spend time on malpractice, I would urge you consider assigning *Simpson v. James* now, whatever your other plans, because the case is only three pages long, it's simple, and it fits right in with the issue of client-client conflicts in the civil context. Another attractive feature is that the conflict did not arise in litigation. Perhaps most important, the case reveals how the fact of a conflict can be used to help establish liability even though, strictly speaking, it wasn't the conflict itself that led to the damages but the conduct that the conflict supposedly inspired. This is discussed at **page 317**. Finally, the case permits easy discussion of two traditional conflict issues -- waiver and consent and client identity -- that are addressed in note material. The paragraph just prior to *Simpson* (**page 313**) reminds students that a conflict of interest can lead to disqualification or discipline. *Simpson* shows that it can also lead to damages.

Simpson v. James **(page 314).** Oliver represented both the buyers (Tide Creek and its investors) and the sellers (Simpson and the Joneses) of a restaurant. As security to the sellers, he provided for a lien on the stock and personal guarantees of the buyers. When the buyers did not meet an obligation, Simpson spoke to James, another lawyer at the firm (Oliver having left), who told her that the buyers would have to pay the obligation more slowly than anticipated. He restructured the debt. Eventually, James withdrew from representing the sellers and continued to represent the buyers. The buyers went bankrupt. The jury returned a verdict for plaintiffs. The court sets out the standards for malpractice recovery at **pages 315-316**. Notice that James tried to maneuver himself out of a professional relationship with Simpson.

The note at **page 317** is well worth discussing. Much of the court's opinion and the underlying trial dwelt on the conflict of interest. But what role if any did this play in the malpractice judgment? If, despite the conflict, Oliver and James had performed with reasonable competence, plaintiffs would recover nothing, although the lawyers might be disciplined and be required to disgorge their fee (see **page 791**). Conversely, if the lawyers did *not* act with reasonable competence and caused loss, then they would be liable even if there were no conflict. So why is the conflict relevant? The note suggests that the conflict made the malpractice forensically easier to establish. It also suggests that even the buyers might have a claim against Oliver and James on the theory that a truly independent lawyer would have protected them from giving the kinds of guarantees that ultimately forced them into bankruptcy. Oliver and James would have had (perhaps did have) an impossible time trying to establish that even with separate counsel for each party, the contract of sale would have looked exactly the same. It's a zero sum game for the lawyers. That's the message.

Take a look at the *Re* case **(page 318)**, where a district judge granted summary judgment on a malpractice claim on the ground, first, that the lawyer's conduct could not be negligence as a matter of law and, second, that the plaintiff could not prove "but for" causation as a matter of law. Yet in a thorough but questionable opinion she also concluded that the same conduct could establish breach of fiduciary duty (on the theory that the firm had a conflict because referrals it received from the firm of an adverse witness (not a party) accounted for 2-3 percent of its business) and damages, under the lower burden of proof required to prove damages when a fiduciary duty breach is shown. The Second Circuit granted interlocutory appeal, but then dismissed and the case settled. Anyway, *Re* neatly brings home how an alleged conflict may make it easier to establish a claim. The case is particularly unnerving given the facts from which the judge concluded a jury could find a breach.

Consent and Waiver (page 319). This note makes the point that clients can consent to concurrent conflicts, although an objective standard of reasonableness circumscribes the authority to consent. This is paternalism, of course. Why can't a truly informed client consent to all conflicts? A second point to stress is that to the extent we recognize consent, the rules are merely default rules that can be displaced by private ordering. California's rules facially permit consent to any client so long as the consent is written and the client is informed. The Rules, however, work on the theory that some conflicts are so egregious that the justice system has an interest in forbidding consent. The Restatement, as noted here, posits that the scope of allowable consent depends on the client's sophistication. The note also distinguishes consent, a voluntary and knowing act, from waiver or estoppel, a legal effect the law infers from conduct or inaction.

Ethics 2000 would amend Rule 1.7 to articulate the fundamental standards differently **(page 322)**. Comments recognize the possibility of prospective consents, with a caution, and address when consent once given can be withdrawn.

Is There a Client-Lawyer Relationship? (page 322) That issue returns once again. Because the existence of a relationship is so important to the existence of most professional duties, and because clients are not always who they once were, I think it's worthwhile to assign these pages. They summarize three cases, one involving a brief telephone conversation which constituted professional advice, one establishing that a lawyer for a trade association may (for limited purposes) also represent its members, and one (*Fund of Funds*) where there was imputation of a professional relationship when a lawyer was hired as the "understudy" to a conflicted firm. In *Glueck*, the court identified loyalty and confidentiality risks to the trade association member. The *Hughes* case may be the most instructive. Advice given in a brief telephone conversation was professional advice and could constitute malpractice. Here the lawyer gave his advice with no investigation. Further, the client could reasonably consider herself a client since the lawyer had previously represented her. Finally, the lawyer failed to tell the client of his conflict. The note ends with the now-resolved problem of the lawyer who serves on the board of a legal services organization while representing a client who is adverse to a client of the organization.

"What Kind of Consent" (page 325)

I like this problem because it requires students to identify the content of a consent to conflicts among three individuals who want to hire Gello to help them launch a small business. I have students draft the written consent. It's not clear if it'll be a corporation or general partnership or something else. To determine if consent is acceptable, and with what forewarning, the student needs to know something about the individuals' investments (are they all putting up the same amount of cash) and reputation (is one the real business getter)? Are they reasonably sophisticated? For example: One of the partners may be putting up most of the capital so their interests may differ on whether that money is invested as debt or equity. Or one of the partners may already be in this business and have most of the contacts (and the tradename). Their interests may therefore differ on what happens – who takes what – in the event of a dissolution of the partnership. Is there a reason why on particular decisions unanimity should be required? Does any partner have the right to make particular decisions in his or her sole discretion, perhaps because the decision will most seriously affect that partner (*e.g.*, the major investor)?

Note that the problem doesn't tell the student to ask these questions. Gello just wants a consent. But the job of the drafter is not merely to follow her instruction but to satisfy herself that this a consentable conflict, which it probably is. Beyond that, Gello cannot advocate for a particular resolution of competing interests and must say so. She can only advise and let them resolve the question. So the clients are not getting a level of advocacy they'd get from separate lawyers. This may benefit one or the other. Something must be said about confidentiality. The clients should know that there will be no privilege between them if there is a dispute. Further, Gello should establish the ground rules for sharing information -- *i.e.*, that she will want to be free to tell any of them what she learns in representing them, including what she learns from others of them (otherwise it's not so clear that could do so, possibly forcing a withdrawal). Gello should explain that if there is a dispute between them, she'll probably not be able to represent any of them. (Later, in Chapter 9 , students will see at least one court's view that if the business entity Gello creates is a corporation, then on its formation she will represent the corporation *retroactively* to the possible exclusion of the individuals, who may cease to be recognized as ever having been clients. See **page 554**.) Gello should probably suggest, in the written consent, that the individuals consult independent counsel.

4. The Insurance Triangle (page 326). These cases present a variation on concurrent conflict questions. A lawyer is paid by an insurance company to represent its insured. Problems arise because the obligation to defend is "broader" than the obligation to indemnify, meaning that the insurance company has to provide a lawyer if the allegations against its insured overlap, in some degree, with the scope of coverage, even though they are not congruent. A related problem arises when the complaint asserts multiple theories of recovery, some of which would require indemnification and some of which would not. These issues are present in *Goldfarb* **(page 326)**. Dr. Goldfarb was a dentist. His patient alleged that he sexually abused her during treatment. The plaintiff alleged intentional acts causing unintended injury and intentional causation of injury. For the latter, she sought both compensatory and punitive damages. The insurer would be liable for compensatory damages only and then only on the first theory. But the insurer was obligated to defend because it was unclear how the jury would decide.

In the note material following **(page 329)**, the second full paragraph asks the student to understand what may be the best strategy of each of the patient and Goldfarb in the trial between them. (The principal case, of course, was the insurance company's effort to relieve itself of the obligation to defend.) The strategy decision of the patient is interesting. She probably stands to get a higher judgment if she can prove intentional injuries. Then she will be entitled to both compensatory and punitive damages. But Goldfarb will not then be entitled to indemnity from the insurance company. So the plaintiff will want to know whether Goldfarb is in a position to pay a large judgment. The patient will also be influenced by whether substantive law allows her to get punitive damages even in the case of non-intentional injuries. Goldfarb prefers to be found liable for compensatory damages on the first theory, which is the last thing the insurer wants. Given these intersecting and conflicting goals, it is important that the lawyer paid by the insurance company to defend Goldfarb appreciate that Goldfarb, not the company, is his client. But under these circumstances, the insurance company needs to be able to participate in the underlying case through its own counsel or have some appropriate opportunity to present its position. The same lawyer can't represent the insurer and the insured.

The lesson here is to understand the dilemma if a single lawyer were asked to represent the interests of both the insurer and the insured. In addition, students should understand that the insurer's responsibility to provide a defense will, because of the conflict, require it to pay for a separate lawyer for the insured. The insured will have the right to choose that lawyer, but see *Finley* at **page 332**.

As the footnote on **page 329** explains, no conflict arises where the question of coverage and the liability issue are not "intertwined." At **page 331**, the note cites the California *Cumis* decision and the statute adopted thereafter. The statute states that there is no conflict simply by virtue of a demand for punitive damages or "solely" because the complaint seeks money in excess of the policy limits. As for punitive damages, putting aside situations like the one in *Goldfarb*, the mere assertion of a demand for punitive damages on a single theory of recovery should not ordinarily create a conflict. The lawyer will behave the same in any event. No course of conduct will ordinarily advantage the insurer but not the insured or vice versa. The one prominent exception to this is settlement. If the claimant is willing to settle for the face amount of the policy, but will seek punitive damages, which the insured will have to pay, if the case goes to trial, the interests of the insured and the insurer will diverge. But what does that have to do with the lawyer? Ordinarily, it is for the insurance company to decide whether to settle. A bad faith failure to settle might subject it to liability, but that's another matter. Our concern is whether the lawyer has multiple strategies with the insured favoring one and the insurer another. Similar points can be made for the situation in which damages exceed the policy limit but the alleged wrong is incontrovertibly within the terms of the policy.

Now having said all that, we have to recognize that these questions are highly fact specific and there may be, in certain instances, different ways of structuring a defense, different themes to emphasize or avoid, such that there will be a right to separate counsel in any event. Consider a claim of copyright infringement or invasion of privacy. It is clear that the claim is within the policy. But what will be the defense? The insurer may want to assert that the insured acted intentionally because it had a right to do what it did. The insured might fear that if the jury concluded that the insured did not have that right, then the assertion of intentionality will subject it to higher damages or punitive damages. So the insured might wish instead to de-emphasize the claim of right and assert that it acted in good faith, even if, perhaps, wrongly. That defense might result in a judgment against the insured, but the judgment might then be within the policy limit and without punitive damages. (P.S. I was involved in such a case, so it could happen.)

I do not here get into the intense debate (at the ALI and elsewhere) over whether the insurance company in the ordinary case, where there is no reservation of rights, is a client of the lawyer along with the insured and, if so, whether it is an "equal" client or a "secondary" client. The ALI debate focused on Section 134 comment *f*, which as of this writing will almost certainly continue to cause ripples until finally adopted, and probably even thereafter. The insurance companies want to be fully equal clients but some practitioners and theorists, including for a while at least the Reporters, seem to prefer to view the insurance company as being in a subordinate position. Anyway, I made a decision not to address this debate in the note material and instead to cover the conflict problems that arise when there is in fact a schism between the interests of the insurer and insured. However, the "insurance company as client" issue does surface modestly in the next problem.

"The Insurer Would Want to Know" (page 332)

Big problem. Begin anywhere. (1) Brett presumably did a conflicts check and got a necessary consent before representing the firm and Tipton both. Even when she thought the problem was only negligence, the substantive law may, *e.g.*, provide the firm or its other partners with claims against Tipton, which Brett can't assert and which her conduct in the litigation (or just time) may eradicate. On the other hand, since the damage claim is less than the insurance coverage, both the firm and Tipton, so far as Brett knew, were fully covered (though that would not be so as to any deductible, where the firm could have a claim over).

(2) Anticipating problems, Brett should have provided for an exist strategy or a prospective waiver in the event she had to stop representing the firm or Tipton.

(3) This becomes pertinent now because Brett has gotten information about Tipton that Tipton may not want the firm to know and which could certainly induce the firm to contemplate claims over.

(4) Can Brett share Tipton's information with the firm without asking her? Yes. The duty to inform wins out over the duty of confidentiality where the information does not come from Tipton and maybe even if it does. See the note at **page 306**.

(5) So Brett can tell the firm without even consulting Tipton. (If she could not, if we were to assume that Tipton gave Brett this information in confidence and that doing so prevented Brett from revealing it, then Brett would have to withdraw from representing both parties.) The firm may not wish to take action adverse to Tipton. If it does, if for example it wants to seek indemnity from Tipton, then Brett cannot be its lawyer and will have to withdraw to avoid a successive conflict of interest. But maybe the firm doesn't want to do this. Putting Tipton's

conduct out there will alert the insurance company and sacrifice the policy, which does not cover intentional wrongdoing or punitive damages. It will also alert the plaintiff.

(6) But does Brett have an obligation to tell the insurance company? If the insurance company is not deemed a client (see **page 329**), then the answer surely is no. But if it is a client, Brett would either have to give it this information or withdraw from representing it. Notice of that withdrawal will tip it off. Nor is it clear that if she did withdraw that she could continue to represent Tipton or the firm. This is a hard problem. Brett has discovered a coverage issue and so the insured needs it own counsel. But the insurance company doesn't know that. Perhaps this is an argument against recognizing the insurance company as a client. But if the jurisdiction does so, probably the best advice that one can give Brett is to resign from representing everybody without saying why. The insured should be able to share information with the lawyer appointed to represent it without fear that doing so might alert the insurance company to a coverage defense.

C. THE ADVOCATE-WITNESS RULE (page 333)

In *MacArthur* (**page 334**), Judge Sofaer describes the operation of the advocate-witness rule under the Code. The note uses his opinion as a way of identifying the four policies the rule purportedly advances. The advocate-witness rule is meant to protect both the client whose lawyer should be called and the other side. The Model Rules make some salutary changes (**page 334**) in the operation of the rule. *MacArthur* reveals the problems posed for law firms that represent all aspects of a client's affairs. The changes in the Rules, which do away with automatic vicarious disqualification in these circumstances, ameliorate the problem. The application to prosecutors is discussed at **pages 337**. In *U.S. v. Prantil*, 764 F.2d 548 (9th Cir. 1985), the court reversed a conviction where the trial judge had refused to disqualify a prosecutor whom the defense lawyer had sought to call as a witness. The prosecutor had knowledge of the underlying facts because of his participation in the investigation of the defendant. (The prosecutor had also expressed his personal opinion of the defendant's guilt at trial.) Perhaps the most famous case disqualifying a defense lawyer under this rule is *United States v. Locascio*, (**page 336**).

The imputed disqualification of the advocate-witness rule in the Code makes little sense. The Rules properly address the matter as a conflicts problem under Rule 1.7. For example, if a lawyer will have to cross-examine his or her own partner and argue that the partner should not be believed, then imputed disqualification is appropriate since the lawyer will be in an obvious conflict position. But if the partner's testimony does not have to be attacked, disqualification of the entire firm seems unwise. The jury will know where the partner works. And despite what Judge Sofaer says about the impact of the rule on a firm's ability to handle all of a client's matters, the rule as he describes it would in fact seem significantly to restrict such endeavors.

CHAPTER VI

SUCCESSIVE CONFLICTS OF INTEREST

A. PRIVATE PRACTICE

Analytica, Inc. v. NPD Research, Inc. (**page 339**) contains a nearly straightforward application of the substantial relationship test. The work Schwartz & Freeman did for Malec and NPD was substantially related to the work it was hired to do for Analytica under the test as Judge Posner states it in the first full paragraph on **page 340**. The note at **pages 343-348** discusses various articulations of the substantial relationship test and its elaboration over time. The note also discusses the meaning of the word "matter" and "other values," including the value of counsel of choice. Obviously, the easier the test is to satisfy, the greater the number of disqualifications and the greater the restrictions on the work of law firms, the free choice of counsel, and (sometimes) the mobility of lawyers. On the other side of the ledger is protection of client confidences and the former client's need for comfort in this regard. Note these two important twists in *Analytica*: Schwartz & Freeman argued it was not NPD's lawyer. The court rejects this claim, looking to the realities of the firm's work and "client" expectations, and not formalism. This point is pursued in the note at **pages 352-354** as part of the book's continuous attention to the issue of client identity in different contexts. The court posits that it is unimportant whether NPD or Malec was the client because NPD had a right to expect the firm to protect its confidences. That right included a "right not to see [the firm] reappear within months on the opposite side of a litigation. . . ." (**page 342**.) A second aspect of the case worth noting is the $25,000 fine against the firm for resisting the disqualification motion. (**Page 343**.) Finally, not only was Schwartz & Freeman disqualified, but the firm (Pressman and Hartunian) that it had hired as trial counsel was also disqualified. The taint traveled. See also on this point **page 350**.

Make note of the reference at **page 340** and note * to the opportunity for screening when a lawyer changes firms (a lateral lawyer). Here that opportunity does not arise because a "constant" firm (no change in personnel) changed sides. The issue of imputation after a lateral move is addressed in Chapter 6B, with a later Seventh Circuit case.

The "Substantial Relationship" Test (page 343). The book sets out Judge Weinfeld's original articulation. Compare Judge Posner's language at **page 340**. Judge Posner states that a lawyer will be disqualified if the "subject matter of the two representations is 'substantially related,'" and then restates this to mean: If the lawyer could have obtained confidential information in the first representation that would have been relevant in the second. Has Judge Posner flipped the test? Didn't Judge Weinfeld envision that a substantial relationship between the matters was indicative of the existence of the relevant confidences? Judge Posner seems to say that the existence of relevant confidences is indicative of a substantial relationship. However, he then goes on to compare the matters factually.

Points made in this note include: The comparison should be between the facts of the two matters rather than the legal issues **(page 345)**; even "one confidential communication" will for some courts require disqualification **(page 344)**; courts may forbid a lawyer familiar with a former client's method of litigating a particular kind of case from thereafter suing that former client in that kind of case **(page 346)**; and distaste for tactical use of disqualification motions has led some courts to require proof that the trial will be tainted and not merely proof that the representation is unethical. Other courts have rejected this view **(pages 347-348)**.

The Successive Duty of Loyalty (page 348). This note reveals that it is not only confidences that the substantial relationship test means to protect, but also the former client's expectation of counsel's loyalty. Even if counsel knows no confidences, the former client has a right to expect that he or she will not attempt to undo the work performed for the former client. The existence of this independent and continuing duty of loyalty raises two questions. Will it, like the threat to confidentiality, lead to imputed disqualification if a conflicted lawyer moves to a new firm? The Model Rules say no. **(Page 371.)** The second question is whether the loyalty obligation will disqualify a lawyer from representing a client against a former client where the parties were once co-clients of the same lawyer on the substantially related matter. In the latter instance, there is arguably no threat to the adverse party's (and former client's) confidences on the theory that multiple clients cannot assert the attorney-client privilege in subsequent disputes between them. So the lawyer can be made to reveal all anyway. The issue is identified at **pages 349-350**. Despite *Allegaert* and *Christensen*, both of which involved special facts, the clearly dominant view is that the prohibition against subsequent adversity does not allow a lawyer for one of two co-clients thereafter to appear adversely to the other on a substantially related matter because the duty of loyalty is broader than the duty of confidentiality or the privilege.

In my view, the cases, like *Brennan's*, that ordinarily forbid the subsequent adverse representation against the former co-client are right, again absent unusual circumstances. Although information may not be at risk, I believe the former co-client has a right not to expect his or her former counsel to be the enemy in the area of the former representation. Certainly, we can appreciate that if a client in a co-client situation knows that, in the event of a rift, the lawyer can choose to represent either against the other, the client will be cautious and less forthcoming. This is not good. It is one thing for a lawyer for former co-clients to be a "stakeholder" of information, it is another to be an advocate who, possessing that information, seeks to harm his or her former client in the area of the former work. The E2K Commission appears to reject

Allegaert (**page 350**) while the Restatement would recognize it in narrow circumstances (**page 349**).

The Consequences of Disqualification (page 350). How far does the status travel? As we saw in *Analytica*, it traveled from Schwartz & Freeman to trial counsel (who also appealed the disqualification but whose appeal was dismissed as moot). For the reasons stated here, the disqualification will not necessarily carry over to co-counsel. The second question is whether disqualified counsel can share her work product with successor counsel. Courts divide here too, but the sensible rule seems to be to allow it if there is no identifiably tainted item. Of course, making this inquiry can cause the very invasion of confidentiality that the substantial relationship test, with its purportedly neat lines, is supposed to avoid. Texas would allow ex parte review of the item (**page 351**).

Malpractice Based on Successive Conflicts. Echoing the material on the place of concurrent conflicts in malpractice is this brief note identifying recent cases that recognize a claim when a lawyer engages in a successive conflict (**page 351**). Students should know that disqualification and discipline are not the only dangers. Unclear is what the damages would be? The cost of a disqualification motion? Disgorgement of fees?

Who Is a Former Client? (page 352) Here are various cases raising the client identity issue in the successive conflicts situation. Notice how courts do not stand on ceremony but are rather quite practical. People or companies that give confidential information to a lawyer, directly or indirectly, in the expectation that the information will enable the lawyer to do work that, directly or indirectly, aids the supplier of information will find a sympathetic judge if the lawyer later appears on the opposing side of a substantially related matter. In paragraphs (4) and (6), however, the moving party went a bit too far in claiming this expanded protection. Paragraph (7) raises the issue of the initial interview which is not followed by retention. Does it nevertheless create an attorney-client relationship? One danger here, if it does, is that prospective clients, especially in smaller communities, can seek to "conflict out" all the lawyers that the adversary might wish to retain. I have heard this happening in matrimonial cases. To my mind, the decision is highly fact-specific. It should turn on precisely the kind of information that the client gave the lawyer. It might be necessary to have an ex parte hearing to do this.

Note especially in paragraph (6) that a nonclient can enjoy confidentiality if it bargains for it as part, for example, of a settlement agreement. Note, too, in paragraph (7), courts have rejected efforts to claim client status based on a discussion with a CLE instructor; and work in lecturing a company's staff on employment discrimination law. This is quite sensible. In neither event was the lawyer performing a lawyer-client service.

Take a look at the Fried Frank case in note 5 on **page 353**. The court gave three theories for concluding that the firm had an attorney-client relationship with Dart. The Restatement uses this case for illustrative purposes in §132, illustration 8. However, as the Reporter's Note says, the Restatement prefers to view the law firm's obligation to Dart under a principal-agent rationale. In this view, First Boston, as Dart's agent, hired Fried Frank as the subagent, creating fiduciary obligations in the firm to Dart. The implications of this construction are that traditional imputation rules, and prohibitions against screening, that are present with lawyer-client conflicts, would not apply. See comment g(ii).

The E2K Commission has proposed a new rule **(page 354)**, which would allow screening of a disqualified lawyer who is disqualified only by virtue of an interview with a prospective client. It is not clear whether the House of Delegates will accept this new rule.

Like a Hot Potato (page 354). It may not be Shakespeare, but Judge Aldrich got a lot of mileage from this little phrase. This note is self-explanatory. For my money, I think the courts are a bit too aggressive in dumping on law firms that, when faced with a conflict, try to wiggle out of it by dropping a client. Sometimes the tactic is indefensible, as when a law firm fires a client to take a new client or matter that it could not accept concurrently but could accept successively. At other times, the law firm's motives are more complex. I think they were so in *Picker* **(pages 355-356)**. The opportunity to merge arose then and there and might be gone by the time MH&S finished its work for Varian. It is not beyond possibility, is it, that Varian dug in its heels to gain a little leverage in the negotiation with Picker? Anyway, if Varian is truly uninjured by MH&S's withdrawal, and if Picker is willing to pay the cost of new counsel's start-up time, why honor Varian's refusal to waive the conflict? After all, the matters were unrelated. There were no threats to Varian's confidences. Jones Day was willing to screen the lawyers working on the two matters. And the likelihood of disloyalty was more theoretical than real. Or am I wrong about that? Is the client's (let's assume) good faith interest in pure loyalty superior to the firms' opportunity to merge?

Anyway, one can think of other situations in which the law firm deserves even greater sympathy. Some are identified at **pages 356-357**. In paragraph (1), two clients on unrelated matters got into a tiff and the firm wanted to drop one so it could represent the other against it. Here, the firm wants to take a *new* matter but for an *old* client. No, said the district judge in *Stratagem. Truck Insurance* is the same. I agree. In the following case (paragraph (2)), however, the conflict "devolved" on the law firm when, by operation of law, the client became successor in interest to the firm's adversary on another matter. The firm didn't do anything wrong here. To refuse to allow it to drop a client so that it may continue to represent another (i.e., *old*) client in an extant (i.e., *old*) litigation would punish that other client. Balancing the equities and recognizing the firm's "clean hands," we should let it withdraw. And that's what the court did. In the two cases cited in paragraph (3), conflicts "devolved" as a result of *client* mergers. Both courts recognized the legitimacy of permitting withdrawal though the *Gould* court, while denying disqualification and distinguishing *Picker*, also said that the firm should have moved more swiftly to correct the situation. In *Oxford* cited at paragraph (4), the court decided that the client in the analogous position to Client One was a current client of the firm even though the firm had done no work for it for a year. This case brings home of the importance of "termination" letters. See also the termination cases at **page 106**.

A final point worth discussing is how a savvy client, perhaps an industry giant, can exploit the "hot potato" rule by trying to neutralize powerful law firms, something it can do by continuously retaining many of them for many different and diverse services, no matter how minor. A firm would have to explore the possibility of anticipatory conflict waivers -- or waivers of the right to assert the "hot potato" rule -- if it wanted to protect itself. The note concludes with a cross-reference to **page 373**, detailing a case in which a firm avoided disqualification not by dropping its client like a "hot potato," but by firing the lawyer who worked for that client and who took the client with him.

Standing and Waiver (page 358). The important point here is that clients can freely waive successive conflicts but not concurrent ones, where waiver is circumscribed by a standard of objective reasonableness. This is because if the firm is no longer representing the client, the risk of disloyalty (as usually conceived) is nil. The only remaining risks are to confidentiality and the particular brand of disloyalty present in successive conflicts matters. Clients can waive confidentiality so they should be able to waive successive conflicts. As for the successive requirement of loyalty, clients can also give up the value of the work a former lawyer once performed for them.

The Appearance of Impropriety (page 358). I think it is important for students to understand this phrase and the influence it has had in the world of lawyer regulation. Although it is dropped from the Model Rules, some states that adopted the Rules retained it, the phrase remains in the Code which continues in many states, and courts continue to quote it even when (as in *Heringer* and *First American Carriers*, **page 359**) the Rules in the particular jurisdiction have *not* retained the "appearance" language.

Conflicts and Class Actions (page 359). Courts are reluctant to apply traditional conflicts rules in class action situations because of their potential for enormous disruption. This position only emphasizes the fact that conflicts rules, and attendant disqualification remedies, cannot be viewed categorically, but rather their wisdom has to be balanced against competing interests in representation and efficiency in litigations. This provides further support for the argument that the "hot potato" rule should not be applied mechanically but that, rather, the legitimate (as opposed to the mercenary) interests of law firms and the representational interests of other clients must be evaluated.

"Divorce and Default" (page 361)

This question gives students a chance to apply the substantial relationship test to an unremarkable fact pattern -- unremarkable except that the first and second matters are in different areas of law and the parties differ. Clarissa will have learned a lot about Patrick's finances in the divorce matter and would likely have learned facts that could be used (including to impeach him) if there is a trial in the foreclosure case. Here the matters are different if we look at their names -- divorce and default -- but they have a subject in common -- financial worth. Under Judge Weinfeld's original formulation, disqualification would be appropriate if the other elements of the test are satisfied. Under the articulation of the Second Circuit in *Cook* (**page 347**), it might not be. Which is right?

Users of the fifth edition will notice that the facts in this problem have been changed to make it a little easier. Previously, the lawyer in Clarissa's position represented the wife, not the husband. On the facts as now written, students will have to deal with the fact that the new matter involves different legal issues and different parties. But the facts from the prior matter – divorce – are likely to be quite relevant to the new matter. Those facts concern Patrick's finances and, therefore, Slipshod's finances since the two are so closely related. And although the new matter is against the company, not Patrick, that close identification between the two should also affect our judgment. In other words, isn't Patrick in the very position that we want to prevent? His former law firm is in possession of relevant confidential information that it can now use in a new matter adverse to him via his company.

Judge Posner would have no trouble in concluding that the test is satisfied although the second matter is different from the first (default rather than divorce). It is a bit harder to ignore the fact that the second adversary is not the former client (Slipshod rather than Patrick). But here is a place where formalism should not reign. For all practical purposes, Patrick is Slipshod. He is its president and largest shareholder. Furthermore, Clarissa had him sign an agreement providing for a lifetime support payments to Leila. So far as the problem suggests, that obligation is not dependent on Slipshod's success. If Slipshod goes under, Patrick will still have the support payment obligation. Indeed, Leila will be even more reliant on these payments because her equity interest in Slipshod, also obtained in the separation agreement, will become worth little or possibly nothing.

This situation can be analogized to the situation where the representation of one affiliate of a corporate family gives the lawyer access to confidential information about another affiliate of the client. The lawyer will thereafter not be allowed to act adversely to the latter, over objection of the former, if the information is relevant to the adverse matter. See **page 359**.

"Do I Still Owe the Record Store?" (page 362)

This problem, largely unchanged from the fifth edition, has always worked well. It gives students a chance to identify whether or not particular work is adverse to a former client and substantially related to the previous work.

Representation of the landlord would be forbidden (paragraph 1) because Lopez would be attacking the scope of a lease covenant she earlier bargained over for Wallace. The risk is that if Lopez can expect to be retained to challenge the meaning of the lease term when the representation ends, she may be tempted to accept a weak clause now. A duty of loyalty that survives the end of the attorney-client relationship aims to prevent present disloyalty motivated by the hope of future gain. In addition, the lawyer may have to be a witness on the meaning of the lease. See Chapter 5C. Next, and I think most important, we respect the client's desire in any event not to see her lawyer argue for an adverse construction of a document the lawyer drafted for the client. Finally, let's not forget that any ambiguity the lawyer failed to clarify in the lease may be the basis for a malpractice action against the lawyer. So the last thing the lawyer would want to do is argue for an interpretation adverse to the former client.

Paragraph (2): If we assume, as I think is most likely, that Lopez's work did not require her to counsel Wallace on bus routes or pedestrian traffic, then while it is true her help may lead to a loss of business, she owes Wallace no duty not to do the work. The answer might be otherwise if, incidentally to her legal work, she did help Wallace compute prospective sales in light of pedestrian traffic -- perhaps as part of her effort to identify a workable credit and cash flow position or in counseling him on the best location to choose. This is debatable. In any event, there has to be some limit. Whether this would cross it could make for good discussion.

Finally, we are confronted with the work for Eloise Case, who wants to open a competing store across from Bill Wallace's store. On the one hand, Lopez has a great deal of information about Wallace's operation that a prospective competitor would like to know. Even if Lopez does not reveal this information, can she avoid using it? What consideration should we give to Wallace's anxiety that Lopez will use it, even if unintentionally? On the other hand, the work is not legally adverse to Wallace. It is only economically adverse to Wallace. Comment [1] and [2] to 1.9 as currently written, coupled with Comment [3] to Rule 1.7, would seem to permit this economically adverse representation as a matter of legal ethics. On the other hand, the *Maritrans* case, cited at **page 347**, disqualified a law firm on the following facts. The firm had done labor negotiations for Client A. The firm then appeared to do labor negotiations for Clients B, C and D, which were competitors of Client A (and of each other). The negotiations for B, C, and D were with different unions, not the union that represented Client A's employees. However, the court concluded that the risk to Client A's confidential information (the terms of its labor contracts) was too great, especially as labor costs were a critical factor in pricing for a highly competitive industry. The court acknowledged that the state's legal ethics rules might not forbid the successive work for Clients B, C, and D, but held that the state's fiduciary duty law did forbid it. *Maritrans* has not been followed in other American jurisdictions. But that doesn't mean that Wallace doesn't have a legitimate concern that the courts should recognize. Or does recognizing that concern create too broad a test for disqualification? A prohibition against representing economic competitors if the secrets of one would be relevant to the work for the other will seriously discourage lawyers from specializing in the legal problems of a particular industry. Coupled with imputed disqualification rules, it can also have a significantly limiting affect on the work of all lawyers in a single office. Yet if we don't forbid the work for the competitor, how do we protect against misuse of the relevant confidential information? Do we ask the client to trust the lawyer? That seems to be the situation today. Of course, a sophisticated client can choose counsel to avoid the problem. Will Coca Cola hire a firm that does work for Pepsi? Can't Ford require agreement that any firm it hires will not do work for G.M.?

The following problem appeared in the fifth edition but does not appear in the sixth edition. However, I offer it here for use in class or perhaps, as you might embellish it, on an examination.

"Opponent Becomes Advocate"

Striker suffers side effects from a medical treatment, consults Remington, who does plaintiff's medical malpractice work, and sues Cavallo, the doctor. Striker loses. After stewing over his loss for a while, Striker comes to believe that Remington was negligent, and he wants to sue him for legal malpractice. He consults Wiggley, the lawyer who defended Cavallo in the medical malpractice case, because he figures Wiggley knows the underlying case and Remington's mistakes better than anyone. Wiggley is interested in Striker's case, which would be against Remington and not against Cavallo. Can Wiggley take it?

My analysis of this problem in the teachers manual for the fifth edition was as follows:

This question is based on California Opinion 93-133, which concluded that Wiggley cannot represent Striker against Remington. If the rule is formally applied, one might argue that Wiggley can take the case because his former client, Cavallo, will not be the defendant. He is not suing his own client. However, Striker's case against Remington is "adverse" to Cavallo in a certain way. Establishing Remington's malpractice could tend to establish Cavallo's negligence. In other words, Wiggley will be arguing that Striker should have won, which means that he should have been able to prove Cavallo's medical malpractice. Cavallo won't like that. Further, of course, Wiggley has presumably a great deal of confidential information about the underlying matter. This information would be relevant on the issue of Remington's legal malpractice because

106

it could tend to establish Cavallo's medical malpractice, something that Wiggley will argue Remington should have been able to uncover. Last, in proving damages, Wiggley would have to show that but for Remington's negligence, Striker would have recovered a certain sum from Cavallo. Here again, Wiggley has incentive to emphasize Cavallo's misconduct and the degree of harm Cavallo caused Striker. This he should not be permitted to do. This question shows that the substantial relationship test cannot be applied literally. One might look at it as a general principle without clear boundaries. The principle can be applied in circumstances not literally within the four corners of the test.

B. IMPUTED DISQUALIFICATION AND MIGRATORY LAWYERS (page 362)

Here we are introduced to the issue of imputation when lawyers travel from one private office to another. This raises the question of screening. Will it be allowed? The Model Rules say no but several, though still a small minority, of jurisdictions allow it. The Seventh Circuit is in that minority. The issue was signaled in *Analytica* (page 339), cited again at note 3 on **page 365**. In many ways, *Cromley* (**page 363**) is an unremarkable case in which the Circuit applied its own precedent to permit screening. The case shows the students what a careful screen should look like and how the Scariano firm planned for Weiner's arrival. The full paragraph at **page 366** explains what the Circuit expects by way of a screen.

The question of screening -- should we allow it, what should we require -- is discussed in the note material beginning at **page 368**. But first, I ask the students to wonder why *Cromley* failed to address two preliminary questions (**page 367**), after signaling unaddressed issues at **page 363**. Didn't Weiner drop Cromley "like a hot potato" to further his own career goals by joining the Scariano firm? Didn't Weiner have an obligation to Cromley to continue with her matter to its conclusion? How, after all, does Weiner's conduct differ from the conduct condemned in *Picker* (**page 355**)? The other question I ask students to ponder is this: Why wasn't it improper for Weiner even to begin to negotiate his new partnership with the Scariano firm while representing a client adverse to that firm? After all, if the Scariano firm's own client in the matter would be greatly advantaged if Weiner were gone, the firm, eager to please its client, could "sweeten" its offer to Weiner to get him to jump. Or so Ms. Cromley might surmise. What ever happened here, isn't this a danger we should recognize? Should we allow Firm A, opposing Firm B in a major litigation with a lot at stake, to offer a very attractive partnership package to the lawyer at Firm B most knowledgeable about the case and most responsible for handling it? Imagine a $50 million case handled by a lawyer at Firm B whose partnership draw is a half a million dollars. Should Firm A, in the middle of that case, be able to offer that partner a $1 million deal if he or she would join Firm A right away? Of course, the lawyer would be screened, but isn't there something wrong here anyway? Authority cited on **page 367** supports a *yes* answer.

The role of presumptions in the operation of the substantial relationship test is extensively discussed in the notes following *Cromley* (**pages 368-377**). Among the matters covered are: (a) explanation of the presumptions and their effect; (b) arguments for and against the rebutability of each of the presumptions; (c) how the presumptions may be rebutted when rebuttal is recognized. I call your attention to the following interesting variations:

(a) Oregon and Massachusetts permit screening but provide more formidable assurance that the screen has been respected. The use of multiple affidavits is described at **page 374**.

(b) *Silver Chrysler Plymouth* (**page 370**) sets out, cogently, the reasons to allow rebuttal of the first presumption (of shared confidences). The New York Court of Appeals, in *Solow* (**page 372**), chose to follow *Silver Chrysler Plymouth* but the opinion could be read to do so only where the firm the migratory lawyer left is not "small" and "informal." While it may be harder to rebut the presumption of shared confidence when a firm is small, should the presumption be conclusive in that circumstance? What is small? The New York court seems to have backed away from this condition in *Kassis* (**page 369**).

(c) At **page 370**, I explain why most jurisdictions and the Model Rules choose not to allow rebuttal of the second presumption. Essentially, the consideration on the other side is the suspicion of the former client that the lawyer was not truly screened and that its confidential information found its way into the enemy camp.

(d) Just as a lawyer can taint a firm to which he or she moves, so can the taint dissipate when the lawyer leaves. Rule 1.10(c). The District of Columbia, however, has made it harder to shake the taint. By using the conjunction "or" in lieu of the conjunction "and," D.C. would forbid a firm to accept an adverse substantially related matter even after the "tainted" lawyer has gone if that lawyer had handled the other side of that matter while at the firm. What is the theory here? That a former client should not have to be in a position to guess about whether its former firm still has its confidences in its file room? That the former client, irrespective of confidences, has a right not to be opposed by its formal law firm on a substantially related matter? That unlike the converse situation described in *Silver Chrysler Plymouth*, there is no countervailing interest in lawyer mobility? (The broader D.C. disqualification rule would not apply if the departed lawyer had done the substantially related adverse work *before* coming to the firm.) The New York Court in *Solow* opted for a distinction based in the size and formality of the departing lawyer's former firm (**page 370**), which distinction probably did not survive *Kassis* (**page 369**).

(e) I find the *Hartford Accident* case rather amusing (**page 373**). The firm effectively fired the lawyer whose presence created the conflict, anticipating that he would take the conflict-creating client with him, which he did. Listen, it's a jungle out there. This avoided the "hot potato" problem. The client chose to leave because the lawyer left. The client was not "fired". In *Hartford Accident*, the departing lawyer had represented the client before coming to the firm and while there. He still represented the client after leaving it. This persuaded Judge Walker that the client was not prejudiced. It still had its "longtime counsel."

(f) The note beginning at **page 373** describes what courts will look for in deciding whether presumptions have been rebutted. We have already seen that *Cromley* well describes what a good screen should have. Failure to screen immediately can have dire consequences **(page 374)**.

The Ethics 2000 Commission **(page 372)** would have allowed "timely" screening, but that position was tentatively rejected at the ABA meeting in August of 2001.

Nonlawyer Conflicts (page 374). This brief note should be of great interest to students because of the possibility that a court will count their summer associate work as a basis for a lateral conflict. That can create a whole lot of headaches for firms hiring new lawyers who worked their summers at other firms. And it can create dilemmas for the lawyers, too. The footnote on **page 375** reveals one firm's awareness of the problem. The balance of this note identifies the same risk for other nonlegal personnel and when a firm speaks to an expert whom the opponent has already consulted.

At **page 376**, I excerpt Judge Low's concurring opposition to the term "Chinese Wall." The term is freely used and perhaps not self-evidently an ethnic or a derogatory reference. But Judge Low, who is of Chinese ancestry, thought it so and I believe students should be aware of that sentiment.

"You Turned on Us" (page 377)

If Monk worked on the actual toaster case now being handled by KGR (paragraph (1)), then KGR would be disqualified unless screening is allowed. (See below for the issue of whose rule applies.) It's the same case and Monk will have worked on it. However, if a new toaster case comes in after Monk has left his former firm (paragraph 2), the plot begins to thicken (or should I say "to thin"). First, the new case will be for a client to whom Monk owes no loyalty and whose confidential information Monk does not have. A precise application of the rule would let Monk work on the matter along with his new firm. And yet, one might ask whether Monk has any obligation to his former firm, if not to its later clients. If he worked on Admiral cases, whether toaster cases or otherwise, he will have acquired a great deal of information about how his former firm prosecutes those cases -- its strategies, its settlement postures, information in its files that would be generically useful for all Admiral cases. Even if Monk has no ethical obligation to other clients of his former firm, current or subsequent, on whose cases he did not and will not work, does he have an obligation to his former firm? If so, it will reside in some theory of fiduciary duty. Should it matter that Monk was an associate, not a partner? Obviously, if the fiduciary-based disqualification is broad, migratory lawyers will not easily be able to oppose their former firms. Yet here, at least, the disqualification would be narrow: products liability cases against Admiral, or perhaps those cases if based on Admiral toasters, because (we assume) Monk will have worked on a toaster case. And where the basis for excluding Monk is fiduciary duty to the firm, not a client, perhaps screening at the new firm should be allowed. In *Greene v. Greene*, 391 N.E.2d 1355 (N.Y. 1979), the court disqualified a law firm from representing a plaintiff who was suing another law firm for breach of fiduciary duty where two members of the plaintiff's firm had been partners at the defendant firm and had had some involvement in the underlying activities. This is, of course, a different situation, but not wholly inapposite.

Still not convinced? We can imagine a situation in which a firm puts an enormous amount of its own resources into a certain kind of litigation. Perhaps it develops a computer program and a great deal of factual data on that type of litigation. Surely it has a proprietary interest in this information, which may have been developed without any particular client's matter in mind. The information is rather developed at the firm's expense to help it across many matters. A lawyer with familiarity with this information, perhaps the very lawyer who supervised its development, then leaves the firm. Wouldn't we say that that lawyer has a fiduciary obligation to the firm to protect the information? And if so, shouldn't that lawyer be disqualified from opposing the firm in an area in which the information is relevant? Of course, as stated above, the disqualification under this theory might be personal, not imputed to other lawyers in the new firm, so long as the migrating lawyer is screened.

What if Monk's work on the matter was only to research venue issues? If he had received no confidences in order to do that, if the issue had been presented to him as one of pure law, the substantial relationship test might not apply. He would have the chance to show as much. See *Satellite Financing Planning Corp. v. First National Bank of Wilmington*, 752 F. Supp. 1281 (D. Del. 1987); *Laker Airways Ltd. v. Pan American World Airways*, 103 F.R.D. 22, 39 (D.D.C. 1984).

Can Monk be screened if he is disqualified? Here is where the Rules and some jurisdictions disagree with other jurisdictions, including the Sixth and Seventh Circuits. The Rules would not allow screening where the migratory lawyer is moving from private practice to private practice. Some jurisdictions, however, would allow screening. Class discussion on whether screening should be allowed in this instance will be worthwhile. What are the effects on migratory lawyers of disallowing screening? On lawyers who are specialists? On lawyers in small communities? On lawyers at the start of their careers? Is screening such a great risk?

Ought it be allowed under some circumstances (compare *Kassis* at **page 369**) and not a matter of categorical prohibition?

It might also be worthwhile discussing whether Monk could well have received confidential information about the matters although he never formally worked on them and billed no time. That could be enough to disqualify him. Are cases informally discussed over lunches among litigators at the prior firm? Was he ever stopped in the library and presented with a set of facts and a question by a colleague? The burden is on Monk to prove that he has no confidences. How can the opponent of Monk contest his assertion of nonaccess without revealing the confidences he allegedly has and which it wants to protect? For example, if Monk was at a litigation lunch at which one of the products liability cases was extensively discussed, will it suffice to negate Monk's declaration of nonaccess for a lawyer at the prior firm to say only that much? Or will the lawyer have to explain what was discussed? If the latter, won't the prior firm be revealing what it wishes to conceal? If the former, the court will have to accept the witness's characterization of the discussion.

A lawyer who had to establish another lawyer's access to confidential information while the other lawyer was at a prior firm once complained to me about how difficult that task is to perform while keeping the client's information secret. In other words, even though, here, the burden would be on Monk, the opponent would wish to introduce some evidence to contradict Monk's credible assertion that he had no access. It can be done, perhaps, but only delicately. The opponent must worry about eliciting too much detail, thereby revealing confidences and possibly waiving the privilege. See also the *Decora* case at **page 345**, which envisions that the former firm might be able to reveal the alleged confidential information to the judge ex parte as a way of establishing that information is at risk.

This brings us to paragraph (3). Can these other firms disqualify Monk from opposing their clients? As we know from our discussion of the common interest privilege (**page 306**) and from *Trinity Ambulance* (**page 352**), there are grounds for arguing that Monk was the lawyer of these other plaintiffs too, at least for conflicts and confidentiality purposes. Assume that Monk worked on the Admiral matters, attended the meetings, and had actual access to the pooled confidential and tactical information. What then? *Trinity Ambulance* and other cases cited at the note at **page 352** would, I think, require his disqualification, on motion of the *other* plaintiffs, and his new firm's disqualification too unless screening were permitted.

While the New York opinion in *Kassis* and the Restatement would allow screening depending on how much information Monk had, imagine how difficult it would be for the prospective new firm to learn that. Using the *Kassis* test, the new employer might ask applicant Monk if he had ever worked on a particular case. Yes, he would say. Is the information you have "significant or material," the firm would ask. How is Monk to answer? Sure, if he did all the heavy lifting, he'll say yes, but what if he did "some work." He can't be more specific. Will the new firm take a chance? I doubt it. It does not want to risk getting kicked off its cases because a court later concludes that screening is forbidden given Monk's knowledge. So a balancing test, while it sounds fair, is often not workable in practice. Firms will be extra cautious and err on the side of refusing to make an offer.

One interesting problem here is this: How would Monk's new firm even know to check for conflicts arising out of the common interest arrangement? If for example the toaster oven case of Monk's former firm had settled but some of the common interest plaintiffs' cases were still pending, Monk's new firm can hardly be expected to ask Monk if he ever worked in such a common interest arrangement. It would look at its database and see that it had no case against Monk's current firm (the one he's leaving) and think itself safe.

But whose rule applies? Students often answer this question by applying the Model Rules, perhaps because they've been instructed to do so, but since we know that tolerance for screening (and perhaps other rules) varies from place to place, we need to know whose rule applies, at least for paragraph (1). Monk is now in Illinois. Let's assume he is now a member of the Illinois bar. But the litigation may be pending elsewhere. The firm he's in has many offices. Monk used to be in Indiana, which may or may not be where the case is pending. Monk may not have joined the Admiral litigation at his new firm. So whose rule applies? It seems to me it would be the rule of the court in which the matter is pending, on motion by Monk's former firm to disqualify the lawyers from his current firm who are defending Admiral in that action (including Monk if he's joined the defense team). But it's interesting, isn't it, that both Monk's former and current state may permit or forbid screening, yet if the action is pending in a jurisdiction that has a different rule, KGR, the new firm, will be bound by that rule. That's how I read the fairly bright line Rule 8.5. The E2k's proposed revision would reach the same result.

"The Verdict Is Unconstitutional" (page 378)

The problem posits that Byon never received Melany's confidential information. So the question is, can he now appear adverse to Melany on the exact same matter? The answer is no. Rule 1.9(a) says nothing about confidential information although generally when two matters are substantially related, it is confidential information that will be at risk. But there is still the continuing duty of loyalty. (**Page 348**. See also the *Sullivan County* case at that page.) Byon cannot turn around and seem to undo the very ruling he successfully achieved for his client. Furthermore, neither can his firm. Imputed disqualification will exclude it. However, as I read the comments to 1.9 and 1.10, if Byon is now at a new firm, that new firm can handle the matter even though Byon cannot. If disqualification is based solely on a surviving duty of loyalty, that duty is not imputed to a new firm. See **pages 371-372.**

C. GOVERNMENT SERVICE

Armstrong v. McAlpin **(page 380)** is a leading case on the ethics of the "revolving door," notwithstanding that it has been vacated on jurisdictional grounds. It states, in part, the position adopted in Rule 1.11. The District of Columbia's version of Rule 1.11 is, as you might expect, substantially more detailed, especially as regards the notice requirements and precautionary measures when a former government lawyer is screened by his or her private firm. New Jersey also varies its version of Rule 1.11, in part by retaining "an appearance of impropriety" standard. New York does the same. DR 9-101(B)(1)(b). In *Brown v. D.C. Board of Zoning Adjustment*, 474 A.2d 37 (D.C. Ct. App. 1984), the term "matter" as used in DR 9-101(B) is defined in terms of the "substantial relationship" test.

Three points students sometimes miss in the area of the "revolving door" are (a) the difference between "confidential information" and "confidential government information" **(page 385)**; (b) that beyond the special rules for former government lawyers in private practice, the government also enjoys all of the traditional rights of a regular client so that even though conduct might not be forbidden by Rule 1.11, it might be forbidden by another rule **(page 388)**, *but see* the next paragraph; and (c) that there are statutory restrictions that overlap and sometimes significantly extend the ethical limitations **(page 386)**.

ABA Opinion 97-409, which unnecessarily and inadvisedly to my mind, concluded that Rule 1.11 is the sole test of the permissibility of a former government lawyer's post-departure work. (Note: The restriction on the imputation of the former government lawyer's conflicts to his or her new colleagues -- governed by Rule 1.11, not Rule 1.10 -- was not an issue in the opinion. In that circumstance, screening is allowed.) According to the ABA, Rule 1.9(a) and (b) does not apply, though Rule 1.9(c), which requires protection of confidential information, does. This result was reached despite contrary language in the comment to Rule 1.11. The Committee seemed to think that Rule 1.9 and Rule 1.11 were contradictory and that it had to choose one or the other to answer *all* questions that may arise when a government lawyer becomes a private lawyer. I think that was error. It was and is certainly possible to apply either Rule's resolution to a particular issue, as the underlying policy dictated. Under the opinion, a lawyer who would personally be disqualified from opposing a former client because of work she did in a private capacity may not be if the former client is the government though the work is identical. I doubt the courts will embrace this Opinion but we'll see. However, the E2K Commission adopts it in substantial part **(page 389)**.

One remarkable consequence of the ABA Opinion, which comes up in "Investigating Landlords," **page 389**, is that a lawyer who drafts legislation or a rule for a government entity can then attack its validity in private practice or argue for a narrower construction than she knew the government intended. This is so because the word "matter" in Rule 1.11(d) does not include drafting. To prevent the lawyer's post-departure effort to undermine the rule or statute, one would have to rely on Rule 1.9(a), but the ABA Opinion says that Rule does not apply to former government lawyers. Can you believe it? Or am I missing something?

What was the reason not to allow the lawyer in *General Motors* to represent the City (**page 384**)? So what if he made use of his prior information? The Rules now allow the former agency to agree to this successive representation, which one must assume it will if the lawyer is effectively on the "same" side. The persons making the decision whether to agree may themselves someday be interested in agency waiver. On the other hand, where "confidential government information" is involved (*e.g.*, here relating to G.M.), it seems proper that the representation should not be allowed, as the Rules establish. The cases on disqualification of prosecutorial offices are noteworthy (**page 386**). The note at **pages 387-389** discusses the meaning of the words "matter" and "substantial responsibility" as these are used in the opinions and the Rules.

New Jersey and West Virginia, perhaps alone, do not allow government agencies to consent to what would otherwise be a revolving door conflict. This is inconsistent with Rule 1.11. (**page 385**.)

"Investigating Landlords" (page 389)

In her investigation and preparation for the hearings, Ho likely acquired confidential government information about landlords. If so, and if she is suing such a landlord on behalf of a tenant, she could be disqualified under Rule 1.11(b) if the information could be used to the "material disadvantage of" that landlord. The city cannot waive. If she does not have confidential government information about the landlord she is suing that could be used to its "material disadvantage," she can sue but she needs the permission of the city under Rule 1.11(a) if the two matters are substantially related. Are they? I don't think so. The investigation and drafting of the legislation is different from the fact-based claim that a particular landlord is violating one of its provisions. Otherwise, Ho will be the only lawyer in town who will not be able to represent tenants in actions under the law without city permission. If Ho is disqualified because she has confidential government information about the landlord within the meaning of Rule 1.11(b), she can be screened by a firm she thereafter joins.

With regard to representing a landlord sued under the statute, Ho may have confidential government information about it, but if it's about her own client, Rule 1.11(b) is inapplicable. Rule 1.11(a) is also inapplicable if the matters are not the same, and one would think they would not be the same here if they were not the same when Ho was going to represent the tenant.

When representing a landlord, it is possible that Ho will have to attack the validity of the statute or in some other way undermine her labors for her former client, the city. (If she does attack the validity of the statute, the city might intervene to defend it.) Could she be disqualified under Rule 1.9(a)? The city as a former client enjoys a surviving duty of loyalty which, it could fairly be argued, would be compromised on these facts. Ho would be attacking the validity of the very law she drafted. But see below.

One policy reason for disqualifying Ho from a representation in which she has to attack "her" law is the reason for creating a duty of surviving loyalty in the first place. We don't want Ho writing the law in a way that will lend itself to attack by landlords later on if she secretly hopes to be retained by them. (She'd be foolish to do this for malpractice reasons too.) On this analysis, Ho could not represent a landlord if she were going to attack the validity of the law, but rather would have to wait until the statute's constitutionality were upheld in another case argued by another lawyer. This Rule 1.9(a) analysis won't work under Rule 1.11(a), because the word "matter" in Rule 1.11(a) is defined in Rule 1.11(d) not to include drafting. The 1982 draft of the Rules anticipated in the comment to Rule 1.11 that "matter would include drafting of legislation." That definition was deleted.

However, as stated above, if Rule 1.9(a) does not apply to Ho post-departure work, as ABA Opinion 97-409 **(page 388)** surprisingly concluded, and despite comment [2] to Rule 1.9, then there is nothing in the Rules to stop Ho form attacking the constitutionality of the statute she drafted or for arguing for an interpretation narrower than she was instructed was the legislative aim. (She might still worry about adverse publicity and malpractice.) The E2K Commission's proposal would reach the same result **(page 389)**.

Assume the ABA is wrong. What about imputed disqualification if Ho thereafter joins a firm? Then, she would continue to have a surviving duty of loyalty (but only that), which would prevent her from attacking the constitutionality of the statute she drafted, but that duty would not be imputed to her new firm. It's not even clear that she would have to be screened under Rule 1.11 because now we would be operating under Rules 1.9 and 1.10, not 1.11, and loyalty duties of migratory lawyers, standing alone, are not imputed.

One issue on which the text of Rule 1.11(b) is silent is this: Assume Ho got confidential government information about a landlord while in private practice and *retained* by government to do her study. Thereafter, can her firm take a case against the landlord and screen Ho, as it could have done were she to have acquired her information about the landlord while employed by government and had then moved to the firm? The government is not the opponent -- the firm is not attacking the law -- so Rule 1.9 is inapplicable. But Ho would surely be disqualified, though retained not employed, and Rule 1.10(a) might then operate to disqualify the whole firm even though, had Ho done her work as a government employee and then moved to the firm, she could have been screened. Shouldn't we apply the screening authorization of Rule 1.11 to this situation, too, in order to encourage lawyers like Ho to accept public service requests even as they remain in private practice? Rule 1.11 comment [2] can be read to reach such "specially retained" lawyers and place them under Rule 1.11 for imputation purposes.

PART III

SPECIAL LAWYER ROLES

CHAPTER VII

ETHICS IN ADVOCACY

The ways to teach the issues in this chapter may be as many as there are teachers of the subject. For many, those issues are the heart of the course. Okay, that's overstated but the point is valid. I don't believe that this is because the issues here are <u>likely</u> to confront our students in the course of their careers. So many of the issues are litigation oriented, for one thing, and so many students will not be litigators. Even those who do litigate will find that many of the "close" questions, the ones we argue over in class, rarely arise. Nevertheless, I believe the issues in Chapter 7 are important because in thinking about them and addressing them we become most mindful of the need for a concept of what it means to be a lawyer for a client, of the need for a theory of the American lawyer's role and therefore a theory of American justice. So (after some quotes) the chapter begins with a brief but lively introduction to the advocate's beleaguered state (**page 394**) and then moves to five different perspectives on the issues, all of which is prefatory to the body of this chapter and Chapter 8, which focuses on some issues particular to criminal cases.

The quotes that start the chapter, aside from being interesting to read in themselves, tell the student that image and reality, sincerity and disguise, and truth and perception are not polarities peculiar to advocacy. Certainly they occur as well in politics and, in some epochs, religion.

I urge you to assign the introductory matter. It crystallizes the debate by bringing home the advocate's special position. And of course it signals the Johnson-Boswell exchange recounted in Judge Rifkind's excerpt (**pages 400-401**). At **page 395** we have the equally famous assertion by Lord Brougham in Queen Caroline's case followed by Judge McLaughlin's (unfair?) dismissal of it. The introductory matter also draws the ends-means distinction and provides a reading list for further study.

A. FIVE VIEWS ON ADVERSARY "JUSTICE" (page 398)

The selections here, in one way or another, touch upon the role of truth in the adversary process. For Judge Rifkind (**page 398**) and Professor Ball (**page 409**), insistence on trying to discover some kind of real or absolute truth is misguided. Compare Professor Ball's theatrical metaphor, and Judge Rifkind's allusion to literary truth (**page 402**), with Professor Post's essay at **page 412**. For Judge Frankel (**page 404**) and Professor Schwartz (**page 407**), truth is important, but is it important in the same way and deserving of the same prominence for each of these authors? It should be stressed that for Rifkind and Ball truth is not wholly irrelevant and for Frankel and Schwartz truth is not a goal to pursue at any cost. Are we talking about different positions on a continuum? Or are we talking about differences of kind?

The excerpt from Judge Frankel's book extends the debate in another way. How do those students who opt for Rifkind's realism and reject Schwartz's vision of "trial as laboratory" respond to Frankel, who does not accept the claim that confrontation between opposing sides will yield the greatest truth of which we are capable and bemoans the fact that many lawyers spend a great deal of time trying to figure out how to help their clients suppress truth? He describes techniques for doing this. Judge Rifkind would say that Judge Frankel is on the wrong track. We can't have lawyers worry about truth. We can't even have a system that is overly concerned with identifying it (though he hedges here by suggesting that the system we do have is as good as any for this purpose, **page 400**). We have many values to which truth is decidedly subservient (**pages 402-403**). Furthermore, there are social costs in making truth too prominent a goal.

Judge Frankel argues that an emphasis on adversariness is not the only way to resolve disputes (**page 404**). Here is an interesting thought: Judges Rifkind and Frankel are not describing different systems nor even the same system in different ways. They largely agree on the nature of the adversary system but as good advocates characterize it (and its consequences) differently. For example, Frankel says that trials pay little attention to discovering objective truth in favor of other values. Rifkind to some extent agrees. Frankel says that's bad. Rifkind says that's good. Frankel says the lawyer's job is to go to great lengths to avoid the truth that hurts her client and that's bad. Rifkind agrees with the description of the job and suggests that it's good. In this contest, the facts are not really in dispute, are they? Is this issue then ripe for summary judgment, based on deeper values? See "Which System Is Better?" at **page 417**.

One other angle worth addressing: Judge Rifkind candidly acknowledges that the adversary system tends "to reward most highly those lawyers who are best suited to the adversary process. In consequence, such lawyers have established the norms of performance." (**page 400**) If the system rewards those who perform well at it, and if the same group largely controls the system's rules, is there any chance for serious reform? Frankel makes the point (**page 406**) that even reforms get "turned -- and twisted -- to adversary uses" (referring to discovery). Stated another way, if a markedly less adversarial system were to produce fewer rewards for advocates, is there any realistic chance of its adoption?

Recall the "Karen Horowitz" problem at **page 256**, the one in which the law firm refused to send a female Jewish lawyer into a rural southern courtroom and would even staff cases with a view to jury biases. Given the Ball-Post analogy of trials and lawyers to the theatre and actors, should the law firm's decision be viewed as a wise "casting" choice and entirely appropriate under the circumstances?

I think you have two choices pedagogically. You can assign Chapter 7A for home reading or you can assign it and discuss it in class, perhaps with the benefit of the questions at **pages 417**. I urge you to assign it at least for home reading because it provides a backdrop for much that follows and, because of the skill of the authors, it is engaging reading.

"Which System Is Better?" (page 417)

Which system would students choose? Does it, should it, depend upon one's place in society? Would a student opt for the Rifkind or Frankel model if the student did not know where he or she would sit in society? Do those of us who side with Rifkind or Ball do so because they are "correct" or because we are better off under their visions? What does "correct" mean here? One possibility is that an adversary system lets the litigants, with their advocates, "fight" for what they claim is their due. It respects their autonomy as individuals. It gives them a chance to "stand up" to the system and their opponents. Whether they win or lose, that has inherent value. Is this persuasive? And by the way, since lawyers are as a group likely to be better off under Rifkind's system -- more to sell, if nothing else -- who should be making these decisions? The bar? What about self-interest? The courts? What about professional self-identification and class consciousness? The legislature?

Sometimes students have opted for the adversarial system because, they argue, if information must be shared lawyers will refrain from gathering it for fear of aiding the opponent. I find this hard to credit as a general rule. Passivity can also result in loss of *useful* information. On the other hand, perhaps lawyers will ignore certain leads because the balance of probabilities makes it too likely that they will discover harmful information that they will have to share. Students also argue, with greater force I think, that the cooperative system's rules will be unenforceable. Lawyers and clients will violate the rules and these violations will be hard to detect. Lawyers may instruct clients on the rules before clients say anything, leading clients to screen information before providing it to lawyers. I sometimes point out that under the Brady rule prosecutors now live in (but do not always honor) a system akin to the cooperative system's requirement of information sharing. I also point out that in discovery today, a notice to produce documents, absent privilege or other defense, requires production even of damaging documents. Violation of this duty is also hard to detect, yet we rely on lawyers and clients to comply with it.

In this problem, I envision that the attorney-client privilege would survive even in the cooperative legal system so there can be no argument that clients will refrain from giving information to their lawyers on the theory that that information would then have to be shared. However, facts discovered in the derivative use of this information – like the identity of a witness – would have to be shared.

B. ARE LAWYERS MORALLY ACCOUNTABLE FOR THEIR CLIENTS? (page 418)

This material that will facilitate discussion on whether lawyers can be blamed for their choice of client. In other words, if lawyers are unaccountable within a particular representation when they seek to achieve a lawful goal ethically and legally, nevertheless, can we question their decision to accept the particular client in the first place? Or: If a lawyer spends his or her life defending major drug dealers or foreign dictators or corporate criminals, is it morally defensible to blame them? Or will they have an excuse based on their status as lawyers?

This material begins with the language of Rule 1.2(b), which is odd because it doesn't tell lawyers that they may or must do anything or not to do anything. It only says that by accepting a client they do not necessarily endorse the client's views. So what? Why is that provision in the Model Rules?

The incident I use to raise the question of moral responsibility for choice of clients is Cravath's representation of Credit Suisse **(page 418)**.

Cravath represented of Credit Suisse in connection with claims that it helped launder gold the Nazis stole from Holocaust victims. This event has the advantage of internal protest from Cravath lawyers and an Op-Ed criticism by Ronald Goldfarb **(page 419)**. The introductory note reveals diverse views within the bar and a comparison to Sofaer and Libya.

Students are often concerned about whose work they'll be called upon to do and their perceived inability (or team player reluctance) to decline. Does a lawyer who works on behalf of a bad client avoid taint because he or she is a lawyer? Are there limits on this ability to deny culpability? Remember, no one is saying that the lawyer should be punished for his or her choice of client. The question is whether it is proper to voice moral criticism or whether the lawyer's status leaves him or her immune? Pedagogically, I have sometimes had a set of students write a paper taking a position on Cravath's decision.

C. TRUTH AND CONFIDENCES

The introductory essay (**pages 422-423**) sets out the paradigm of the perjurious criminal defendant but also describes a number of variations, including: the case may be civil or criminal; the perjurer may be a client or a witness; and the perjury can be anticipated, surprise, or completed. **Pages 423-426** review the legislative history of the Code and Rules. (Opinion 353 (**page 426**) does the same for the Canons.) The Code history takes the student through the amendment to DR 7-102(B)(1) and Opinion 341. A student should know this history in order to understand the material that follows. Forgive my chauvinism, but I believe that knowing it is part of being an American lawyer, part of the profession's "cultural literacy." The Rules history reveals how much Rule 3.3 was narrowed from the January 1980 Draft (where it appeared as Rule 3.1).

ABA Opinion 353 (**page 426**) is the ABA's pronouncement on Rule 3.3 generally and in light of *Nix v. Whiteside*. I divide the opinion in two, with *Nix* in the middle (**page 431**). The second half of Opinion 353 is the part that addresses *Nix* (**page 441**). The first half discusses the lawyer's duty on discovering perjury or false evidence. The first half also reviews the obligations under the Canons of Professional Ethics and Opinion 287 (**pages 427-428**). Several points worth underscoring here are: (a) the time limit on the disclosure duty (**page 427**); (b) the way the Committee handles the lawyer's responsibility if the judge directly asks the lawyer for information the lawyer can't provide (**page 427 n.5**); (c) the Committee's view that disclosure of the client's false statement will be the only "reasonable remedial" measure available even though this is not explicitly what the rule requires (**page 428 n.7**); and (d) most interesting, the Committee's willingness to read the word "assisting" in subsection (a)(2) in a "prophylactic" way (**page 428**) and not as "limited to the criminal law concepts of aiding and abetting or subornation." (This issue comes up again at **page 489** and has significant implications.)

Opinion 353 does not require a lawyer whose client has committed a fraud on a tribunal to withdraw (**page 426 n.2**). Opinion 287 did require withdrawal, while Opinion 341 said nothing. Of course, the lawyer cannot aid the fraud. Further, when the lawyer takes remedial measures, she will often have to do something that will make a continued relationship impossible. See **page 429**.

The second note on **page 430** ("Ethics, Lies, and Rule 26") introduces the student to the intersection between the disclosure obligations in Rule 3.3 and disclosure obligations that may exist in discovery rules, including the Federal Rules as amended. When the discovery rules mandate revelation of information and a client has failed to honor that mandate, Rule 3.3 may require the lawyer to correct the failure. Much depends on the precise language of the discovery rule. The note ends with the dissent of three justices from the adoption of certain of the Rule 26 amendments, expressing the view that they are out of synch with our judicial system and "lawyers' ethical duty to represent their clients and not to assist the opposing side." One can make the same argument against the election, in Rule 3.3, to subordinate confidentiality to the duty to correct fraud on the court.

Nix v. Whiteside **(page 431).** We interrupt Opinion 353 to bring you a word from the Supreme Court. The balance of Opinion 353, which addresses the *Nix* issue from the ethics perspective **(page 441)**, then follows. The note material at **pages 445-456** identifies, with interesting reading (I hope), questions still open after *Nix* and Opinion 353. Among the issues you may wish to raise or points you may wish to make in discussing this material are the following:

(a) *Nix* is a constitutional decision. Opinion 353 construes the Model Rules. But as Justice Brennan points out in concurrence, states are free to fashion other ethical rules. So an overhanging question is: should they? Does Opinion 353 reach the right ethical result, even if the conduct it commands would not render counsel ineffective? Some places do not subscribe to the Model Rules' position that the duty to reveal fraud on the court is superior to the confidentiality duty. Among these are New York, the District of Columbia, Illinois, Maryland, Massachusetts, and Washington State. The District of Columbia permits a narrative if withdrawal is denied. Massachusetts allows a narrative if withdrawal is not possible without prejudicing the defendant. So does other authority cited at **pages 445-448**, including New York, Pennsylvania, and Delaware. The *Johnson* case at **page 445** nicely sets out the varying approaches and adopts the narrative approach as the best. What's wrong with the narrative solution anyway? I'm rather partial to it. I realize it's a compromise position, but what's wrong with compromise?

(b) When does a lawyer "know" something? Justice Stevens made this point in his *Nix* concurrence, emphasizing that the Court was in the relatively luxurious position of being able to assume that Whiteside was going to lie. The issue of what "know" means arose in *Doe v. Federal Grievance Committee* **(page 448)**, and is discussed at **pages 448-450**. Take a look at *Wuliger* **(page 449)**, where a lawyer, with only partial success, argued that he had the right to maintain ignorance of the truth of a client's explanation for the genesis of a tape recording, which the lawyer then used. The tape was made in violation of federal law and the lawyer was prosecuted. At **page 450**, the note discusses the propriety of an effort to avoid knowledge. Is there anything wrong with that? Doesn't it undermine the lawyer's duty of competence? ABA Opinion 353 deems it improper.

(c) When a lawyer asks a client to tell her the facts, should the lawyer have to give the client "*Miranda*" warnings about the way in which the client's rendition of the facts will thereafter constrain the lawyer? Perhaps the lawyer should say something like:

"Before you tell me your story, you should know that ethical rules may prevent me from letting you testify contrary to that story and may require me to call material inconsistencies to the attention of the court, should they occur. I will also be generally unable to introduce testimony or witnesses that contradict the facts you tell me are true. Now, tell me your story."

Or is this an invitation to lie? I finally read "the lecture" in Anatomy of a Murder. It works really well here and I've included a section from the book after describing the characters. Biegler doesn't give Manion the warning set out above, at least not explicitly, but he says enough about the law and what it will and will not allow him to do to make it rather clear what he wants to hear. Is Biegler's conduct acceptable? Most lawyers would say it is. But I ask: What legitimate good purpose could it have? We know the illegitimate purpose. **(pages 451-453)**

(d) What should the judge do when the lawyer complies with his obligations to report fraud on the court? The excerpt from "L.A. Law" at **pages 453-454** shows one savvy judicial reaction. But if that's what the judge is going to do in any event, why go through this? Why not just let the jury do its job? And what should the judge do if the lawyer tells the judge that the client has lied and the client denies it? Or if the client complains that the lawyer won't call her to testify because the lawyer erroneously believes she will lie? How can the judge resolve that issue?

Because it may be the only example of this sort of thing we will ever see, and because it happened in a case with which all students should be familiar, I have included Robert Bennett's letter to Judge Wright withdrawing the affidavit of Monica Lewinsky he submitted in connection with President Clinton's deposition **(page 455)**. This is an example of the application of Rule 3.3(v), which was binding on Bennett because the case was pending in the Arkansas federal courts, which had adopted the state ethics rules, which included Rule 3.3. The rule in Washington, D.C., where Bennett actually practiced, would not have required this withdrawal.

D. FOSTERING FALSITY OR ADVANCING TRUTH? (page 457)

Lawyers are forbidden to lie or to use or exploit the lies of others in their representation of clients. But lawyers are not forbidden, at least not explicitly, to mislead or to tolerate (even encourage) the misperceptions of others. This freedom, to the extent it exists, and it exists to some extent, presents some of the most interesting riddles in the course. Let's face it: Tricks for fooling people without actually lying are often the stuff of "how to" books and the speeches of legal raconteurs. The material beginning at **page 457** identifies seven ways in which lawyers may seek to encourage error in others. While none of this material is central to the basic legal ethics course, all of it is interesting. You can pick and choose which portions you might assign in any one year.

1. Literal Truth (page 457). I have somewhat expanded this material in light of the *Jones v. Clinton* case. The purpose of this section is to help students understand that truth is relative, at least in the sense that what we might call a lie in everyday life might be unobjectionable, even expected, in litigation. But how much will even litigation tolerate? The first three entries **(pages 457-459)** provide "everyday life" events in which the speakers speak literal truth but which we would call lies. We then turn to the Clinton testimony in *Jones v. Clinton*. I focus on the meaning of the word "alone," as Clinton tried to define it to avoid a charge that he committed perjury. The material at **page 461** reveals that Clinton's "plea bargain" did not involve a concession that he lied. Probably most people don't realize this. You might say that Clinton confessed to a failure of craft and of mistakenly, but with the best of intentions, saying something false when he intended to say something true.

The *Bronston* case appears at **page 462**, followed by the Sixth Circuit's opinion in *DeZarn*, which was much cited during the impeachment proceedings. *DeZarn* can be juxtaposed with *Bronston*. *DeZarn* holds, in language broader than the facts required, that context can make a literally truthful answer false and therefore perjurious. We end with the risk of contempt if what a person believes is literally true turns out to be false in the view of the judge. **(Page 465)**

2. Cross-examining the Truthful Witness (page 465). This may be one of the most common examples and, surely, at least today, the rules allow it of all but prosecutors if the goal is to make the knowingly true appear false. Should they? What if the cross-examination demeans and degrades a truthful witness? If the lawyer knows the witness is telling the truth -- and we recognize that that is not always so -- why allow the lawyer to degrade the witness, who may be doing his or her civic duty in coming to court in the first place? But if the lawyer does not cross-examine, isn't he or she bolstering the witness's credibility through inaction, especially if the lawyer has cross-examined other witnesses? Also, wouldn't a rule that forbids the lawyer to cross-examine a truthful witness -- or at least forbids the lawyer to attack the credibility of a truthful witness -- encourage the client to lie to the lawyer? Perhaps so, but the rule forbidding lawyers to call perjurious witnesses, including the criminal defendant, might also encourage clients to lie to lawyers. A possible middle ground would be to forbid the lawyer to attack the credibility of witnesses with essentially collateral matters (e.g., incidents in the witness's private life even if otherwise permitted by the evidence rules) when the lawyer knows the witness is telling the truth. See below.

I urge you to benefit from the sharp dialogue between Kornstein and the Rubens. Kornstein responds to the Rubens in a letter reprinted in part at **page 470**. The debate centers on Max Steuer's famous cross-examination of Kate Alterman in the Triangle Shirtwaist Company

126

Fire case. Would Steuer's conduct have been proper -- would it be proper today -- if he knew that Alterman were telling the truth? Is Kornstein too apologetic in his response? Insufficiently apologetic?

Incidentally, notice that the Rubens criticize the "moral vacuum in which many lawyers operate." Kornstein seems in his reply to take this as a criticism of Steuer. But wasn't it intended as a criticism of Kornstein for encouraging a celebration of Steuer's tactic?

Here is a variation on the Kornstein-Rubens debate. The witness has no trouble testifying in conversational English. However, Steuer learns that nine years ago the witness pleaded guilty to receiving money under false pretenses in the third degree, a misdemeanor, in satisfaction of an indictment charging receipt of money under false pretenses in the second degree, a felony. Assume alternatively that the jurisdiction in which the current case is being tried either allows impeachment with the misdemeanor conviction (see Federal Evidence Rule 609(a)(2)) or that, in any event, Steuer can ask about the underlying events, or both. The trial judge has no discretion to exclude the question. The witness served no jail time and has since moved and taken a government job, where she has distinguished herself and risen to a position of high trust. Her employer is unaware of her conviction. If it becomes public, she will lose her job. Further, as it happens, the jurisdiction routinely permits trials to be televised and this one will be. (This additional "fact" is not necessary, but it does tighten the screw.) Steuer lets it be known that if the witness testifies, he will use her prior conviction and the underlying act to impeach her credibility although it will have only modest effect there, if any. Steuer knows (let us assume) that the witness is telling the truth. May he, should he ethically be permitted to, threaten the use of the information on cross-examination and, in fact, use it? Assume the judge has no discretion to forbid its use or is not likely to forbid it.

This "variation" has been turned into an NYU-produced video ("Plea Negotiation"). The video posits a prosecutor's use of information like that described, although it also asks if the same rules would apply to defense use.

3. Appeals to Bias (page 470). Although the number of cases addressing improper appeals to bias in jury argument is sparse, I believe it is a worthwhile topic within this Section while recognizing that the Section itself is only a strong coverage preference, not a mandatory one. Further, the ABA Judicial Conduct Code requires judges to prevent from exhibiting bias **(page 471)**. The two cases here result in reversals of civil court verdicts where the successful lawyer was seen to play to juror bias against, respectively, the Japanese and out-of-state residents.

4. The Boundaries of Proper Argument (page 474). I include material on both "Arguing for False Inferences" **(page 475)**, and the scope of proper argument **(page 474)**. For the latter, I use the Third Circuit's affirmance of a district court's grant of a motion for a new trial

127

based on improper argument of plaintiff's counsel. Among other things, counsel argued his own truthfulness, supplied facts not in the record in his argument, expressed his own opinion that the defendant had concealed information and lied, referred to a crime and a conspiracy that had been removed from the case by a directed verdict, and in view of the lower court, most troubling, disparaged defense counsel including with an implication of "sexual misconduct" between one of the defense counsel and a witness.

I have kept the Subin-Mitchell debate because I find it to be a crisp distillation of conflicting policies. Beginning at **page 478**, Professor Subin argues that the right to present "a false case [is] not absolute." He is right, of course. The defendant has no right to use perjured testimony. Professor Subin wonders why we draw the line there. He would forbid a lawyer who knows beyond a reasonable doubt the truth of a fact to attempt to refute it through the introduction of evidence, impeachment, or argument. The lawyer would be reduced to a so-called monitoring function, which mainly means that the lawyer would be limited to argue to the jury that the state had not proved its case beyond a reasonable doubt. (Why should the lawyer be allowed even to do that?)

Mr. Mitchell **(page 479)** provides a hypothetical in reply and identifies the evidence he would elicit and the argument he would make based on it. He provides an alternate theory of the defense lawyer's role and defends it. In response, Subin identifies a different argument as the one defense lawyers would likely give and criticizes the argument Mitchell would give as well. He also criticizes Mitchell's willingness to elicit the fact that the store manager possessed a lead pipe. The only reason the defense lawyer would elicit this information would be to encourage the jury to draw a false inference, which Subin would not allow.

The questions at **pages 483-485** explore the Subin-Mitchell debate. Question 1 asks students to identify the winner. Most students will, I suspect, pick Mitchell. But then they have to explain why we draw the line at perjurious testimony, an act Subin calls "utterly arbitrary." One possible answer is that perjury is a crime. But this just moves the inquiry a step further along: We could also make arguing for false inferences a crime. A second answer is that a lawyer who argues for false inferences, or who attempts through impeachment or otherwise to encourage the jury to believe a false fact, is not representing something false as true or something true as false. Everything the jury has heard and seen is true "information" (as Mitchell would use the word). The lawyer is only encouraging the jury to use that information one way rather than another. Is this a tenable distinction? Does it stand up when applied to my modification on the Steuer cross-examination above?

Question 2 **(page 483)** asks what if anything is wrong with the alternate argument Subin sets out at **page 482**. Couldn't the defense lawyer go so far as to ask the jury to find as a fact, based on the evidence, that her client walked out with the ornament by accident? Couldn't she say: "I submit the following is what happened, ladies and gentlemen. In the hustle and bustle of Christmas shopping . . . "? This question leads to Question 3 **(page 483)**, which reincorporates

128

Question 1. Most defense lawyers would feel they were entitled to ask the jury to find that the defendant's tears were caused by the lead pipe even if they knew she did not see the pipe. That is a permissible inference from the "information" available to the jury. I think they'd be quite correct in this view. They could not, however, have the defendant testify that she feared the lead pipe if she didn't see it. But then we're back at Question 1: How can we let the defense lawyer argue for the false inference from the existence of the lead pipe but not let her elicit a false statement from the defendant about the cause of her tears? Is that "utterly arbitrary"?

The fourth question asks whether any of the answers the student has given to the first three questions would change if the lawyer arguing for the false inference is a prosecutor rather than a defense lawyer. What about a government lawyer in a civil case? If the answer is that either government lawyer is somehow in a different position, aren't we disabling the government unfairly? Or if the population comes to understand that the government cannot do things that private lawyers can do, won't jurors begin to distrust private lawyers?

One question I have asked my class (in Question 5) is this: If you are prepared to let the defense lawyer argue for false inferences, attempt to disprove a fact they know is true, and impeach truthful witnesses, are you prepared to let the trial judge instruct the jury that the defense lawyer can do this but that the prosecutor cannot? Why shouldn't the jury have all the necessary information? Refusal to give the jury this information would seem to encourage error, or at least duplicity. Alternatively, we can give the defense lawyer a choice. If she wants the freedom to "fool" the jury in these ways, then she has to let the judge tell the jury that the playing field is not level. What's wrong with that?

I further explore these questions with two hypotheticals at **pages 484-485**.

"The Eyewitness" (Part I) (page 484)

The answer to the first question is certainly that the lawyer can employ the impeachment even though he knows the witness is telling the truth. An interesting variation, referenced above, is whether the defense lawyer can let it be known that he plans to use the prior guilty plea to impeach, expecting that that prospect might discourage the witness from testifying in the first place. I think the answer to this is no. The lawyer should not be able to avoid the testimony by, in effect, threatening the witness. On the other hand, it would be virtually impossible to police such conduct since the lawyer might simply contact the witness in an effort to ascertain whether his information is correct.

The answer to the second question is also yes. The witness is telling the truth – he did see the defendant in the Burger King. The lawyer is free to argue false inferences from the true testimony, although Professor Subin would disagree. Professor Subin would also disagree with

129

the answer to the lawyer's first question. He would not let the lawyer impeach knowingly truthful testimony.

"The Eyewitness" (Part II) (page 484)

This question poses the same issue from the prospective of the prosecutor. To what extent is the prosecutor more restricted than the defense lawyer? Can a prosecutor cross-examine a knowingly truthful witness (and you should assume the prosecutor knows the witness is telling the truth) in an effort to discourage the jury from believing the witness? The prosecutor worries that otherwise the witness's testimony will enable the defense lawyer to argue reasonable doubt. This is a tough one. I am inclined to believe that the prosecutor may not impeach a knowingly truthful witness in this way. So the Subin world would actually exist for prosecutors and possibly for government lawyers in enforcement proceedings. But this is a close question and many may disagree. As for letting the prosecutor argue that the witness's testimony is wrong, the prosecutor may want to do this even if she doesn't cross-examine the witness with the conviction. For example, she may want to point out discrepancies between the video and the defendant's appearance. If, again, you assume that the prosecutor has no doubt that the defendant was in the Burger King, may she nevertheless attempt to persuade the jury to discount the eyewitness? The problem has the prosecutor say that she believes that the defendant was in the Burger King. This is obviously less strong than knowing beyond a reasonable doubt. You might want to play with the difference. If the prosecutor only believes but does not know, it is easier to let her impeach and argue for the contrary inference. But what if she knows? And even if she only believes that the witness is wrong, would that be enough for her to be able to use the two-year-old conviction since there is no evidence here that the witness is being suborned? Could the prosecutor let it be known that she is prepared to cross-examine the witness with the conviction in an effort to discourage the witness from testifying in the first place? I don't think so, just as I don't think the defense lawyer has a legitimate basis to do that.

5. Exploiting Error (page 485). This wonderful Michigan opinion, which could be an exam question, has the lawyer exploiting the error of a crime victim about the time the crime occurred. The crime victim misremembers, but the time he does remember is the time for which the client has a valid alibi. The lawyer is free to call the alibi witnesses and argue his client's innocence even though he knows that the client is guilty and the victim is wrong about the time of the offense. In the Michigan opinion, the defense lawyer is exploiting error by the prosecution's witness. Perhaps the harder question is this: Could the defense lawyer call a witness who is telling the "truth" but is wrong, so there is no actual perjury? If a lawyer can help a client tell the literal but misleading truth, why can't the lawyer call a witness who is telling the truth as the witness remembers it even though the lawyer knows the testimony is wrong? Or does

130

that conduct fall on the wrong side of the line? Just asking the question gives some added ammunition to Professor Subin's point that the place we now draw the line is "utterly arbitrary."

6. Silence (page 487). Watch this category. It may grow. Given the "prophylactic" view the ABA Committee took in Opinion 353 of the word "assisting" as it appears in Rule 3.3(a)(2), lawyers may have significantly more affirmative obligations than anyone assumed when the Rules were adopted. (Interesting question of governance comes up here: If the Committee's gloss were on the table before the House of Delegates when it adopted Rule 3.3, does anyone believe the House would have passed it?) The smattering of judicial authority gives lawyers duties to speak up in various contexts **(pages 488-491)**. Discovery rules may as well.

One of the video vignettes I use, "Pinocchio's Lawyer," plays with the issues of silence and literal truth. When showing "Pinocchio's Lawyer" to an assemblage of lawyers in Florida, one member of the audience told me about the *Diago* case **(page 487)**, which certainly tests the conventional reaction to "Pinocchio's Lawyer." The case is very brief but essentially the client did not reveal, when examined, that he had been in an intervening accident, which might explain some of his injuries. However, the trial judge refused to vacate a $1 million judgment in plaintiff's favor after the defendant, learning of the intervening action, so moved. The appellate court excoriates the trial judge. But what did the plaintiff do wrong? He didn't lie. In footnote 2, the appellate court cites the language in the comment to Rule 3.3 that silence can sometimes be an affirmative representation. It might also have looked at the definition of "fraud" in the Terminology section. It says that fraud "denotes conduct having a purpose to deceive" and excludes a mere "failure to apprise another of relevant information." Which was this?

The first paragraph on **page 491** explains the relationship between confidentiality and reporting duties under the ethics codes, on the one hand, and discovery rules on the other. See also the discussion of "Ethics, Lies, and Rule 26" at **page 430**.

"Carl's Deception" (page 491)

This is an "on the one hand, on the other hand" set of questions. On the one hand, no one has committed perjury. Carl lied (*if* we assume Tanya has "knowledge" that what he said was knowingly false) but he did not lie under oath. His expert witness gave an opinion based on false assumptions, but she believed that her opinion was true. She was under oath but she didn't lie. Consequently, in this view, Tanya has not introduced "false" evidence within the meaning of Rule 3.3(a)(4). Nor, from this perspective, has the client committed a "fraud" upon the tribunal within the meaning of DR 7-102(B)(1) because he did not perjure himself.

On the other hand, perhaps Tanya does now know that the psychiatrist's testimony is "false" in the sense that it provides an opinion based on assumed (and stated) facts that are false. Without those facts, the opinion would be different and so the opinion is not true. Further, the client may have committed a "fraudulent act" within the meaning of Rule 3.3(a)(2) and also a "fraud" on the court under DR 7-102(B)(1) (if read more broadly). Given the ABA's reading of "assisting" in Opinion 353 to have a "prophylactic" dimension, Tanya has an obligation to correct this fraud on the court. In Rules' jurisdictions, these obligations are superior to the lawyer's confidentiality duties. They are as well in many Code jurisdictions, although not in all.

Two questions are whether Carl *has* lied and whether the lawyer "knows" that Carl lied if he did. His "sister" might be lying or wrong, or might not even be his sister; but then she's got the photo albums and a lot of persuasive detail. What does "know" mean in this context? Are we prepared to say that the lawyer does not "know"? If we are, do we require the lawyer to confront Carl with his sister, or at least with his sister's information, to see if he confesses or maintains his position? Or can Tanya, if she reasonably believes she doesn't "know" that Carl lied, now choose to avoid pinning things down? For Carl to have "lied" he would have to know what he said was wrong. To make the issue incredibly complex, what if Carl wrongly believed the truth of his story?

Students answer these questions in many ways. Rightly so. A majority believes that Tanya does not "know" that Carl lied. The "sister" may be an imposter. After all, the state did not discover any subterfuge. There may be other explanations for Carl's reaction in prison than his recognition that he has been found out. Perhaps Carl is angry at Tanya for showing up with the "sister" without consulting him. Maybe he saw it as an act of betrayal. Many students believe that Tanya should have proceeded with her summation and have ignored the visitor's story. Some think Tanya had to check it out but not in the way she did. We work through all this permutations. I'm inclined to conclude that Tanya did not have a duty to pursue the "sister's" story at that point (eve of summation), should not have taken her to the jail in any event, does not know Carl lied even after she did (though this is close), and should have summed up as planned. But in the end, it is useful to make the assumption that Tanya knows Carl lied. Then what?

Assume we are in a jurisdiction in which Tanya, though she knows Carl lied, does not have a superior duty to reveal the lie to the court. Nevertheless, she may not exploit the false statements, may she? Rules 1.2(d), 3.3(a)(1), 4.1(a). That would mean that she cannot argue the psychiatrist's conclusion to the jury in summation because that conclusion is based on Carl's lie and the lawyer cannot help Carl reap the benefit of his lie. But if Tanya does not argue the conclusion to the jury in summation, she might just as well not argue at all. That's all Carl has. The jury was impressed with his abused childhood. The lawyer has to drive that home or give up. Pretty strong incentive not to "know," not even to talk to the sister if the lawyer has any inkling. Can the lawyer not talk to the sister if *that's* his motive?

132

This question was first printed (in different form) in the third edition of the casebook and then, truth follows fiction, I read *People v. Bertagnolli*, 861 P.2d 717 (Colo. 1993), which censured a lawyer on the following facts. The lawyer represented an accident victim in arbitration. He called a psychiatrist to testify that the victim had suffered certain brain damage. After the close of testimony, but before argument, the psychiatrist wrote the lawyer to say that after further testing, he concluded that he had erred in his testimony. The psychiatrist requested the lawyer to correct the testimony. The lawyer did not. Instead he asked the arbitrators to credit it.

E. FRIVOLOUS POSITIONS AND ABUSIVE TACTICS (page 492)

This material covers 4 pages (**pages 492-496**). Difference of opinion exists over how much time, if any, should be spent on the issues addressed here. Some of us believe the burden falls to teachers of civil procedure. Plausible. Some of us have a deep interest in Rule 11 and like provisions because they facilitate discussion about the role of lawyers and their duties to "the system" as contrasted with their duties to the client. A legal ethics casebook editor must decide how much of this stuff to include. One can get into the interstices of Rule 11 issues and, by golly, they are many. Or a teacher may wish instead to focus on the grand question: Should there be some *objective* standard of reasonableness, enforced with the threat of sanction, for the litigation positions lawyers take? We are still debating that question. You will have to decide, of course, how much time you want to spend in "Rule 11 Land." Some years it may be an hour or so. Some years you might skip it altogether. My editorial decision assumes that few of us will want to spend more than part of a class on judicial sanctions.

Without attempting to summarize all this material, essentially it does the following:

(1) It identifies the three "ages" of Rule 11: 1983; 1983-1993; and post-1993.

(2) It summarizes the major Supreme Court decisions under Rule 11 as it existed in 1983-1993 and the changes worked by the 1993 amendment.

(3) It identifies the obligations and powers the amended rule envisions.

(4) It identifies other rules that enable federal judges to impose sanctions and alerts students to the existence of state rules.

(5) It notes the much-discussed Washington Supreme Court decision in the *Fisons* case and cross-references a fuller article about that case. In *Fisons*, a state version of Rule 11 was used to sanction a major Northwest law firm despite the fact that about ten legal experts testified that the discovery answers of the firm were proper. See headnote [9] of the case.

F. DILATORY TACTICS (page 496)

Closely related to the prior material, yet distinct, is the problem of delay and dilatory tactics. The evolution of the Model Rules on this issue is latent with ambiguity and inconsistency. The material rehearses these matters. The question to ask at the end of the day is this: Should a lawyer ethically be permitted to encourage delay, as an end in itself and through otherwise legitimate procedural means or inertia, when delay is in the interest of the lawyer's client? Or should a lawyer, instead, have an obligation to expedite litigation, even when speed does not serve the client's interest, consistent with the client's *other* procedural and substantive rights (e.g., to discovery, or to a change of venue)? The profession has chosen the former response.

G. HARDBALL (page 499)

Hardball is one of those issues that has of late caused the profession to question its "professional" credential. The increase in the use of hardball tactics has also caused something of a crisis of conscience. In this edition, I have substituted the *Mullaney v. Aude* case which affirmed a monetary sanction against a male lawyer for calling his female adversary "babe" during the deposition. This case is useful because it raises issues of gender bias and because the court directly acknowledged how gender references might be used to through the other lawyer off balance (**pages 503-504**). The court also uses the term "hardball" (**page 504**). Finally, the court's rejection of the male lawyer's effort to defend his use of the term "babe" is cogent and amusing. This case ties in with *Matter of Jordan Schiff* at **page 861** and with Professor Duncan's article at **page 868**.

H. MISSTATING FACTS, PRECEDENT, OR THE RECORD (page 505)

This material also overlaps the material on Rule 11 and other sanctions. Students should be aware that courts react harshly to such practices. Is there a double standard here? Given the many ways in which lawyers can foster falsity when presenting a case to a jury or to a judge as trier of fact, why are courts so intolerant of similar efforts to distract or mislead in legal arguments?

I. THE OBLIGATION TO REVEAL ADVERSE LEGAL AUTHORITY (page 507)

Thonert shows that violation of this obligation can carry disciplinary sanctions. Remarkably, the case the lawyer failed to cite here was one he himself had argued. Emphasize how narrow the obligation appears to be. Compare the rule as adopted with the rule as proposed **(page 507)**. Why wasn't the proposed rule accepted? Does it have a problem? Students should understand that legal authority is not a "confidence" and so there is no Rule 1.6 or Canon 4 problem with its revelation. The obligation requires revelation only of "legal authority in the controlling jurisdiction." Furthermore, the authority must "be directly adverse" to the lawyer's position. A good example of a violation of the rule is revealed in Judge Messite's opinions in the *Massey* cases **(page 509)**. The note material discusses *McCoy* **(page 510)**, which upholds a Wisconsin statute that requires appointed lawyers who seek to withdraw to inform the court of the legal basis for their conclusion that their client has no case. This goes rather far. Criminal defendants who retain lawyers do not suffer the same fate.

CHAPTER VIII

REAL EVIDENCE

Previous users of this book will note that I have significantly modified Chapter 8. It now deals solely with the issue of real evidence -- that is, a lawyer's responsibility when coming into possession of objects. These may be legal to possess or not. The issues may arise in civil or criminal matters although generally they arise in criminal matters. It is with regard to real evidence that students might be most in the dark, mistakenly assuming, for example, that privilege protects the real evidence itself as opposed to communications about it. The two principal cases in this chapter are *In re Ryder* (**page 513**) and *People v. Meredith* (**page 527**). *Meredith* has appeared in every edition of this book. *Ryder*, the older case, is new in this edition. I reread it in planning Chapter 8 and decided that the facts were just too good to summarize. And if we accept that Ryder's motives were benign, as the court seems to, the lessons here are important.

Essentially, Ryder took a sawed-off shot gun and the bank loot and put it in his own safe deposit box after removing it from his client's box. He tried to get advice about what he should do. His advisor told him to return the money (at the time he didn't know about the gun) from his client's box, but instead he simply transferred the money, and the gun which he then discovered, to his own box. He claims he would have ultimately returned the money at a time that it would not have hurt his client for him to do so.

The court rejects the argument that Ryder's conduct is protected by the attorney-client privilege (**page 517**). It accepts that Ryder "intended eventually to return the money to its rightful owner," but it emphasizes that "no attorney should ever place himself in such a position"(**page 516**). The money belonged to the bank and Ryder was not entitled to hide it in order to help his client get acquitted (**page 517**). Further, it was illegal for Ryder to take possession of the sawed-off shot gun (**page 517**).

Note that Ryder did nothing to suggest that he was merely going to examine the money and the gun before turning it over. So far as it appears, he was going to keep both until the case was over. The ABA takes a position that a lawyer in Ryder's position could keep the item "for a reasonable time . . . to test or examine the items for defense purposes." (**page 527**.) It bears stressing that the items Ryder concealed either belonged to someone else or were illegal in themselves to possess.

The note following *Ryder* **(page 518)** posits three variations – the client puts the murder weapon on the lawyer's desk; the lawyer preparing for a civil litigation discovers harmful e-mail messages; the murder defendant tells the lawyer the location of the buried bodies of other victims (an actual case, "The Buried Bodies Case" from Upstate New York – see **pages 531-532**). The ensuing part of the note identifies the several interesting variables that can arise here. It then introduces the student to the "Nixon tapes" history. I find that as years go by, I have to be more explicit about these events.

The note at **page 520**, from the Yale Law Journal, is still useful to describe the intersection of the ethics rules and the law – and the significant dependence of the former on the latter in most jurisdictions. The legislative history and the different approach in a few other jurisdictions are described at **pages 523-524**. However, it is important to note that even in jurisdictions that make the ethical obligation congruent with the legal obligation, the legal obligation itself can be rather broad, as it is in New York or under the federal obstruction statute **(page 524)**. So anyone who thinks that the ethical obligation is narrow because it imposes no greater burden than the law does should think again. While the legal obligation might not be very intrusive for nonlawyers, lawyers are particularly situated to come into possession of evidence encompassed by the legal obligation. And as the *Lundwall* case shows **(page 524)**, that circumstance can arise in civil as well as criminal cases (although in *Lundwall* the defendants charged with obstruction were not lawyers).

The note at **page 524** gets deeper into the Nixon tapes issue. This is inherently interesting stuff, made more so by the excerpt from Leonard Garment's autobiography **(page 525)**.

We now turn to *People v. Meredith* **(page 527)**, in which the lawyer did give the prosecutor the incriminating wallet. But the case goes further and asks whether the lawyer had to reveal, or permit the investigator to reveal, the location of the wallet. As such, *Meredith* is a case at the borderland between the obligation not to conceal real evidence and the attorney-client privilege.

Meredith is about as good as a case as one could hope for to discuss these materials. What was the evidence that was destroyed in *Meredith*? The location of the wallet. It seems odd to talk about location as something that is destroyed. The amicus's hypothetical explains why it is not odd **(pages 532-533)**. Is the result in *Meredith* salutary? What will happen the next time a lawyer meets up with the same situation? No doubt she will examine the wallet and leave it where she found it. Chances are that it will then be picked up by the trash collector and never seen again, depending on where the container is located and the local practice. By allowing the lawyer to remove it and hand it in, the prosecutor at least gets the wallet, if not the location. If instead we require the lawyer to reveal the location in a form admissible in evidence, and despite the attorney-client privilege, we encourage the lawyer to leave it where she found it. So what have we gained? On the other hand, it may be pretty likely that, without the lawyer's removal, the authorities would discover the evidence. This may induce the lawyer to take it and turn it in

138

(assuming it cannot be connected to the defendant, as the wallet could not, once removed) or keep it. Do we want to encourage that kind of behavior. On *Meredith's* particular facts, indeed, the police may have eventually come to the "burn barrel" behind Scott's house and located the wallet. Students generally think *Meredith* reaches the wrong result. I think it reaches the right result. By "destroying" the location, the lawyer did destroy something of significant evidentiary value. The wallet has almost no value absent location and a great deal of value in light of its location. But does this argument prove too much? How can I then resist saying that the lawyer who turns over an object with evidentiary value received from the lawyer's client can decline to identify its source? See the note at **page 537**.

Meredith cites most of the major cases in this area, including *Ryder* (**page 533**), *Morrell* (**page 532**), and discussed in the following note), and *Belge*, the buried bodies case, at **page 531**. You may be aware of the Public Television videotape "Ethics on Trial," which portrays the *Belge/Armani* case in a very dramatic way. It is worth showing in class.

The Turnover Duty (But How Broad?) (page 534) This note introduces the fact that the turnover duty, recognized for contraband and the fruits and instrumentalities of criminal conduct, can also apply to documents. In *Matter of Grand Jury Subpoenas* (**page 532**), the duty applied to telephone bills. But note that the law firm did not reveal those bills on its own. Rather it waited for a subpoena and then, unsuccessfully, asserted privilege. One might ask why it wasn't a violation of the federal obstruction statute for the law firm to retain the telephone bill until subpoenaed. True, the bill itself was not contraband or otherwise illegal to possess, but it was evidence of a crime and the law firm did conceal it in the sense that it had the phone bill in its possession, where the authorities were much less likely to look for it. Yet it does not appear that there are any prosecutions against lawyers for taking possession of such otherwise innocent items pending subpoena.

At **page 535** I include a discussion of the *Morrell* case because it involved a document, probative of guilt but not in itself illegal to possess. Also, the lawyer got the document not from the client but from a friend of the client. However, the court seems to say that Cline, the lawyer, would have been obligated to give the document over to the police regardless of the source. Remember, this is "mere evidence" of the crime. Not a weapon, not contraband, not someone else's property. But remember too that this case arises in the context of a challenge to a conviction based on ineffective assistance. If all the court had to decide was that Cline's conduct in turning the kidnap plan over to the authorities did not render him constitutionally ineffective, it did not have to say that the Cline was obligated to hand over the plan. At one point it suggests that he was, but at another it suggests only that he could reasonably have so concluded.

The note "Moving Pictures" (**page 536**) is here because the criticism of the Simpson lawyers' conduct is biting but almost certainly wrong. The lawyers transformed Simpson's house to appeal to the visiting jury, but at this point, the house was in Simpson's control. The authorities had released it. So surely Simpson, through his lawyers, was free to redecorate. One wonders what the judge would have done if the prosecutors had insisted that the house remain as it appeared at the critical time and that the original pictures be restored. Supposedly, it shouldn't matter what pictures the jurors saw in the house. But the lawyers thought it did matter and probably it did, to some extent.

Does the Source Matter? (page 537) The hardest case is presented if the lawyer receives the contraband or the fruit of the crime from the client himself. While she may not be able to keep it, does the prosecutor then have a right to introduce the source? Analytically, the answer should be yes. Just as the lawyer in *Meredith* made it impossible for the prosecutor to find the wallet in a relevant spot (the garbage can behind the defendant's house), so too a lawyer who receives the evidence from a client directly makes it impossible for the police to discover it on the client's person. But if we extend *Meredith* to this situation, will lawyers then have to tell clients: "You can leave that here if you want but I'll have to give it to the police after examining it and they will be entitled to establish in court that I got it from you. In fact, you would even have to get a new lawyer if I have to testify. However, since you just asked, you should know that you may [or may not, as the case may be] legally destroy the item." The *Morrell* court **(page 535)** seemed to think that Cline would have had to hand over the kidnap plan even if his own client had given it to him, but that case is ambiguous, especially given the context in which the issues arises (claim of ineffectiveness). So far, the case law seems to reject an extension of *Meredith* to require the lawyer to reveal when his own client is the source of incriminating evidence, although he lawyer will still have to hand over the evidence, whether as in *Meredith* it is contraband or the property of another or simply probative of the criminal conduct.

Spoliation of Evidence (page 537). This note introduces students to the spoliation concept and the fact that spoliation can lead to a negative evidentiary inference, and some places may serve as the basis for an independent cause of action.

CHAPTER IX

LAWYERS FOR ENTITIES

The hard questions in entity representation concern confidentiality and conflicts. These questions are hard because of the difficulty in identifying the client. At one level, of course, it is not difficult at all. The client is the entity, as *Weintraub* (**page 555**) makes clear. There, former officers of a bankrupt entity could not block the trustee's decision to waive the attorney-client privilege for communications that took place while the officers were in control. But saying that the entity is the client, while formally correct, does not solve all the practical problems. Entities can work only through agents. When the entity is a closely held corporation (see **page 566**), formal distinctions between the entity as such and its constituents are particularly unhelpful. When the entity is large, matters are complex in a different way.

The introductory note (**pages 541-545**) presents the student with some of these problems. The student is also asked to recognize a distinction between business decisions and legal decisions. The first are for managers and the second are for lawyers. What about when a business decision risks legal liability? Is the decision to run that risk for the manager as well, once properly advised by counsel? A decision to breach a contract belongs to management. A decision to engage in conduct that constitutes a business tort may as well. At what point can counsel try to "take it away" from management? At what point can counsel go to higher management? Outside the organization? The easiest situation is when the management decision amounts to self-dealing in violation of management's fiduciary duties to the organization, or when the conduct is a crime or fraud. But how sure does the lawyer have to be? How serious does the self-dealing or other misconduct have to be? Beyond self-dealing, even if management's conduct on behalf of the organization is only tortious, if the tort "is likely to result in substantial injury to the organization," within the meaning of Rule 1.13(b), the lawyer is obligated to take further action.

Note that 1.13(b) imposes obligations on a lawyer when, among other things, constituents of the organization act or refuse to act "in a matter related to the representation." Does that mean that when a tax lawyer discovers that corporate constituents are causing the entity to pollute the environment, she need do nothing?

The introductory note also identifies the relevance of these questions. It summarizes a Fortune article on corporate crime, adds some more recent examples of bad conduct and quotes Judge Sporkin's rhetorical questions in *Lincoln Savings & Loan Ass'n* (**page 543**).

The first principal opinion is *Tekni-Plex* from the New York Court of Appeals (**page 545**), followed by *Jesse v. Danforth* as a note at **page 554**. The two cases present interesting bookends. *Tekni-Plex* addresses loyalty and confidentiality obligations for a company when it merges to into a new company. *Jesse* addresses the loyalty and confidentiality duties of a lawyer for persons who hire him to form a corporation after the corporation is formed. Does the lawyer continue to owe anything to the individuals that incorporated the entity or only to the entity?

Tekni-Plex concluded, citing *Weintraub*, that the loyalty and confidentiality duties of the acquired company's lawyers were owed to the "new" (merged) company, except to the extent that these arise out of the actual merger negotiations itself, where the acquiring company had to view the lawyers for the acquired company as adverse to it, since they were negotiating the terms of the acquisition. I think this is entirely right. A different result can be agreed upon if the parties wish, but the "default" rule should be that the new owners can command the loyalty and secrecy of the company's counsel in matters in which it had represented it. However, it is also true that the merger negotiations should be recognized by all as not for the benefit of the anticipated "new" company but for the benefit of the sellers. This is also what *Flanzer* (**page 550**) held. *Tekni-Plex* is complicated by the fact that the company had only one shareholder when it was sold (Tang), who understandably viewed the law firm as *his* law firm and made an independent claim to its loyalty and confidentiality. That claim was recognized as possibly legitimate, depending on further facts, but only as regards the firm's work in the merger negotiations.

Before proceeding to say a word about *Jesse*, let me emphasize that these cases, though a touch difficult to unravel, so neatly interlock. Unraveling the facts and the issues will go a long way toward enabling students to understand the complexities of lawyerly duties in corporate representation.

Who Is the Client in Entity Representations? (page 553). In *Jesse*, a law firm was suing a couple of doctors for malpractice. The law firm also represented a professional organization. of doctors that owned an M.R.I. The defendant doctors were shareholders in the professional organization. One was its president and the immediate contact between the plaintiff's law firm and the entity. Before the firm sued the doctors, it did a conflicts check and turned up nothing. The introductory paragraph asks why not. The answer is that the client in the firm's records was the entity and not the doctors.

Among the questions here are: Who is the client of the firm? The court has no trouble saying it is the entity and not the doctors. So the firm is not suing its own client. Easy enough, but here there is an additional fact. The doctors were among the group that retained the law firm to form the corporation. Of course, this occurred before there was a corporation. Who was the client then? It could only have been the doctors. There had to be a client and there was not yet an entity. The court's gloss on Rule 1.13 is to say that the entity becomes a retroactive client, displacing the doctors, once it is formed. Confidential information given to the law firm pre-incorporation becomes the entity's information after incorporation.

The only exception is where the incorporators provide information to the firm "not directly related to the purpose of organizing an entity." **(page 554**.) That was not true here, even though the doctors had consulted the law firm pre-incorporation for advice about the effect of incorporation on their own tax status. The firm had given the doctors questionnaires which called for their personal financial information. Tough luck. The information was directly related to the purpose of organizing the entity. This does seem to push the boundaries a bit. I myself have nothing against the retroactivity theory in general, but is it really right to say that information about the incorporator's personal financial situation, provided in connection with requests for tax advice, also and retroactively becomes the corporation's information? Why doesn't the court ask what a reasonable lay person consulting a lawyer under these circumstances would assume? In *Analytica* **(page 339**), Judge Posner said that NPD would be deemed a client because it provided confidential information to a law firm. As a result, the law firm was disqualified from a subsequent adverse matter. Didn't the doctors here do the same? Would the Seventh Circuit dispense with the formality of technical client status, as it did in *Analytica*, and deem the doctors clients for conflicts purposes?

In an analysis not included, the court also rejects the argument that the firm has a conflict because it is suing the president of its corporate client, although on a matter unrelated to the corporation. The argument is: If the malpractice claim is successful, the doctor defendants could lose their license and that would hurt the corporate client. The court says this does not establish the "direct" adversity to the corporate client that the conflict rules require. Perhaps not. But how about the argument that suing the president of one's corporate client is adverse to the client in the sense that the result can harm the client, possibly fatally? What difference should it make that the work is not legally adverse to it? Didn't the corporate client have a right not to see its own law firm sue its president, the very person who served as the intermediary between the client and the law firm? Or did this issue not get raised because the doctors had no standing to raise it? In any event, the claim should probably lose or the scope of disqualifications will be expansive.

One argument on behalf of the Wisconsin Court is the need to avoid the limitations that would be imposed on a lawyer if incorporators who provide information, even personal information but solely to enable the lawyer to form the corporation, thereby become clients of the lawyer. Even if they are only former clients after the corporation is formed, the lawyer may be limited in what he or she can then do for the (now current) entity client. Otherwise, the entity, to have unconflicted counsel, would have to change lawyers following incorporation. Of course, that issue does not arise here.

The note then goes on to identify other cases in which the "who do you represent" issue arose. See especially the (extreme?) position in *Innes* **(pages 556-557**), where the court found no professional relationship though corporate counsel actually represented a corporate constituent for whom he appeared in court. One begins to feel sorry for the corporate employee.

The note also cross-references the uncertainty of the scope of privilege in government lawyer work, arising out of the Eighth Circuit's opinion concluding that Kenneth Starr could subpoena to the grand jury the notes of White Counsel in conversation with Hillary Clinton. **(page 558**.) Finally, the note identifies the dangers to the entity if its lawyer is also deemed a constituent's lawyer and it also asks about "Miranda warnings" so corporate agents are not misled. **(pages 558-559**.)

Members of Corporate Families. (page 559) This material was previously in Chapter 5, whose subject is concurrent conflicts. I have moved it here since it raises more than merely conflict issues, although those predominate. The note is really self-explanatory. The question is "When does the representation of one member of a corporate family translate, at least for certain purposes, into the representation of other members of the corporate family?" The *Sprint* case at **pages 559-560** shows just how broad the scope of the conflict rules might reach if the representation of one company automatically constituted the representation of all of its affiliates. ABA Opinion 390 **(page 560**) rejected that view. Its most important conclusion was that a lawyer could be adverse to a nonclient member of a corporate affiliate even though success in the adverse work could have dire economic consequences to the client member of the corporate family. In other words, economic adversity all by itself was not enough to create client identity or a conflict. Dissenting members of the committee took the opposite position. Since the last edition of this book, the Restatement seems to have sided with the dissenters **(page 561**) through an illustration set out at **pages 561-562**. So this may still be a front-burner issue. The *Travelers* case at **page 560** presents a cogent application of the standards adopted in the ABA opinion.

General partnerships are treated like corporations most places and Rule 1.13 will apply. **(page 562**.)

Some courts seem to distinguish between the lawyer's duty to share information with partners and the lawyer's duty of loyalty to the partnership, which might not prevent the lawyer from acting adversely to a partner. Obviously, if a lawyer's representation of a partnership meant the lawyer represented every partner, the partnership could never hire a lawyer to sue a partner. On the other hand, should we be more willing to let a partnership hire a "new" lawyer to sue a partner (or to defend an action by the partner against the partnership), than we might be to let the partnership's longtime counsel represent the partnership against the partner? The theory would be that longtime counsel might have developed a relationship of trust with each partner.

Privilege and Conflicts in Shareholder (and Other Fiduciary) Actions (page 563). In a derivative action, a constituent group of indeterminate size is invoking the rights of the entity against various others, possibly including officers of the entity and, nominally, the entity itself. The privilege and conflicts issues here are difficult. Can a single lawyer represent the entity and the defendant officers? At the outset, especially if the case looks weak, it makes sense to permit it and save costs. Otherwise, separate counsel should be used. If a single counsel represents all defendants but then a conflict emerges, that lawyer may have to withdraw from all representations. See Rule 1.13(e). A second question is whether the constituent group should have a right to confidential information. *Garner* is the leading case, holding that on a proper showing the stockholders should be permitted to discover privileged information. The *Garner* rule has been extended **(page 565)** to nonderivative shareholder actions and to cases in which plaintiffs charge a defendant with breach of fiduciary duty. However, notice the disagreement between the Ninth Circuit and the California Supreme Court over whether trust beneficiaries can use *Garner* to get confidential information from the attorney for the trust. The California court, concluding that they cannot, relies on the statutory nature of the privilege in the state, which it has no power to alter.

Is Sexton's criticism of *Garner* in light of *Upjohn* well-founded? It would seem that *CFTC v. Weintraub* **(page 555)** strengthened *Garner* when it rejected the argument that corporate officers would hesitate to confer with corporate counsel if their communications were subject to discovery following bankruptcy. One could also say that the prospect that communications between a corporate lawyer and an officer may be discoverable in a shareholder action will not have a deleterious effect on corporate communications. *Shirvani* rejected *Garner* after *Weintraub*, holding that the crime-fraud exception was sufficient to protect shareholders **(page 566)**.

Closely Held Entities (page 566). This is like Newtonian physics. The rules break down when you deal with very small particles or immense space. Einstein, phone home. While some courts continue to insist that the rules are the same no matter how small the entity (see *Pelletier* at **page 570**), other courts are obviously uncomfortable with a regime that requires them to ignore size entirely. See *Rosman v. Shapiro* **(page 570)** and *Fassihi* **(page 571)** which circumvented (?) the problem by finding a fiduciary relationship between the corporate lawyer and one of the two shareholders.

The *Murphy & Demory* case **(page 567)** is a real treat. It is the transcript of a bench opinion by a trial judge in Virginia, finding a major American law firm to have engaged in malpractice. The firm, in several dramatic ways, favored one of two owners of its corporate client over the other, to the possible detriment of the entity. These ways are listed in the third paragraph of Judge Roush's opinion. I include the case especially because it is not filtered by appellate review. After the decision, the parties settled. I ask students how it could happen that a lawyer knowledgeable in the jurisdiction's ethics rules -- she wrote a book about them -- could have made these mistakes. One conceivable answer, often true whether or not true here, is personality. Corporate constituents can be demanding people. If they are strong personalities, and perhaps if they account for a large amount of the business that the outside lawyer brings to his or her firm, it may be hard to resist. This case also has the nice fact that discovery produced E-Mail from junior associates alerting the partner to the danger. I tell my students to assume that E-Mail never disappears. Even when you click on "garbage" you later find all of your trashed E-Mail in a file called "garbage," easily retrievable.

Granewich (**pages 569-570**) also involves a shareholder in a small company suing company counsel. The court upholds the claim that the lawyers violated their fiduciary duties to the plaintiff and, separately, assisted the other shareholders in violating their own fiduciary duties to him.

B. Retaliatory Discharge and Whistleblowing (page 571). The third edition of this book contained the Illinois Supreme Court's opinion in *Balla v. Gambro, Inc.* This edition (like the fourth and fifth) contains the California Supreme Court's decision in *General Dynamics* (**page 573**). *G.D.* discusses *Balla* and I felt no need to include it as well. In my view, *Balla* is inexplicable, a disaster, illogical and bad policy. Now, you may disagree. But even if you want to write an opinion with the same result, it could be done better. Let me say a word about *Balla* and then about *G.D.*

Why am I offended by the Illinois Supreme Court's opinion? Is it simply because it makes no sense? Is it because it is callous? I don't know. Here, a court rule commands a lawyer on pain of discipline to reveal a client's conduct that physically endangers others and then, when the lawyer does, the court tells him to get lost. Heartless. It would be fine if the lawyer were in private practice and the lost client represented three percent of his billings. Balla was a one-client lawyer. It seems to me the Illinois opinion encourages ignorance as the economically dependent lawyers's best solution to the dilemma it creates. Some additional points:

(1) The court sees no need to extend retaliatory discharge protection to Balla. He <u>had</u> to report the dangerous condition. This really sacrifices the lawyer, doesn't it? If Balla were only *permitted* to notify the FDA, the result would have to change, wouldn't it, because then the court would want to encourage him to do what he would not be obligated to do. Yet it seems to me that it is precisely because the lawyer must report that the court should protect him.

(2) The argument that corporate officers will not be forthright if lawyers have retaliatory discharge claims makes only partial sense and none at all in this context where the lawyer was required to report. It is the requirement, more than anything else, that will impede communication. Anyway, for years lawyers have been permitted under DR 4-101(C)(3) to report future criminal activity yet no one has discerned a failure in corporate officers to seek legal advice.

146

(3) The American Corporate Counsel Association's decision **(page 572)** to side with the company -- to identify with the master rather than the lawyer -- can only be explained by its membership's deep need to be "real lawyers." Outside counsel don't have retaliatory discharge claims so ACCA's members should not either! But ACCA's members are in a different position, aren't they? They have one client on whom they are economically dependent.

(4) Should outside lawyers have these claims? No one has argued for it. The economic realities are obviously different. Indeed, if a retained lawyer were discharged under similar circumstances, it would be hard to know how to determine damages. Future fees? The harder problem concerns law firm associates. Although they are not strictly speaking one-client lawyers, they are economically dependent upon their firms. What if a firm tells an associate to act unethically, or to remain silent when there is a duty to speak, but the lawyer declines and is fired? If we give in-house counsel retaliatory discharge claims, don't we have to give that salaried associate the same claim?

(5) The majority seems to think that permitting the claim here would impose the economic cost of the rule on the company and not on the lawyer, where it presumably belongs. But the economic cost of having to pay a retaliatory discharge claim would flow from the client's illegal conduct, not the lawyer's revelation, wouldn't it?

(6) The argument for more protection for lawyers is that courts write the rules governing the behavior of lawyers and should therefore see lawyers as within their special province. Even if the courts are reluctant to create a retaliatory discharge claim for others, and if the legislature fails to do so, courts should still feel free, given their inherent power over lawyers, to protect lawyers when they comply with the rules the courts themselves impose.

Several points should be made about *General Dynamics* **(page 573)**. The case nicely reviews the "sociology" of the profession -- the growth in the number of in-house lawyers -- as well as their economic dependency on a single client. It makes the point that although a client has the absolute right to fire a lawyer (with certain exceptions not here relevant), that doesn't mean that the client doesn't have to "pay" for exercising that right. The lawyer might not be entitled to get the case or the job back, but he or she might have a right to money damages. The court disposes of the lawyer's breach of contract claim -- based on an implied-in-fact provision -- at **pages 578-579**. The claim is simply that G.D. had created "a reasonable expectation that the plaintiff would not be terminated without good cause."

As for the retaliatory discharge claim sounding in tort, I do wish the court had been a little clearer, but here is what I understand it to say. Where a rule governing the lawyer as a lawyer mandates certain action or forbids certain action, a lawyer will have a retaliatory discharge claim if he or she is fired because of compliance with that rule. **(page 581.)** The court then discusses *Balla* at **pages 581-582** and, if too politely, disposes of it at **pages 582-583**. Last the court goes on to ask whether a lawyer will have a retaliatory discharge claim where the lawyer was terminated not "for refusing to violate a mandatory ethical rule," but in those situations "in which in-house counsel's nonattorney colleagues would be permitted to pursue a retaliatory discharge claim and governing professional rules or statutes expressly remove the requirement of attorney confidentiality." **(Page 584**.) The answer will be yes because the attorney will be able to pursue a retaliatory discharge claim on these assumptions without violating confidentiality. Conversely, if information the lawyer will have to reveal in pursuing the claim will breach the lawyer's confidentiality obligations, confidentiality wins. The suit must be dismissed. **(page 585**.) But the court quickly declares that that will "seldom if ever" happen. The reasons it will seldom happen are two: often, the underlying facts will establish that the client's conduct was criminal or fraudulent and so the relevant information will not be confidential **(page 585**); or even if the information is confidential, trial courts have many procedural devices at their disposal to protect the information while permitting the case to advance **(page 586**).

The note material following *General Dynamics* **(page 587**) identifies other cases that have addressed its issue. The line up seems to be in favor of recognizing the claim, at least to some extent. Massachusetts allows it **(page 587**) as does Montana **(page 588**). However, an intermediate Tennessee appellate court endorsed *Balla* and the Illinois Supreme Court has continued to embraced it **(pages 593-594**).

On the issue of the use of client confidences to establish the retaliatory discharge claim, see *Kachmer* at **page 589**, where the in-house lawyer's claim was discrimination. The court seems to suggest that Rule 1.6's exception for "self-defense" is broad enough – it's broader than the Code's -- to allow the lawyer to pursue her claim even if doing so *will* require use or revelation of confidential information. The court is textually correct, isn't it? That same language is broad enough to allow us to reach the same result whatever the nature of the lawyer's claim. After the book went to press, ABA Opinion 2001-424 agreed that a discharge claim is a "claim" within Rule 1.6(b)(2). The problems this can create are stunning.

Read the final paragraph on **page 589**, which describes a (not so) hypothetical situation in which a lawyer whose job may be in trouble allegedly because of poor work charges discrimination and says her work is good. Does the work then become open to tribunal review? Does the jury evaluate it? Will the company's adversaries in other matters have access to this record?

Douglas, at **page 590**, identifies the risks to a lawyer who brings a discrimination claim and, in the course of doing so, reveals confidential information outside the four corners of the claim. The court holds that the lawyer's conduct will obliterate her claim even if it was otherwise meritorious. This is a very strong ruling. An effort to rehear the case en banc failed over several dissents.

The Rights of Associates (page 592). Here I briefly summarize the saga of Howard Weider who persuaded the New York Court of Appeals, no friend of retaliatory discharge claims for anyone (unless legislatively created), to create a right of action for a law firm associate (Weider) who alleged he was fired after insisting that his firm report the derelictions of another firm lawyer to the disciplinary committee. Alas, the court recognized only a right of action for breach of contract. The firm, said the court, impliedly promised that it would not fire its associates for their compliance with the ethical rule at issue here. The court stresses that it was not about to imply every ethical rule into contractual relationships among lawyers.

The problem with a breach of contract claim, of course, is that the damages are less and punitive damages are nonexistent. The court declined to recognize a tort action. The *Kelly* case at **page 593** extended *Weider* by applying its logic to the conduct of a law school graduate not yet admitted. As stated, the Illinois Supreme Court has continued to embrace *Balla*, even extending it to the situation of an associate who claimed retaliation for reporting illegal practices within the firm.

The Ethics of Whistleblowing (page 594). This note takes the student through the legislative history of Rule 1.13, with particular focus on (I) a lawyer's obligation to take corrective measures in the face of constituent harm to the entity; and (ii) a lawyer's authority to protect the entity by revealing information to outsiders. As you can see, both the obligation and the authority were significantly narrowed between the first and final drafts of Rule 1.13.

CHAPTER X

NEGOTIATION AND TRANSACTIONAL MATTERS

More lawyers negotiate than litigate -- even litigators negotiate about the litigation -- yet negotiation has received little attention when compared with the millions of words spent on litigation. The introductory note (**pages 597-600**) makes this point and others. It identifies the critical provisions of the Code and Rules on negotiation ethics. And it highlights (**page 599**) the Rule 1.6 comment permitting a "noisy withdrawal" as consistent with the lawyer's confidentiality obligations. New York has put a like (but not identical) authority in DR 4-101(C)(5). A central question, posed here (**page 599**), is whether lawyers have any greater responsibility in negotiation than do other negotiators. In other words, is it enough for a lawyer to obey the law or must the negotiating lawyer do more? If the answer is that she must do more, why? Two possibilities are that lawyers carry a certain status that will encourage the reliance of others and that only lawyers have the power to put an agreement into binding form.

It is worth discussing why the ABA chose to make the duty of confidentiality superior to the duty to correct fraudulent or criminal conduct in a negotiation, see Rule 4.1(b), but opted for the reverse priority in the event of fraud on a tribunal or fraud in a nonadjudicative proceeding. See Rules 3.3(b) and 3.9. Maryland, Mississippi and New Jersey, for example, subordinate Rule 1.6 to the corrective obligation of Rule 4.1(b). The Texas version of Rule 4.1(b) says that a lawyer shall not "fail to disclose a material fact to a third party when disclosure is necessary to avoid making the lawyer a party to a criminal act or knowingly assisting a fraudulent act perpetrated by a client."

Do lawyers get immunity? (page 600). The following case attempts to address the question whether the status of being a lawyer entitles one to enhanced protection against charges of actionable conducting arising in negotiations. It soundly holds that the answer is no. However, there is a dissent and a Fourth Circuit case (cited at **page 608**) which is more protective of lawyers in these circumstances.

Rubin v. Schottenstein, Zox & Dunn (**page 600**) I have added this en banc Sixth Circuit opinion. Rubin and Cohen sued the law firm (as well as its clients, who settled) for securities fraud and common law and constructive fraud in connection with their investment of about $150,000 in a business. Rubin and Cohen, through their counsel, and at the suggestion of the control persons of the company seeking the investment (MDI) spoke with Barnhart, MDI's counsel. Neither the MDI control persons nor Barnhart revealed that MDI was already in default on its bank loan and that the Rubin and Cohen investment would also constitute an act of default. Rubin and Cohen invested and lost all their money.

The substance of the discussion with Barnhart is at **page 601**. So this can be seen as a negotiation. It is an exchange of information with a view toward making an investment. Barnhart is encouraging the investment. He makes certain statements about MDI's status. There are two ways to look at these statements. Either what he says is true but incomplete and what he leaves out makes what he has said misleading. Alternatively, Barnhart's statements are misrepresentations. The court concludes that Barnhart could be liable under Rule 10b-5. It rejects the defense summary judgment motion. It finds that Barnhart's failure to reveal the default status, even if everything else he said was true, could be a violation of the rule. Separately, a jury could find that Barnhart affirmatively misrepresented MDI's status.

As for the reliance required under either theory, the court holds that Rubin and Cohen could reasonably have relied on Barnhart's statements because they were material and because there were no facts, or ready access to information, that would undermine the reasonableness of the reliance. The court points out that the amount of the investment was relatively small, which was a reason for Rubin and Cohen to choose not to spend additional money checking on Barnhart. The court might have required a different level of diligence if the transaction involved substantial sums of money **(page 604)**.

At **page 605**, the court says it finds "least persuasive" the defendants' argument that as attorneys they should be "treated differently" from other defendants in securities-fraud cases. Apparently the defendants relied on their confidentiality obligations. The court acknowledges that ordinarily a party to a transaction cannot rely on the opposing lawyer's view of the state of the law (unless of course it is in an opinion letter directed to the opposing party). However, here Rubin and Cohen relied on "factual representations." The court refused to say (on this summary judgment motion) that an opposing party could not as a matter of law rely on the factual representations of counsel. Saying that "would allow an attorney to mislead investors with impunity. We cannot endorse this perverse result. Admission to the bar, if anything, imposes a heightened, not a lessened, requirement of probity."

Finally, but important for our purposes, the court also denies summary judgment on the state law fraud claims, the elements of which tract common law fraud, as well as a constructive fraud claim.

I frankly don't understand how the court could have reached any other result, although a panel of the court did reach a contrary result and there is a dissent. Judge Kennedy says that "an attorney for a party's duty to disclose is fundamentally different from a lay person's duty to disclose material facts." Kennedy accepts that Barnhart made misrepresentations but thinks that plaintiffs' reliance on them was reckless. Kennedy points out that Rubin was a sophisticated investor represented by sophisticated counsel and had access to the relevant information. There is other evidence that plaintiffs acted in haste. So while Kennedy disagrees on the reasonableness of plaintiffs' reliance on Barnhart's misrepresentations, he does not seem to take issue with the proposition that, if there were reasonable reliance, the misrepresentations were actionable. At **page 608**, I set out another part of the Kennedy opinion that discusses two cases in which the lawyers won. The *Schatz* case has been roundly criticized in the literature, but it is worth summarizing to present a different point of view. The *Roberts* case is clearly distinguishable from *Rubin*.

It is worth taking a minute to contemplate the situation in *Rubin*. Obviously, it was a great benefit to MDI to have Barnhart give plaintiffs and their counsel information. By virtue of being a lawyer, Barnhart had a certain credibility. Yet his firm then argued that by virtue of being a lawyer it should enjoy special protection against liability for securities fraud. The majority rejects this result as perverse. Judge Kennedy and the Fourth Circuit in *Schatz* are attracted to it. The argument in favor of the argument is that the opposing party should have recognized that Barnhart's sole loyalty was to help his client achieve its goal and therefore should have been inherently suspicious of anything he said, as well as his silences. This works less well when the allegation against a lawyer in Barnhart's position is an allegation of misrepresentation as opposed to a mere failure to reveal. It is hard to argue that a lawyer's status entitles him to misrepresent. It is easier to argue that a lawyer's status should put opposing parties on notice that a lawyer may not be revealing everything he knows. In fact, that argument would often work outside the securities area. However, in the securities area, Rule 10b-5 may impose a duty to reveal when silence is misleading. Even outside the securities area, the comment to Rule 4.1 states that "substantive law may require a lawyer to disclose certain information to avoid being deemed to have assisted the client's crime or fraud." The comment also says: "Misrepresentations can also occur by failure to act." Compare Comment [2] to Rule 3.3: "There are circumstances where failure to make a disclosure is the equivalent of an affirmative misrepresentation." Paradoxically, the increased value to clients by virtue of a lawyer's credibility in negotiation will be lost if lawyers do have some extra protection against fraud claims for what they say in negotiations. That extra protection (once established) could easily lead opposing parties to discount the trustworthiness of the lawyer's statements. So in a way upholding liability in a case like *Rubin* also facilitates negotiation by giving lawyers greater credibility. It also makes negotiation more efficient by encouraging the parties to rely on the statements of opposing counsel without having to independently verify them.

May or must lawyers warn victims of a client's fraud? (page 609.) This brief note distinguishes between a duty to avoid fraudulent conduct, the issue in *Rubin* and the duty to warn. If the substantive law requires a warning, the ethics rules, including confidentiality duties, will not interfere. If the ethics rules permit a warning, a lawyer similarly will not be able to rely on a confidentiality obligation for failing to warn. Here we get introduced to the "noisy withdrawal"

153

concept and the comment to Rule 1.6 (a concept that is continued but relocated in the E2K recommendations). See **page 621**.

Legislative History and State Variations (page 609). I set out earlier versions of Rule 4.1 and show that some jurisdictions will require a lawyer to warn a victim of a client's fraud even if doing so means the lawyer must use confidential information.

The note at **page 610** discusses the meaning of "fraud," as used in the Model Code and Model Rules. The Rules' definition of "fraud" contains a certain ambiguity that should be kept in mind as you discuss the issues here. What is the relationship between "fraud" within the meaning of the Rules or Code and in the substantive tort or criminal law? One possibility is that the definition in the Rules or Code is meant to be narrower than the substantive law definition. In other words, conduct is fraudulent within the meaning of the ethical document if it is fraudulent under substantive law and, in addition, satisfies the definition of "fraud" in the Terminology section of the Rules. Another possibility is that conduct may be fraudulent within the meaning of the ethical document whether or not it is actionable under the substantive law. In other words, if particular conduct has "a purpose to deceive" then it will be unethical for a lawyer to aid it even though, for one reason or another, the conduct will not result in injury or be actionable even if it does. (The E2K proposal negates this second meaning **(page 611)**). A related possibility is that "fraud" in the Code and Rules is both narrower *and* broader than substantive law definitions.

Note the use of the word "merely" in the definition of "fraud" in the Rules' Terminology. The definition would seem to say that conduct "having a purpose to deceive" is "fraudulent" within the meaning of the Rules even if the conduct is a "failure to apprise another of relevant information" so long as the conduct is not "merely" such a "failure" but is rather a "failure to apprise" motivated by "a purpose to deceive." Is that the right reading?

Also of interest is the definition of "assisting." (See **page 611**.) Recall the discussion of 87-353 **(page 489)** which seemed to give "assisting" a rather broad sweep in the context of litigation. The same broad definition could apply in the context of Rule 4.1(b). Even though a lawyer who discovers a "fraud" cannot reveal it under that Rule, because of the superior obligation of Rule 1.6, he or she cannot "assist" the client's conduct either. If "assist" is defined broadly, the obligation to withdraw will be broad too. Massachusetts has opted for a broad definition of "assist" in its Rule 3.3 but a narrower one in Rule 4.1.

ABA Opinion 366 (page 612)

I decided to use this opinion in this edition because, though dense, it is the best single description of a lawyer's duties when client fraud permeates a transactional matter. The opinion also applies the "noisy withdrawal" provision, concluding that in some instances a noisy withdrawal may not only be permissible, it will be mandatory if being "noisy" is the only way to ensure that the lawyer's previous work (if unwithdrawn) will not aid the client's future fraud. This conclusion required quite an interpretive feat for the majority, given the legislative history of the Rules and the failed efforts to amend them (discussed in the opinion) and given the absence of mandatory language in either Rule 1.6(b) or Rule 4.1. Instead, the Committee uses Rules 1.2 and 1.16, both of which do have obligatory language. But that was a stretch. Logically, possible, perhaps, but historically disingenuous. I personally think the dissent's view is the intellectually honest one, though I'd support a rules change to achieve the majority's objective. You have to read the majority opinion carefully to follow its reasoning. Essentially, the committee is saying that the mandatory obligation in Rule 1.2(d) (not to assist a client fraud), or the one in Rule 1.16(a)(1) (essentially, to withdraw from a representation if failure to do so will result in a violation of a rule), may have the effect of mandating a noisy withdrawal under the comment to Rule 1.6. This is because withdrawing without "noise" might be ineffective to effect a true withdrawal and avoid assisting the client's fraud. That, in turn, is true because the lawyer's statement is still out there upon which the other party may rely. The noisy withdrawal, in short, may be mandatory if it is the only way to satisfy the mandatory obligations of Rule 1.2 or Rule 1.16. All of this is best summarized in the full paragraph on **page 617**. I included only a small part of the dissent. I will not try here to trace the majority's argument further than I have because I'd probably wind up writing an explanation as long as the opinion. If nothing else, this opinion should alert students to the fact that the issues here are conceptually complicated, divisive, and not intuitively evident.

The questions following the opinion **(page 619)** are meant to help students sort out its meaning. I think questions like these are useful because they force close reading, which is a critical lawyerly skill.

Question (1) requires the student to work through the logic of the majority and the criticism of the dissent. As I say, the majority view is not illogical (though it is not inevitable either), only highly technical and historically inconsistent. For the dissent, the obligatory language in Rule 1.2 and 1.16 look to assistance in *future* fraud, not a client's use of a lawyer's prior (and blameless) work product in a future fraud. The lawyer, by withdrawing, will not be participant to any future fraud. In other words, for the dissent, the prohibitions are against the lawyer doing something in the future. The client's use of the lawyer's work product does not entail the lawyer doing anything in the future. The language of the rules are all future tense verbs.

The answer to question (2) appears above. If the lawyer "knows or has reason to believe" that her work product will be used to advance a client fraud, mere withdrawal will not satisfy the lawyer's obligations under Rules 1.2(d) and 1.16(a)(1). "Disavowal of work product...may be necessary, in order to make the withdrawal effective." **(Page 617.)**

Question (3): The majority says that its interpretation of the Rules does not go as far as failed amendments would have gone. **(Page 617.)** The dissent, in text not included here, charged that the majority was legislating a position that the true legislative body, the House of Delegates, twice rejected in effect (even if in broader form). As it happens, E2K has proposed to keep the noisy withdrawal language but put it in the comment to Rule 1.2 **(page 621)**, and this decision has been tentatively approved by the House of Delegates. Similar language appears in the comment to Rule 4.1. Whether the noisy withdrawal language survives final adoption of the commission's recommendation's is yet unknown. It likely will because lawyers, I believe will want the authority provided by the noisy withdrawal language to protect themselves against civil liability in difficult situations.

Question (4): The dissent's fear that the opinion can serve as the basis for increased discipline or civil liability **(page 619)** is half-legitimate. First, by making a "noisy withdrawal" obligatory, a lawyer's failure to be "noisy" when noise is required is grounds for discipline. But I don't see this as a real danger absent an extreme situation. Civil liability is a danger, however, because plaintiffs who sue lawyers can now point to support for an obligation and thereby surmount a defense motion to dismiss or for summary judgment. The opinion gives plaintiffs leverage in settlement of claims against law firms and lawyers. *But see Cavin* on **page 620** for the use of the opinion *defensively* in a criminal case, although the court appears to have misunderstood the opinion (no big surprise given its lack of clarity).

Questions (5) is rhetorical.

"The Case of the Substandard Plumbing Lines" (page 621)

This question requires the student to work through the reasoning in ABA Opinion 366. As for future work on Birchwood, the inquirer cannot continue to represent Klunk on the project unless everything is cleared up. I reject the idea that the lawyer can remain on parts of the work that do not involve fraud. I doubt the work can be divided so neatly. It's one big project. The client can hardly be trusted. Even if discipline is not a risk, civil liability is. The problem doesn't say how many of the homes with substandard plumbing lines remain unsold. Selling any of them now, given the certificate with ST. DRED, would be fraud. The lawyer's certification in that filing is no longer true, nor is the lawyer's certification to the bank that Klunk's company was not in violation of any laws nor in breach of any contracts. Even selling new homes with proper plumbing lines might be fraud under applicable laws since those purchasers have an interest in the legality of other homes in the development. If several dozen homes have substandard plumbing lines, that can easily affect property values throughout the development. Those other purchasers have a right to rely on the filings with ST. DRED. So the inquirer must withdraw if he has not already done so.

The real question here is not what the inquirer should not do in the future but what the inquirer has to do about what he has already done in the past. Is it enough simply to refrain from doing any additional work? The inquirer has done three things – the certification to ST. DRED, the certification to the bank, and the master contract. The last is easiest. The master contract does not have his name on it and therefore in no way is his credibility behind any language in that contract. He has made no representation in it. No one reading it will even know of his existence. I don 't think the fact of the master contract, if that is all there were, would require the inquirer to do anything.

The representations to ST. DRED and the bank present a different issue. They are both now wrong but were not wrong when made. Klunk is probably now in violation of land use or environment laws and in breach of contract, too. These facts differ from the ABA opinion because, there, the lawyer's representation was false when made (though the lawyer did not know it).

Must our lawyer withdraw the representations to ST DRED and the bank? That will surely shut Klunk down. The lawyer must, says the ABA, if failure to do so will mean the mandatory withdrawal will be ineffective because Klunk will continue to be able to use the lawyer's representation to advance his fraud on purchasers, the bank, and possibly ST. DRED (or the State). So this seems to be a logical extension of the opinion even though the representations were true when made. A true-when-made representation must be withdrawn, in order to effect a proper withdrawal, and avoid aiding client fraud, because the recipients of the opinion and home buyers will continue to rely on it. This is not an inevitable conclusion. One may disagree with the opinion's identification of a mandatory noisy withdrawal. Or one may not think that it applies a to statement that was true when made. After all, the recipients of the opinion should understand that subsequent events can change the accuracy of the representation. Surely, though, a noisy withdrawal is at least permissible. The lawyer's interest in protecting himself against potentially massive civil liability (which may have to end in a generous settlement to avoid risk of enormous damages) counsels a noisy withdrawal even if only permissive.

"The Case of the Complex Formula" (page 622)

This problem is not unlike those in Chapter 2C, on autonomy in the professional relationship. Can a lawyer be a "nice guy" if it seems to work to the disadvantage of a client, at least in the immediate term. The answer is yes. A factually close ABA opinion (86-1518) supports this conclusion. See the discussion of this opinion in connection with the problem "Ms. Niceperson" set out at **page 93** of the casebook.

Negotiating Settlements in Litigation (page 623). The balance of this chapter addresses whether and how different rules may apply to negotiation of settlements once matters are in litigation. There seems to be some stricter obligation sounding in candor to the court, but it's not clear what it is or when it applies. It's easy to accept such an obligation when a court is required to approve the settlement, especially in a matter involving a minor. But what is the duty in other cases, including ones like *Virzi*, next discussed. Note cases following *Virzi* provide other examples which do not, however, do much to clarify the rule. A final note **(page 628)** discusses use of threats of criminal prosecution in negotiating civil liability.

Virzi v. Grand Truck Warehouse & Cold Storage Co. **(page 623)**. The issue here was whether in settling a lawsuit the plaintiff's lawyer had an ethical duty to advise the court and opposing counsel that his client had recently died. Among the cases the court discusses is *Spaulding v. Zimmerman* **(page 624)**, where the defendant in a personal injury action learned through the examining physician that the plaintiff's physical condition was worse than plaintiff or his physicians knew it to be. Nevertheless, the defendant settled without revealing this information. When the plaintiff learned of his condition, he moved to vacate the settlement. The motion was granted. While there was no duty to disclose defendant's knowledge during negotiations, one arose when the parties sought the court's approval of the settlement. In *Spaulding*, the plaintiff was a minor and court approval was required.

The *Virzi* court relies on various ethical provisions and on Rule 25 of the Federal Rules of Civil Procedure, none of which *textually* compels the result. It is hard to say what *Virzi* stands for. Where does the court's "duty of candor" come from and what is its breadth? Excessive candor can violate a lawyer's duties to his or her client. And how is this amorphous duty of candor to be reconciled with adversary justice? Does the duty in *Virzi* and *Spaulding* arise only because, in each case, the court approved the settlement? If court approval were not necessary, these holdings would not strictly apply. If a negotiation were not in connection with the settlement of a litigation, or if settlement is reached before a case is filed, these holdings would likewise not be binding. How far do they extend? Should the fortuity of court approval be determinative?

What does *Virzi* stand for? (page 626) Here are four questions based on actual cases. You can use them to test the limits of *Virzi*.

(1) The referee found that the lawyer had a duty to disclose the additional policy and that failure to do so violated DR 1-102(A)(1) and (4). In addition, failure to correct the hospital's misimpression was a violation of DR 7-102(A)(5). The court accepted the referee's conclusions without discussion and suspended the lawyer for six months. The lawyer filed "a conditional admission with this court, acknowledging that his conduct constitutes a violation of DR 1-102(A)(1) and (4)." Is *Virzi* correct, and *Addison* wrong, on the ground that by continuing with the proceeding in <u>Virzi</u> after the client's death the lawyer implicitly represented that the client was still alive, whereas in *Addison* the lawyer made no representation at all?

(2) In *Kath*, the court vacated the settlement. After an extended factual recitation, the court said that the "sole issue in this case is whether appellees' attorney had an ethical duty to advise the court and the appellants' attorney" of the facts. "We hold that he had such a duty." The court then quotes liberally from *Virzi*, DR 7-102(A), and Rule 3.3. It quotes from Judge Rubin's article in 35 La. L. Rev. 577 (1975). It states that counsel had learned information contrary to what Q had stated at his deposition. And it concluded: "We hold that appellees' counsel owed a duty of candor and fairness to disclose to opposing counsel and the court" this new information. Unfortunately, the opinion is not any more detailed than this.

(3) The motion was denied on appeal. The Circuit held that contract law did not require reformation. It also held:

> The district court concluded that the appellant had both a legal and ethical duty to have disclosed to the appellee its factual error, which the appellant may have suspected had occurred. However, absent some misrepresentation or fraudulent conduct, the appellant had no duty to advise the appellee of any such factual error, whether known or suspected.

The court then went on to quote the Fifth Circuit as follows:

> An attorney is to be expected to responsibly present his client's case in the light most favorable to the client, and it is not fraudulent for him to do so. . . . We need only cite the well-settled rule that the mere nondisclosure to an adverse party and to the court of facts pertinent to a controversy before the court does not add up to "fraud upon the court" for purposes of vacating a judgment under Rule 60(b).

How does this determination square with *Virzi*?

(4) "The Practice" did a really fine show based on this case. The court refused to vacate the conviction. Information about the death was not exculpatory evidence within the meaning of *Brady*. The prosecutor was not obligated to share with the defense particular information demonstrating the weakness of the prosecutor's case. The prosecutor had no affirmative duty to

reveal "tactical data." There was no proof here of "affirmative misrepresentation." The court did say, however, that it was not deciding

> what the rule might be where in the course of plea negotiation a particular defendant staunchly and plausibly maintains his innocence but states explicitly and creditably that as a matter of balanced judgment in the light of the apparent strength of the People's proof, he wishes to interpose a negotiated plea to reduced charges to avoid the risk of a more severe sentence likely to attend conviction after trial; failure of the prosecutor to reveal the death of a critical complaining witness might then call for a vacatur of the plea. Silence in such circumstances might arguably be held to be so subversive of the criminal justice process as to offend due process.

Many who read *Jones* have a visceral disagreement with it. I did at first, but on reflection I think it's correct. Why should the defendant have a *right* to learn about the state's loss of a witness. The defendant will learn at the trial that the witness is not available when he is not called. Why should he have a right to learn sooner? Sure, it'd be strategically useful to know, but that's not a good enough reason to give him a *right* to know. Assume the prosecutor has two good eyewitnesses to a crime, as the defendant knows because they both picked the defendant out of a lineup. A week before trial, the more certain of the two dies. A day later, the lawyers are negotiating a plea. Must the prosecutor tell the defense lawyer that the stronger eyewitness died? Must the prosecutor keep the defense lawyer informed as an ongoing investigation affects the strength of her case, in either direction? I don't think so. *Jones* is an extreme case because the death of the victim meant the prosecutor could not prove guilt. But that's a difference in degree, isn't it? It doesn't call for a different analysis, one that would recognize a right to know when no such right would exist if all that happened was that the prosecutor lost one of two eyewitnesses before trial.

CHAPTER XI

JUDGES

This is a discretionary chapter but well worth occasional assignment.

The introductory note **(pages 631-634)** identifies the ABA's Code of Judicial Conduct as the most influential document on judicial ethics. Two courts have held that the Code of Conduct for U.S. Judges, based on the ABA Code, is not a standard for discipline of federal judges because its directives are aspirational and voluntary. **(page 632)**. It also introduces students to 28 U.S.C. §§144 and 455, both of which deal with recusal and conflicts of interest, and to §372(c), whose focus is federal judicial discipline. The ABA adopted a new Code of Judicial Conduct in 1990, much like the 1972 Code but with some differences, especially in the area of judicial bias. The material on judges first addresses conflict of interest issues, under the statute and the Due Process Clause, and then turns to issues of judicial bias. Notice the questions in the last paragraph of the introductory note on **page 633**. These resurface in the bias materials. As an introductory matter, you might also want to point out that an "appearance" standard receives greater respect in the area of judicial ethics than it does in the area of lawyers' ethics. See **page 632**. This is because judges (unlike most lawyers) wield public power, which requires greater public confidence in what they do and how they do it.

I have added a brief section on ex parte communications **(page 634)** because I think students should know they are generally forbidden. I have used the material from the Rosenberg prosecution and allegations of ex parte communication between the trial judge and Roy Cohn.

What judicial conflicts violate the Due Process Clause? (page 635). The reach of the Due Process Clause, so far as it can be discerned, is addressed here. The issue also arises in criminal cases and may be covered in courses on constitutional law or criminal procedure. See, *e.g.*, *Ward v. Village of Monroeville*, 409 U.S. 57 (1972). *Aetna* **(page 635)** appears to have turned on the fact that Justice Embry was the swing vote. Justice Brennan thought that should not matter. In his view, it was a violation of due process for Justice Embry even to participate in the deliberations, regardless of the vote. That view has not been followed.

Ethical and Statutory Disqualification (page 637). The *Liljeberg* decision **(page 637)** put judicial disqualification on the map and rather dramatically too. The court applies §455 which in many ways, but not all, parallels the ABA Code of Judicial Conduct. The case is remarkable for the majority's insistence on the appearance of impartiality even while it purports to accept the lower court's findings of fact on what Judge Collins knew and when he knew it. In affirming the lower court's ruling, which vacated a declaratory judgment that benefitted Loyola (though it was not a party), the majority relied on a conjunction between §455(a) and Rule 60(b) of the Federal Rules of Civil Procedure.

Part III of the opinion concludes that §455(a) was violated notwithstanding that Judge Collins lacked knowledge of the factual basis for his disqualification. This is the most controversial portion of the opinion. The factors set out at **pages 644-645**, the Court concludes, "might reasonably cause an objective observer to question Judge Collins' impartiality." Most notably, perhaps, the Court says that although it credits the lower court's finding of fact that Judge Collins was unaware of the University's interest, it was nevertheless "remarkable that the judge . . . completely forgot about [this] interest." **(Page 644.)** The Court emphasizes that "advancement of the purpose" of §455(a) "does not depend upon whether or not the judge actually knew facts creating an appearance of impropriety, so long as the public might reasonably believe that he or she knew" **(pages 641-642)**. Judge Collins should therefore have recused himself on March 24, when he regained actual knowledge of the basis for his disqualification. The Court also states **(page 645)** that Judge Collins' "interest" constituted a violation of §455(b)(4), which disqualifies a judge who, as a fiduciary, knowingly "has a financial interest in the subject matter in controversy or in a party to the proceeding."

Section 455(a) does not alone secure the respondents the relief they seek. Rather, the Court does a separate analysis under Rule 60(b) to decide if vacating the judgment is the appropriate remedy for the §455(a) violation before it.

Liljeberg is interesting for the critical tone of the majority opinion and the extensive relief it upholds. It is questionable whether the Court actually believed that Judge Collins was unaware of Loyola's interest. Justice Stevens used the word "remarkable" twice and the phrase "unfortunate coincidence" to describe Judge Collins' ignorance of the disqualifying fact. Yet despite the Court's apparent incredulity, the case formally assumed ignorance and the relief proceeded on this assumption. Twice the Court referred to the danger of public suspicion about the integrity of judges. At **page 642**, it wrote that the particular fact that Judge Collins said he forgot might nevertheless be one "that people might reasonably suspect that he does know." And then at **page 644**, it wrote: "The problem, however, is that people who have not served on the bench are often all too willing to indulge suspicions and doubts concerning the integrity of judges." The Court concluded that allaying these suspicions, even if erroneous, is the aim of §455.

The note material at **pages 649-663**, while extensive, gives students a great deal of information about the kinds of conflicts that will prevent a judge from sitting, including conflicts that may arise from the work or interests of a law clerk **(page 660)**. The notes also address the old "duty to sit" concept and its rejection in the statute, although the Tenth Circuit at least still seems to embrace it. **(Page 656.)** Several interesting aspects of this material deserve mention.

First, §455(f), added in 1988, allows judges to continue to sit in matters, despite a financial interest, if the interest was discovered only after the matter was assigned to the judge, the judge had devoted "substantial judicial time to the matter," and the interest could not "be substantially affected by the outcome." This provision will be especially important in class action litigation. This enactment overturns the unavoidable holding of *In re Cement & Concrete Antitrust Litigation*, discussed at **page 658** and in note 8 of *Liljeberg*.

Second is the scope of the judge's duty to reveal information that could serve as the basis for disqualification. *Liljeberg* took Judge Collins somewhat to task for failure to reveal his Loyola connection once he became aware of it. The 1990 ABA Code explicitly requires revelation of reasonably relevant information **(page 662)**. *Liteky* **(page 652)** does, too. The 1972 Code did not except in conjunction with an invitation for a waiver. See §3(D). Section 455(e) is in accord.

Third, on the issue of waiver, notice the dramatically different provisions of §455, the 1972 Code and the 1990 Code **(page 662)**. The statute permits waiver of conflicts falling under §455(a) but not conflicts falling under paragraph (b). The 1972 Code is the reverse! The 1990 Code permits waiver of <u>all</u> conflicts. Waiver provisions have been criticized for the reasons described on **page 663**. Is this criticism valid? I know of at least one case in which after the presiding judge in a long-running matter died, and a new judge acceptable to both sides was substituted, counsel discovered that that new judge, more than a decade earlier, when in private practice, was a partner at a firm that had briefly represented one of the sides to the dispute. The judge himself had nothing to do with it, had no access to it, had no memory of it, and was actually housed in a firm office in a different city from the office of the partner who did handle the case. Yet, literally read, §455 required the judge's recusal. No waiver was possible.

The *Liteky* decision **(page 652)** is worth notice. I find the opinion a bit opaque but I think I'm comfortable with the result. The question was whether or not the so-called "extrajudicial source doctrine" applied to §455(a). That is, can a judge be disqualified under this section if the reason that the judge's impartiality might reasonably be questioned relies on information the judge learned as a judge, rather than extrajudicially? As I read the opinion, Justice Scalia says there's not much doctrine to the doctrine. But in the end it seems that a judge's impartiality might reasonably be questioned even based on "facts introduced or events occurring in the course of the current proceedings, or of prior proceedings. . . ." **(Page 652.)** Justice Kennedy seems to think that the *Liteky* majority undermined *Liljeberg*, but I don't see how.

Next, I call your attention to the Third Circuit's decision disqualifying Judge Kelly in the *School Asbestos Litigation* (**page 653**). This is a factually interesting situation. In the end, Judge Kelly was disqualified because he attended a conference (unfortunately underwritten by the plaintiffs' lawyers from partial recoveries) in which he was exposed to a one-sided presentation of the "science" in the case, much of it from experts the plaintiffs intended to call.

New to this edition is the material on judicial seminars at **page 653**. These seminars are often sponsored or funded by frequent federal court litigants with a decided interest in a particular judicial philosophy (generally pro-big business or anti-environmental protection, in the view of their critics). They often occur in comfortable resorts. Summarized is a report on this issue (**page 654**) and a Second Circuit case trying to set standards for judicial attendance at these seminars.

"Conflicts in Bush v. Gore" (**page 663**). Given the topicality, I couldn't resist inserting these issues. Various news articles raise questions about whether Justices Scalia, Thomas or O'Connor had conflicts in *Bush v. Gore*. I thought not. I just don't see that §455 would forbid any of them from sitting, although some students might disagree based on §455(a).

Judicial and Courtroom Bias (page 664). This is rich material, signaled in the introduction to this chapter. The 1990 ABA Code of Judicial Conduct attempts to address some issues of courtroom bias and judicial membership in exclusionary organizations. The drama of exclusionary memberships has also played before the Senate Judiciary Committee, which on occasion gets nominees for federal judgeships who have spent their private professional life as members of exclusionary clubs.

The *Iverson* case (**page 664**) reveals a judge who not only had a stereotypical view of young women who marry older men, but who had no hesitation in expressing that view in language that would conventionally be characterized as sexist. The appellate court unanimously reverses his decision on the validity of the antenuptial agreement, but one judge, concurring in the result, concludes that it was unnecessary for the majority to decide that the trial judge was actually biased since his comments "gave the appearance of his lack of impartiality." This case is here not only for shock value, although it has some of that, but more because it should spark good discussion. The note material following (**page 668**) gives other examples of judges who made biased comments from the bench.

The note at **page 669** reviews the case of Judge Santora, whose statements were made off the bench, in an interview with a newspaper. As a result, he was removed as Chief Judge of the intermediate appellate court and reprimanded. One question here is whether that penalty violated Judge Santora's First Amendment rights. I cite the *Jeffries* case, which resulted in a money

164

judgment for Professor Jeffries, affirmed by the Second Circuit, but vacated and remanded by the Supreme Court and since dismissed by the Circuit. Should Professor Jeffries' comments be protected as free speech? If so, why not Judge Santora's? I ask the students whether neither should be protected or whether both should be protected. The school removed Jeffries as a head of a department, but not from his tenured position. Santora was removed as chief judge, but not from the bench. Should he have been removed from the bench?

Matter of Bourisseau **(page 672)** offers one further brief example of judicial bias, revealed in an off-the-bench comment. The following note explains what the Code of Judicial Conduct now requires of judges in connection with judicial bias and in connection with membership in exclusionary organizations **(page 673)**.

"The Judge and the Boy Scouts" (page 675)

Can a judge who is active in volunteer efforts for the Boy Scouts of America, which do not permit homosexual men to serve as scout masters, sit in a case in which a class is challenging discrimination against lesbians and gay men in state hiring practices? The judge was randomly chose for the case. The Boy Scouts' policy is constitutionally protected. The single question would be whether or not a judge who is active as Judge Claremont is here, appears biased or, in the language of the rule, whether his "impartiality might reasonably be questioned." I think the answer is that the judge is not subject to recusal. Or put it another way, if Judge Claremont declined to step aside, no circuit court would overturn that. We can push the issue by hypothesizing that Judge Claremont is very active in the local Boy Scouts chapter or possibly even in the national organization. We can assume he voted to maintain the exclusionary policy. Then it becomes harder. The more ardent and visible he is in favor of the policy, the greater the appearance of bias. On the other hand, Judge Claremont can believe that as a matter of privacy the Boy Scouts should have a constitutional right to exclude gay men without thereby necessarily being bias against gay men or thinking that the state, whose hiring policies are being challenged, should have that right. Anyway, this could make for a good discussion.

PART IV

AVOIDING AND REDRESSING PROFESSIONAL FAILURE

CHAPTER XII

CONTROL OF QUALITY:
REDUCING THE LIKELIHOOD OF PROFESSIONAL FAILURE

This is the first of three chapters about rules whose purpose is to prevent or remedy professional failures of lawyers. Chapter 12, as the introduction states, is mainly about prevention. Chapter 13 is mainly about remedy. Chapter 14 deals with a special kind of preventive rule -- the rule that forbids lay investment or managerial authority in for-profit law firms. That rule, which may be partly on its way out, has significant financial and distributive consequences. Chapter 14 also covers the contiguous topic of law firm ownership of ancillary businesses.

The introductory note **(pages 679-681)** tells students to ask two questions as they review "preventive" rules: How can we know the extent to which a particular rule actually does assure competence and whether that assurance is worth the cost of the rule? Are the motives behind the rule benign or are they partly influenced by the profession's interest in controlling the availability, and therefore the price, of legal services? The note ends with a longish excerpt from a Posner opinion that applies a sort of economic analysis to the limitations in Indiana's motion admission rule. The same sort of reasoning is useful in addressing other hurdles to bar admission and well worth assignment.

A. ADMISSION TO THE BAR (page 682)

Licensure is perhaps the paramount rule of exclusion. Its purpose is to limit entry into the profession to those who, by virtue of education, proven competence, and character, will predictably provide competent services. The predictive value of licensure is much debated. Is the price of the ticket of admission commensurate with our confidence in its predictive value? Or asked another way: Is the entry barrier too high given what we get? If it is too high, we are excluding people from the "supply side" of the law business without adequate reason. Perhaps the error is in having only one kind of license -- lawyer -- when we should recognize licenses for legal technicians or paralegals, too. See Section F on unauthorized law practice.

This inquiry pushes us to an anterior inquiry: How sure do we have to be and how do we know? Courts have not required states empirically to justify bar examinations or educational requirements or to demonstrate that a slightly easier examination or educational requirement would not serve the competence goal while excluding fewer applicants. In other words, when it comes to bar examinations and educational requirements, a "fit" need hardly be proved. Courts are insistent on some proof of a relationship when the entry barrier is based on character. And they are still more insistent (to the point of invalidation) when the entry barrier is a residential requirement. It might be worth asking why the level of judicial deference varies so.

1. Geographical Exclusion (page 682). *Piper* **(page 682)** knocked out residency requirements, even nondurational ones. (A durational residency requirement is one that forbids admission to a jurisdiction's bar until the applicant has lived in the jurisdiction for a minimum period of time. A nondurational rule merely requires that the applicant be a resident of the state when he or she is admitted.) *Piper* could have been decided as Justice White would have decided it -- on the ground that Piper lived so close to the New Hampshire border -- but it was not. Justice Rehnquist makes some good points in his dissent about the state's interest in a resident bar, and I push those points in the first note following *Piper*, which is called The "New Jersey" Problem **(page 688)**. The "New Jersey" Problem recurs throughout the material; it is essentially this: What is a small state to do? New Jersey, sandwiched between New York and Pennsylvania, or, more particularly, between New York City and Philadelphia, does worry about invasion. I use New Jersey emblematically. At **page 688** I recount the battle between New York and New Jersey over motion admission. New York would routinely admit New Jersey lawyers on motion, but New Jersey would not afford the same courtesy. Consequently, New York adopted a reciprocity law that denied motion admission to lawyers from states that did not admit New York lawyers on motion. The expectation might have been that New Jersey would back down, but it did not. The plight of smaller states or states adjacent to dominant financial and legal markets will intensify as modern communications makes a truly (inter)national bar (lawyer anywhere advises client anywhere) increasingly feasible.

The note ends at **pages 689-690** with discussion of rules in some jurisdictions that require lawyers to maintain offices in the state. This seems to be a way to discourage out-of-state lawyers from gaining admission to a state's bar, especially as the office must be a real office, not a mail drop. One wonders how effectively this is enforced. Surely in-state lawyers who then relocate do not find their bar membership withdrawn.

2. Geographical Restriction (page 690). Whereas *Piper* concerns geographical exclusion -- if you don't live here you can't join us -- *Friedman* **(page 690)** has a geographical restriction -- if you don't live here, you can still join us (after *Piper*), but you have to jump through hoops that in-state lawyers can avoid.

Friedman is a simple case. Justice Kennedy, who wrote the opinion, sides with the libertarian wing of the Court, as he did in *Went-For-It* (**page 998**), *Shapero* (**page 1007**) and *Gentile* (**page 948**). Friedman lived in Maryland and worked in Virginia. To gain admission to the Virginia bar she would have had to take the bar examination. If she had lived in Virginia and worked in Virginia, she could have been admitted on motion. So Virginia treated a lawyer who lived and worked in the state differently than it treated a lawyer who worked in the state and lived elsewhere. This enabled the Court to find that the Virginia rule violated the Privileges and Immunities Clause because non-Virginians were disfavored. Compare *Goldfarb* below.

The note at **page 695** asks what the states can do after *Piper*, *Frazier* and *Friedman* to discourage out-of-state lawyers. One thing they can do is bite the bullet and admit lawyers living outside the state but practicing in it on motion. Alternatively, they can eliminate *all* motion admissions and require lawyers living anywhere to take the bar examination, as many states now do. Do students think *Friedman* can be read more broadly, as stating a requirement under the Privileges and Immunities Clause for states to grant *motion* admission to lawyers admitted anywhere and working anywhere? We are not likely to see that rule. In *Goldfarb* (**page 696**) the same Circuit that had voted for Friedman (and which was thereafter affirmed by the Supreme Court) earlier rejected Goldfarb's slightly different attack on the Virginia statute. Goldfarb was in a position converse to Friedman. He lived in Virginia but worked in Washington, D.C. His attack on the Virginia motion admission rule failed. Why should a state be entitled to require Goldfarb to take its bar exam when it is not entitled to require Friedman to do so? Is it simply because the Privileges and Immunities Clause protects non-residents like Friedman and not residents like Goldfarb? Does Goldfarb now have an Equal Protection argument?

The state of the law now seems to be this: A lawyer admitted in state A has a right to take the bar exam in state B. If state B recognizes admission on motion of lawyers who move to state B, the state A lawyer who practices in state B (full time? half time?) also has a right to admission on motion. That's *Friedman*. However, if the state A lawyer moves to state B while continuing to work in state A, or continues to live and practice in state A, or has always lived in state B while practicing in state A, he or she can be required (so long as *Goldfarb* remains valid) to take B's bar exam.

Tough Questions Department: What about the lawyer admitted in state A, who works in state B, and gains admission on motion in state B under *Friedman*? Her employer then moves to adjoining state C. State C must now admit her on motion (if it otherwise recognizes motion admission), but can state B "unadmit" her unless she takes the state B bar exam? The only reason she enjoyed motion admission in the first place was the location of her job in state B, which is now gone.

3. Education and Examination (page 696). Because of likely student interest, I have included a few pages on education and bar examination requirements for admission, including the generally unsuccessful efforts to challenge them.

4. Character Inquiries (page 698). One could go on and on about this subject. Inclusion is appropriate for many reasons. Not least among them is student interest. One can, of course, also question the efficacy or wisdom of character inquiries, although the issues are not so simple as might first appear.

In re Mustafa (**page 698**) can provoke intense debate. Some of my students thought Mustafa should never be admitted to the bar. Others thought that his law school conduct should not delay his admission one day. I believe the court's resolution -- delay -- was proper but that permanent exclusion would be an overreaction. A critical fact here is that the conduct occurred while in law school, when Mustafa should have known better, and involved the use of funds entrusted to his care.

At **page 701** I provide a note on reasons courts have cited for denying or delaying bar admission. This can be assigned without discussion or discussed briefly. Students have a keen interest in these matters. Note especially application of the ADA to bar admission (**page 703**). Individuals have been denied admission because of failure to pay student loans (**page 704**).

"The Racist Bar Applicant" (page 705)

This of course is an actual case in which Hale was denied admission to the Illinois Bar because of his racist views. The Illinois Supreme Court refused to review the denial of admission. One justice dissented. Is it really possible to predict from Hale's views that he will transgress a disciplinary rule? Further, what if Hale adopted his views after he was already admitted to the bar? Could he be removed? These are questions the dissent asks and the majority never addresses. I haven't yet tried this problem in class so I don't know what the student reaction will be. I myself do not believe that Illinois could properly exclude Hale, loathsome as his views are.

The note at **page 705** identifies the procedural rights of bar applications in connection with the character inquiry.

5. Experiential Requirements (page 706). This note takes up the debate, somewhat muted of late, over whether courts ought to or can require trial experience before admitting lawyers to their trial bars. A parallel question arises for appellate courts.

6. Admission in the Federal System (page 706). Not only do we have more than 50 state and territorial jurisdictions deciding whether to admit lawyers and under what circumstances, but superimposed here is the entire federal system. *Roberts* involved a lawyer who wanted to be admitted in federal court in New Jersey though he was not a member of the state bar. The Third Circuit's conclusion is efficient, but does it make sense? Does it mean that a lawyer admitted in state court must also seek federal court admission? *Kennedy* concerned a lawyer who *was admitted* in federal court in Maryland and wanted to set up a practice there but the state high court had its doubts. Still, it gave Kennedy leeway to show that he would be able to isolate clients with federal problems. The issue here arises again in the context of out-of-state lawyers practicing "in" a state in which they are not admitted. The very word "in" turns out to be ambiguous. See Chapter 12B(2).

B. TRANSIENT LAWYERS AND MULTIJURISDICTIONAL FIRMS: LOCAL INTERESTS CONFRONT A NATIONAL BAR (page 707)

This material (beginning at **page 707**) addresses the problems of lawyers whose practices extend beyond the jurisdictions in which they are licensed. We could be talking about a single lawyer, for example a criminal defense lawyer with a national reputation. Or we could be talking about a large firm with offices in six states and perhaps some foreign countries. The fact is that clients may come from all over. Even local clients have problems that extend far beyond their lawyer's jurisdictions. Many themes percolate in this material, including: the economic interests of a local bar; unauthorized practice of law rules; the changing nature of law practice and firm marketing in a global economy; admission requirements; and the difficulty in identifying the locus of a particular legal matter or the locus of a lawyer's work.

The introductory note (**pages 707-711**) describes the problem and the definitional difficulties, including the ambiguity of the preposition "in." This material also introduces the theme of economic protectionism, which students will have encountered in cases on residency requirements. The first paragraph on **page 709** alerts students to the state interest in the probity of lawyers who represent state residents. This is important. Even if competence concerns are satisfied because the "foreign" lawyer is representing state residents on the law of a jurisdiction in which he or she is admitted, issues of honesty and integrity remain. Licensure gives the state a way to control dishonest lawyers. An out-of-state lawyer is by definition not licensed so threat of sanction in the foreign state may carry little weight.

One way of addressing a "host" jurisdiction's interest in controlling against this behavior by out-of-state lawyers is by giving the host state disciplinary authority over the out-of-state lawyer. Such "long-arm" discipline has been recognized (**page 709**) and would seem to satisfy due process requirements so long as the lawyer has really done something in the host state, physically or even virtually. However, of course, the host state cannot suspend or disbar a person who is not admitted to its bar and so could be a truly useful sanctioning system. Effective long-arm discipline depends on the home state imposing reciprocal discipline against the errant lawyer. However, no home state requires full faith and credit to the host state's recommended discipline. Even the ABA identifies a number of exceptions to any comity obligation (**page 710**).

1. Admissions Pro Hac Vice (page 711). Unfortunately, *Leis v. Flynt* **(page 711)**, the leading case in the area, is a casually reasoned *per curiam* opinion decided by the Supreme Court without full briefs and oral argument. Nevertheless, it is the leading case on a state's power to exclude out-of-state lawyers and so must begin our study. The holding is harsh: A lawyer denied admission pro hac vice is not entitled to a due process hearing. There is simply no right to be admitted pro hac vice in the first place, and that is apparently true even if the jurisdiction recognizes pro hac vice admission and extends that admission to other lawyers. Justice Stevens' dissent relies not only on constitutional theory but also on history. Notably, Justice Powell cited it in his *Piper* opinion some years later even though he joined the *Leis* majority. We ask **(page 717)** whether *Leis*'s importance shrinks given *Piper*. In part it would seem that it does because after *Piper*, it will be easier for out-of-state lawyers to gain admission to the bars of other states, thereby de-emphasizing the importance of pro hac vice admission. But how many lawyers will seek admission to many other states, especially if there is a reciprocity rule? Pro hac vice admission remains an important tool for the national bar. However, its unpredictability, and its unavailability in non-litigation matters, commend it as a partial solution at best, making a separate system of bar admission for national practitioners more attractive.

What About the Client's Interests? (page 717). Mr. Flynt did not assert his own rights in *Leis v. Flynt* because *Younger* abstention would have prevented him from filing a plenary action in federal court. So those rights remain unaddressed, as the *Leis* majority states. *Ford v. Israel* **(page 717)**, however, gives little weight to the client's interests. It upholds the requirement that out-of-state counsel affiliate with a local lawyer notwithstanding that Ford (via his parents) did not have enough money to hire the preferred out-of-state lawyer *and* a local counsel. Judge Posner recognizes the "guild restriction" aspect of the local counsel rule, but finds it a rational way to meet the "tactic of an unsuccessful criminal defendant to complain . . . that he did not have effective assistance of counsel at trial." *Ford* does not answer the big question: If the state does *not* have a local counsel rule and a defendant wants to have out-of-state counsel, or alternatively if the defendant *has* the money to hire *both* local counsel and out-of-state counsel, does the defendant have a constitutional right to do so? At the very least, must a judge who denies pro hac vice admission to the out-of-state lawyer have a rational basis for the denial that focuses on the particular lawyer, rather than a categorical exclusion of all out-of-state lawyers? Cases on **pages 718-719** suggest that there is some limitation on refusal to grant pro hac vice admission to out-of-state criminal defense lawyers (and even civil lawyers) but I question if the Supreme Court would endorse that view. The note also identifies the procedural rights a lawyer admitted pro hac vice has before that permission is withdrawn.

2. Services Other Than Litigation (page 719). Things become more difficult when we are not talking about court appearances. For then there is no procedure by which a lawyer can seek formal authority to behave as a lawyer in a jurisdiction in which she is not admitted. The lawyer takes her chances. While criminal prosecutions of lawyers for unauthorized practice of law are virtually unheard of, the issue of the propriety of a lawyer's conduct may arise in discipline (still rare) or when the out-of-state client refuses to pay the lawyer's fee, the lawyer sues, and the client defends by asserting that the lawyer was not authorized to practice in the state in the first place. In the sixth edition, we include the California Supreme Court's *Birbrower* case **(page 719)**. It has certainly put the issue on the map. Whatever else one might say about the decision, and one could say a lot, it has focused the profession on the problems of lawyers with multistate practices. As you may know, the ABA has appointed a commission on Multijurisdictional Practice (MJP). I am on it. It is expected to issue a final report to the ABA in Spring of 2002, and an interim report in late 2001. It's work can be followed via the web site for the Center on Professional Responsibility (CPR) of the ABA, whose work can be followed at www.abanet.org/cpr/.

Birbrower, Montalbano, Condon & Frank, P.C. v. Superior Court (page 719). Here are the key facts to keep in mind. The New York lawyers made three trips to California. In August 1992, two lawyers went there. The following spring, three lawyers traveled to California. In August 1993, one lawyer went to California. **(Page 721.)** The court says that these lawyers "performed legal services in California for a California-based client under a fee agreement stipulating that California law would govern all matters in the representation." It is important to stress the quadruple California connection: California corporate client (though it was a subsidiary of a client of the firm based in New York); work done in California in connection with an arbitration to be held in California; the arbitration would be governed by California law; the fee agreement would be governed by California law. These factors certainly influenced the court but by how much we do not know and some of its language is broad enough to have supported the same result even if the California connection was not as significant.

The court also says that the firm's work constituted "extensive practice in this state." **(page 724.)** This is highly questionable. Three brief trips across one year would not seem to be "extensive." Perhaps the court is also relying on the firm's "virtual" presence in California from New York, except that the court does not know the extent of that virtual presence if there was any at all.

The firm had two fee agreements with the client, one hourly and one contingent. It is not clear which agreement the firm is seeking to enforce and the court says that its decision does not turn on it.

The arbitration never occurred. The case was settled. While in California, the Birbrower lawyers negotiated with the opponent, made a settlement demand, interviewed potential arbitrators, met with the client's accountants, and gave legal advice **(page 721)**.

As these things happen, the firm and client had a falling out. The client sued for malpractice and the firm counterclaimed for its fee. So it is important to stress that the issue of lawyer UPL arises in the context of a fee dispute, as it often does.

The court went out of its way to stress that the Birbrower lawyers would not have been saved even if they had associated with local counsel because the UPL statute does not envision that exception **(page 721)**. This surely surprised many American lawyers. It was also a gratuitous reference since the firm did not associate with local counsel. But the reference shows the court's willingness to defer to the legislature's judgment about what constitutes UPL by out-of-state lawyers.

The material at **pages 722-724** traces the history of the state's UPL statute and the "tension" between state regulation and interstate law practice.

The Birbrower firm offered various theories why it should be excepted from the rigors of the UPL law. These are often raised in such cases and they lose here **(pages 724-726)** as they often do. Most interesting, perhaps, is the claim that arbitration is not the practice of law (and then preparing for it is not either). The firm has the advantage of a Judge Weinfeld opinion to that affect **(page 726)** which, does not impress the court.

Perhaps the most stunning part of the opinion was the court's conclusion that work the firm lawyers did while physically in New York but "virtually" in California can constitute UPL in California. This is a case that turns on the meaning of a preposition: "in." The court says that "physical presence here is one factor we may consider in deciding whether the unlicensed lawyer has violated" the statute. But the court also says that "one may practice law in the state [in violation of the statute] although not physically present here by advising a California client on California law in connection with a California dispute by telephone, fax, computer, or other technological means." The court declines to identify a more comprehensive list of activities that would constitute sufficient contact to transgress the statute. **(Page 723.)**

Finally, the court holds that the fee agreement is severable and that the firm can get paid for work it did physically in New York and not virtually in California. **(Page 728.)** The dissent **(page 729)** concludes that representation in an arbitration is not the practice of law under California law. It finds the effort to distinguish the New York case "unpersuasive."

Thousands of American lawyers are probably in violation of a state's UPL statute every month and nothing happens. This discrepancy between the law as *Birbrower* viewed it and what really happens has led to a lot of soul searching in the profession in an effort to rationalize the rules and conform them to actual practice. As I say, the case can be read narrowly by focusing on the multiple California connections and it is more likely than not that the court intentionally identified these several times. But we don't know how the case would have gone if one of those connections was absent. What if the arbitration was governed by New York law? What if the arbitration was going to be held in New York but governed by California law and the lawyers made the same trips to California for their California client? What if everything was the same except the client was a New York corporation?

176

A partial defense of the California court: This is a problem. A state certainly has an interest in excluding out-of-state lawyers from continuous and active work physically in the state. We do not have a national bar, where a lawyer admitted anywhere can set up shop anywhere. It would seem therefore necessarily to follow that continuous "virtual" presence, like prolonged physical presence, can also invoke a state's legitimate interest in protecting its residents. This is the focus of the problem at **page 732** ("Practicing Nationally From St. Louis"). If *Birbrower* got it wrong, it was because it went too far. Even with the California connections, the three trips to the state should not have been viewed as "extensive." No one doubts that if the firm had been retained to do the very same arbitration under California law for the very same client but with the arbitration located in New York, and if the lawyers had insisted that the clients come to them rather than go to the clients for the pre-trial work, California could not have declared the lawyers' activity UPL. A lawyer admitted in New York (or anywhere) and competent to do so may give advice on the law of any jurisdiction in the world while the lawyer and the client are physically in the lawyer's home state. That's the oddity of this whole thing. The New York lawyer who gives competent advice on California law in New York to a client who is in New York is guilty of nothing. The New York lawyer who advises a California client on New York law in California, depending upon the amount of time he or she spends there, may be guilty of UPL. The *Ranta* case **(page 733)** concerned a Minnesota lawyer who advised a North Dakota businessman on federal tax law and was deemed guilty of UPL while giving that advice in North Dakota (but not while doing so while physically in Minnesota). In short, states have a legitimate interest in being concerned about extensive virtual practice, just as they have a legitimate interest in being concerned about extensive physical presence, but the facts of *Birbrower* simply do not add up to enough of a presence to warrant the holding.

If *Birbrower* is the problem, what is the solution? The note material beginning at **page 731** identifies many of these themes. At **page 733** I list a number of significant court opinions in the area, mostly about fees, but occasionally about discipline and in one case a criminal prosecution (*Schrader* at **page 734**).

The paragraphs immediately following *Birbrower* reveal the California statute that effectively overrules it at least until 2006. For the reasons given – loss of arbitral business, forcing California residents to travel for arbitrations – the legislature, followed by the court, overturned the opinion in part at least temporarily.

"Practicing Nationally from St. Louis" (page 732) is meant to provide facts that test our tolerance for virtual practice augmented by some physical presence. It is possible, isn't it, for a law firm based in one city, using modern technology and specializing in a particular area, to have a national practice? Some do now. Yet those lawyers will be offering to serve and serving clients nationwide while members of only one state bar. Law firm marketing makes it increasingly possible to establish such a national practice. On the side of the states, they have an interest in protecting their residents from unscrupulous lawyers and in being able to punish lawyers who behave improperly either toward their own clients or others (adversaries, the justice system). Given *Birbrower*, surely states can impede the business plan of our St. Louis firm. But what should the policy be? Should we restrict this activity? If not, how can we respond intelligently to a state's legitimate interests? Perhaps most challenging, is it a legitimate interest that the state wants to protect its local bar against economic invasion? Remember, a state does have some interest in having a strong local bar and in not seeing outside lawyers "cherry pick" the best work. Local lawyers are part of the system of governance in state with integrated bar associations. Local lawyers do a lot of volunteer work. In part this was Rehnquist's position in *Piper* (**page 686**). It has some basis, I believe, and is entitled to respectful response.

Some alternatives. The note at **page 735** describes how some states have attempted to address the particular problem of the lawyer employed by a corporation who gets moved around the country for brief stints in various offices. They use a special admissions rule. Also mentioned here is the Foreign Legal Consultant rule, which allows a lawyer from a foreign country to counsel on the law of his home jurisdiction while physically established in a law office in a U.S. jurisdiction that has such a rule. It is interesting, isn't it, that a British lawyer can have an office in New York and advise on British law, but a California lawyer cannot have an office in New York and advise on California law unless that lawyer gains admission to the New York Bar? The note identifies rules in Michigan and Virginia that seem particularly enlightened and address the special dilemmas of transactional lawyers who have no recourse to pro hac vice admission.

Lessons from the European Community. This interview at **page 736** with Professor Laurel Terry gives students useful information about how the EC countries are handling transnational practice. Their approach is much more generous. While you may not choose to discuss this interview in class, it is well worth assigning (**page 736**).

Ethics 2000 (page 741). The E2K Commission has proposed to expand Rule 5.5 to allow greater freedom for MJP. Note that an expansion of the ethics rule may not be enough to achieve the goal since this activity is also controlled by unauthorized practice statutes that are passed by state legislatures. The Restatement's provision is textually broader than the E2K recommendation. Under the Restatement, the out-of-state work need only "arise out of" or be "reasonably related to the lawyer's practice" in the home state. Under E2K, the out-of-state work must arise out of or be reasonably related to "the lawyer's representation of a client" in the home state. So in the former, the nexus is to the practice and in the latter the nexus is to client representation.

3. Multijurisdictional Firms (page 741). Controversy over multijurisdictional firms has arisen largely in the context of mass marketing legal clinics, like Jacoby & Meyers and Hyatt Legal Services. The note tries to make this point and identifies two cases, from New Jersey and New York, in which local lawyers tried to stop Jacoby & Meyers from using its name. Its name, of course, is one of its most valuable assets. The determination by the in-state lawyers to press their efforts to keep Jacoby & Meyers from practicing under its firm name -- claiming that it would confuse the working class clientele of this firm, who would believe they were actually going to get one of the named partners as their personal lawyer -- does lay bear the economic reality of this material. The local lawyers lost in New York but won in New Jersey! Recall the "New Jersey" Problem at **page 688**. Ultimately, however, New Jersey changed its rule to allow Jacoby & Meyers to use its own name in that jurisdiction. Old established firms don't run into this problem. Why is that?

C. THE ETHICAL DUTY OF COMPETENCE (page 743)

Here is another way competence in minimally adequate performance is ensured, at least in theory. We encountered the duty of competence briefly in Chapter 2B1, where we listed the attributes of the attorney-client relationship. Rarely is a lawyer disciplined for incompetence. And the few who are often guilty of other things as well -- intentional neglect or a pattern of grossly negligent behavior. Incompetent conduct standing alone is usually left to malpractice actions. Still, the courts do insist that a single act of incompetence can be grounds for discipline. Malpractice actions for incompetent representation will only occur in a small percentage of such matters. First, there must be sufficient damage to justify the action. Second, the client has to discover the incompetence. Third, the client has to be willing to retain a new lawyer to sue the former lawyer. Fourth, the client and the new lawyer have to conclude that they can prove the "case within the case" as generally required in malpractice actions. See **page 794**. So it might be thought that malpractice (like discipline) can only work at the extremes. Furthermore, discipline may not be public. Even if it is public, new clients will often not know to inquire about it. Malpractice actions may also not be public. Settlements may be accompanied by secrecy agreements. Verdicts may simply not get attention. Shall we require all lawyers to inform all new clients of all malpractice and disciplinary complaints against them, together with the dispositions? Or does that go too far?

D. CONTINUING LEGAL EDUCATION (page 745)

About half the state now have mandatory CLE plans. These vary in their details. They have been upheld, as *Verner* attests.

E. SUPERVISORY RESPONSIBILITIES (page 746)

This material used to be a Part in a longer chapter called "Special Masks Lawyers Wear." The Part was titled "Subordinate and Supervisory Lawyers." I have now placed the material on supervisory responsibilities here, viewing it as a mechanism for preventing professional failures. The material on subordinate lawyers has been merged with the general duty to report another

179

lawyer's misconduct and appears in Chapter 13D. Supervisory failures can lead to discipline **(page 747)** or malpractice liability **(page 748)**.

The most striking of the Rules' developments may be the creation of a duty in partners and supervisory lawyers to take preventive measure to protect against violation of the ethical rules **(pages 746-747)**. These may include an in-house structure for resolving ethical quandaries, especially when a partner and an associate disagree about the propriety of conduct the partner is about to take, and periodic seminars on ethical requirements.

New York, alone as of this writing, provides for discipline of law firms that fail, among other things, to "make reasonable efforts to ensure that all lawyers in the firm conform to the disciplinary rules." **(Pages 748-749.)**

"I Don't Want to Pry, But..." (page 749)

I have a confession. I am sure that the issues this story raises can engender good class discussion, though I have not yet figured out precisely how to do it. I've finetuned the facts several times. The "clash" here is between the following:

(1) The firm or at least the management of it has responsibilities to ensure that lawyers at it perform competently and ethically. Failure can result in discipline for the supervisory lawyers and also malpractice liability. (The latter should be sufficiently obvious even though students may not yet have studied malpractice in Chapter 13 Reference to civil liability appears throughout the book, including in connection with *Simpson v. James* in Chapter 5.) The firm also has a legitimate interest in client confidence and comfort in working with its lawyers, at least where the possible discomfort is not for an impermissible reason (race, gender, etc.). The firm can rightly worry that if Kitty messes up, failure to take extra precautions in light of the signals it is getting may subject it to harsher civil liability -- not just vicarious liability for her errors, which is bad enough, but independent liability and possibly punitive damages for its independent failure to supervise appropriately. As Spencer says, these concerns are becoming incrementally harder to manage as law firms become larger, more bureaucratic, and as its lawyer population is less homogenous. Spencer's fear of a connection between Kitty's perceived life crisis and the quality of her work, where mistakes can be very expensive, has not occurred. Her work is not stellar but it has been "fine so far." Still, does the firm have to await an error? If it concludes that the signals are sufficient to require closer scrutiny of Kitty's work -- or that a jury might later so conclude in a civil action against the firm -- who will pay for that extra time? The firm cannot reasonably charge a client, can it? And what if it doesn't want to absorb the cost? Can it lower Kitty's hourly rate (and salary) to reflect the time of others in supervising her?

(2) On the other hand, control may interfere with a lawyer's personal autonomy -- in her decisions about how to behave and appear outside work, with whom to associate socially, and

even how to present herself at the law firm. Are dress codes legitimate? Even if so, how restrictive can or should they be? Spencer's purported dilemma can be seen as a surrogate for impermissible bias. Does the firm respond the same way to men who don't quite fit its mold? Even if there are no such men, is the firm's "image" of how a single woman should behave and dress a form of gender bias? Some of my students have suggested that insofar as Kitty has an eating disorder, it's a medical problem and cannot be the basis for negative employment treatment under the ADA and perhaps other law. Some students wondered whether the firm may be biased against Kitty based on her perceived sexual orientation (which some state ethics rules or antidiscrimination laws don't allow).

In the end, this problem should grapple with the clash between increased managerial responsibility at increasingly large law firm, coupled with increased civil liability risks, on the one hand, and personal autonomy of lawyers at institutions whose professional populations are becoming more heterogeneous and diverse. What would the student advise Spencer? How does he or she answer his particular concerns?

F. UNAUTHORIZED PRACTICE OF LAW (page 750)

Unauthorized practice rules address three problems. First, the person offering the legal service may not be admitted to the bar of the state, or indeed to the bar of any state, and therefore the "client" may be ill-served. This risk is reduced, of course, if the lawyer is a lawyer somewhere. A second problem is that the lawyer may be dishonest or lacking in character. If a lawyer admitted in state A advises clients in state B on the law of state A, state B has an interest in insuring not only competence but integrity as well. Last, there is also a conflict risk if a lawyer, though duly admitted to the state bar, renders service to a third person through an entity that is not authorized to practice law. The particular conflict issues that arise when a lawyer works in or with an organization owned, controlled or managed by lay persons is discussed in Chapter 14.

The introductory material **(pages 750-752)** raises the paternalism question, the market question, and the governance question. Paternalism: Should people have the right to use an unlicensed "lawyer" to save money? Market: How can we constrain the bar's interest in expanding the definition of law practice in order to increase the cost of legal services? Governance: Should the courts share with other branches of government the responsibility for defining the practice of law?

Professional Adjusters **(page 752)** rejected plaintiff's action for a fee on the ground that it was selling a legal service though not qualified to practice law. The case is interesting for several reasons. The issue arose in a defensive posture (the client, though it got value, didn't want to pay). The court refused to recognize legislation that would have allowed the plaintiff to engage in the adjustment business. The legislature had not casually authorized firms like Professional

Adjusters to engage in this business. It created a system for written examination and certification under the authority of the insurance commissioner. The court was unimpressed.

Notice how broadly the court defines the practice of law. Plaintiff engaged in law practice merely by submitting a claim to the defendants' insurance carrier. There was no bargaining. The court would have ruled otherwise if plaintiff merely evaluated the loss and reported that value to the client so that the client could then settle the claim. It was the authorization to negotiate a settlement that troubled the court. But don't nonlawyers negotiate deals all the time? How about literary agents? Real estate agents? Sports agents? What is so special about negotiating an insurance loss that it requires a legal education? Distinguish drafting the settlement agreement.

The opinion causes a certain lack of symmetry. An insurance company can employ adjusters or retain independent adjusters. Employed adjusters are free to bind the company in settlement. But individual claimants, although they may retain independent adjusters to advise them, must deal with insurers on their own or through counsel, not through the adjuster.

Of what is the court fearful, especially given the legislature's care? A slippery slope? Is this a patent example of a guild restriction? Contrast *Professional Adjusters* with *Cultum v. Heritage House Realtors, Inc.* (**page 756**). The risk in *Cultum* was that the real estate salespersons would not competently prepare the documents. Nevertheless, the court allowed them to do so but only under narrow circumstances without charge, and provided they "comply with the standard of care demanded of an attorney." So here we see a form of sublicensure. The court allows persons who are not lawyers to provide what is traditionally a legal service without legal supervision, except that the forms had to have been prepared by a lawyer.

The New Jersey Supreme Court (**page 755**) has addressed the practice under which sales of residential property in the southern part of the state were accomplished without the use of lawyers. Brokers did what lawyers do. In the northern part of the state, lawyers were traditional. A committee of the court held the practice in the southern part of the state to be unauthorized practice of law. The New Jersey Supreme Court disagreed so long as brokers conform to certain conditions including notification of both buyer and seller of the conflicting interests of brokers and title companies and of the general risk of not being represented by an attorney.

The Troubled World of Unauthorized Practice (page 757). This note briefly summarizes the reasons why the lay (including the client) community is suspicious of unauthorized practice rules.

Uncontested Divorces (page 758). Here is one area in which the Rules have been repeatedly tested and challenged, especially in Florida, which finally relented and permitted "limited oral communications" between nonlawyers and individuals who wish to complete legal forms approved by the state supreme court in order to secure an uncontested divorce.

182

Will Courts Share Power? (page 759) The book presents a sampling of cases in which courts have and have not been willing to accept modest legislative intrusion on judicial authority to define the practice of law and the identity of those who may engage in it.

Should Paralegals Be Licensed? (page 760) Still incipient, this trend may balloon in the next few years, especially given predictions about the anticipated growth of the paralegal population. In California, at least, paralegal practice seems to exist de facto. Efforts formally to recognize and license paralegals reportedly failed there because both sides opposed the rules -- one side as too generous and the other as too restrictive. Licensed paralegals present a serious threat to many practicing lawyers. They would compete for some of the same work and charge much less. The ABA Professionalism Commission recommended exploration of paralegal licensing (see **page 14**) but its recommendation went nowhere. Opposition was intense. One member of the Commission told a forum I attended that lawyers complained that well more than half their work fell within the categories the Commission contemplated as appropriate for paralegals because the work was sufficiently nondiscretionary. Many students will be able to see the effect of paralegal licensing on the practices they anticipate having. The threat is especially keen in a bad economic climate. Not only will more lawyers be seeking the routinized work, but many paralegals may have no choice but to open their own shops. Do students credit the Bar's assertion that its resistance to paralegal licensing is meant solely to protect clients? After all, as the Texas State Bar President artfully put it **(page 760)**, we wouldn't allow "nurses to perform brain surgery."

Constitutional Limitations (page 761). Although inherent judicial authority to define the practice of law is broad, it does have its limits and some of those can be found in the Constitution. Here, the book collects diverse cases that draw the line. *Sperry* cited the Supremacy Clause in deference to a rule that allowed nonlawyers to practice before the Patent Office. *Johnson v. Avery* concerned the "practice of law" by prison inmates on behalf of other prison inmates. There is, lastly, Norman Dacey's battle with the New York County Lawyer's Association, which wanted to stop him (can you believe this?) from publishing a book telling readers how to avoid probate. Dacey communicated directly with no one. It could not be said he had a "client" whom he was advising. The First Amendment entitled him to sell his book.

See also the decision in *State Unauthorized Practice of Law Committee v. Paul Mason & Associates, Inc.*, 46 F.3d 469 (5th Cir. 1995), holding that bankruptcy standards permitting nonlawyer agents to perform administrative functioning in bankruptcy courts take precedence over any effort by a state to deem such conduct the practice of law.

Quicken Family Lawyer confronts Texas UPL Statute (page 762). This does seem to parody the debate. A federal judge finds that a CD-ROM is engaged in UPL, or more accurately, those who sell the CD-ROM. The CD-ROM certainly raises the stakes beyond what "how to" law books threaten. They have a whole lot more information and can have a "conversation" with the user. But really. It is instructive that Texas, which is not at the forefront of changing the rules in this area, immediately change the rules that supported the district judge's decision, which was then vacated by the Fifth Circuit.

G. SPECIALIZATION (page 763)

Specialization is a way of ensuring competence by encouraging greater knowledge of a particular area of the law. In February 1989, the ABA amended the comment to Rule 7.4 to allow use of such words as "practice limited to" or "practice concentrated in." After the Supreme Court's decision in *Peel* (**page 1017**), the ABA amended Rule 7.4 to permit the use of the word "specialist" and variations on it where the lawyer has been certified as a specialist "by the appropriate regulatory authority or by an organization which has been approved by the appropriate regulatory authority. . . ." Rule 7.4(c)(1). Where there is no such authority, a lawyer can advertise certification as a specialist by an organization accredited by the ABA. Ruth 7.4(c).

CHAPTER XIII

CONTROL OF QUALITY:
REMEDIES FOR PROFESSIONAL FAILURE

This Chapter investigates three prominent mechanisms for remedying professional failures when they occur. The first is malpractice and other civil actions by clients and third parties against lawyers for a variety of professional defaults. The second is discipline. The third is the constitutional guarantee of the effective assistance of counsel.

A. MALPRACTICE AND BREACH OF FIDUCIARY DUTY (page 765)

Closely related to the ethical duty of competence, and some would say nearly as useless for most disgruntled clients, is an action (in tort, contract, something else) for professional malpractice. Clients may sue, even third persons may sue (and sometimes win), for negligent work. Either plaintiff may try to cite an ethical rule in support of her argument that a duty was breached or conduct was improper. Although the texts of the Code and Rules disclaim any intention that their standards may be so employed, they are anyway.

The introductory material (pages 765-767) provides statistics on malpractice cases (the trendline no longer seems up), headlines the alleged "crisis" in lawyer liability, asks whether increased liability will change the behavior of lawyers, questions whether there is a connection between professionalism and the malpractice "crisis," and queries whether increased professional exposure reflects a decrease in the sanctity of professions generally.

1. Liability to Clients (page 767). The recurring theme of client identity is sounded once again here. Even though nonclients can now sue lawyers for professional defaults, at least in some places and under some circumstances, it still helps to be a client. A teacher could hardly ask for a better case than *Togstad* **(page 768)** to introduce the subject of malpractice generally and the lesser included issue of client identity. The result in *Togstad* often surprises students.

Togstad should be used to illustrate (i) contract vs. tort theories of recovery; (ii) the definition of "client"; (iii) the proximate cause element of the claim -- *i.e.*, plaintiffs here had to prove that but for the malpractice they would have won the underlying claim and the amount of damages (compare the possibly different causation requirement when the allegation is breach of fiduciary duty as described at **page 796**); (iv) the difference between errors of judgment and malpractice -- here Miller failed <u>both</u> to inform Mrs. Togstad about the statute of limitations and to do the minimum factual research (checking hospital records and consulting an expert) required before concluding she had no case; and (v) the use of expert testimony on the legal standard of care.

What is the practical lesson of *Togstad*? You might begin by asking students what they would warn colleagues in a firm to do or not do after reading the case: When you decline a case, does *Togstad* mean you should not say why and write a memo to the file stating what you didn't state? Miller would not likely have been found negligent if he had said: "I don't do medical malpractice. It doesn't seem to me you have a case but I may be wrong. I urge you to get a second opinion and you should also realize that you have only ten more months in which to sue." Or was Miller required to do the threshold research before saying even this? (No.) Was he required to warn the Togstads of the statute of limitations even if he said *nothing* else? (Not entirely clear though I'd think not.) These points may also be elicited through the questions about the case at **page 775**. Taking them in order:

(1) Students should understand that an attorney-client relationship was formed even though Mrs. Togstad never retained Miller and no money changed hands. Indeed, Miller was deemed to have a professional relationship with Mr. Togstad who, so far as appears, never met him. What created the relationships was Mrs. Togstad's testimony "that she requested and received legal advice from Miller concerning the malpractice claim." See also the quote from *Ryan* at **page 773** for determining whether a professional relationship exists. Miller tried to characterize the conversation with Mrs. Togstad as one in which she was merely asking his "opinion as an attorney in the sense of whether or not there was a case that the firm would be interested in undertaking." **(Page 772**.)

(2) The first theory of liability was Miller's negligence in assessing the merits of the case without adequate research. The second theory was his failure to advise on the two-year statute where fourteen months had already run. A legal expert testified that under the circumstance he "would have advised someone of the two-year period of limitation." That was enough to support the malpractice on the second theory. The second theory is intriguing. As discussed above, does the court hold that lawyers in Miller's position must always inform the client of the limitations period? Or was it only because Miller told Mrs. Togstad that he didn't believe she had a case? The court seems to think that identifying the limitations period is easy. Often it is. But sometimes it is hard. (From when does the period run? Is the running of the statute suspended under certain circumstances?) Would Miller have been secure if he had said: "There is a statute of limitations on malpractice actions which is normally two years and which may run out in ten months but I'm not saying for sure that it will." Need he even have said that if he had only said "not interested"? While it seems oppressive to require lawyers who simply decline any interest in a case and explicitly decline to give an opinion about its merits nevertheless to investigate the statute of limitations, a lawyer in Minnesota, at least, may be taking a chance if he or she does otherwise. I realize that those were not the facts of *Togstad*. At the top of **page 775** the court seems to say that it is only because Miller did give legal advice ("no case") that he was therefore

obligated to inform the client "of the applicable limitations period." But I wouldn't want to bet on what the Minnesota Supreme Court would do on those facts especially if the statute were about to expire.

(3) The court does seem to give Miller an out here. At **page 774**, it emphasizes that "Miller did not qualify this legal opinion by urging her to seek advice from another attorney, nor did Miller inform her that he lacked expertise in the medical malpractice area." So Miller could probably have told Mrs. Togstad that he had no opinion on the merits of her case and was not interested, that he was not going to seek the hospital records, and that she should consult another lawyer. He ought then to have followed up his response with a letter saying the same thing. This avoids inconsistent recollections. Miller's mistake was to tell Mrs. Togstad "there wasn't a case," without doing the minimum factual research. She predictably "relied upon this advice in failing to pursue the claim for medical malpractice." **(Page 774.)** But if Miller had given my alternate response, could he then have said nothing about the statute of limitations? A good office practice would be to alert the rejected client to the fact of limitation periods, perhaps saying what they "generally" are in the particular kind of case while emphasizing many possible exceptions, and urging the client to see another lawyer "without delay in order to be sure to protect your rights."

(4) The court distinguishes tort and contract theories of recovery at **page 773 n.4**. In *Collins*, cited at **page 775**, paragraph 4,, the Illinois Supreme Court held that malpractice claims can be based on a contract or tort theory. Often it won't much matter, especially when the plaintiff was a client. It may sometimes matter, as it did in *Pelham* at **page 783**, if the plaintiff was not a client.

What Is the Required Standard of Care? (page 776) While errors of judgment do not a malpractice case make, failure to exercise ordinary prudence does. Miller failed that test by ignoring the "minimum research" that an expert said he should have conducted. Students should know that, on facts like *Togstad*, a lay jury could not on its own determine that Miller did not exercise ordinary prudence. An expert was necessary. That will not always be true. See **page 787**. This note provides various articulations of the malpractice standard, including the higher standard of care required of lawyers who hold themselves out as having special expertise in a field of law.

Fraud (page 777). Ordinarily, it would not make sense to point out that a lawyer may be liable to a client for the lawyer's fraud. But *Baker v. Dorfman* is such a neat case, I decided to spend a half page recounting the facts. This is a situation of resume padding in an effort to persuade a client to retain a lawyer. When the lawyer messes up, not only is he liable for lost claims but also for fraud, including punitive damages.

Breach of Fiduciary Duties (page 778). In *Togstad*, Miller did not exercise ordinary prudence because he did not do minimal research and did not advise Mrs. Togstad of the limitations. A lawyer may also disserve a client by breaching fiduciary duties to the client. (The theories of recovery are not always kept distinct.) Stealing client funds is a prime example. Using client confidences to compete with the client is another. If you covered *Simpson v. James* in Chapter 5, students will already have seen an example of what was labeled malpractice based in a concurrent conflict, but which can be viewed as a breach of the fiduciary duty of loyalty. As students move through the malpractice material, they will encounter theories of liability based on lack of prudence and other theories based on breach of fiduciary duty. They should be alert to the difference. One issue that has arisen in my classes is the identity of the line between legal malpractice and breach of fiduciary duty. Negligence is the former. Misuse of client confidences is the latter. A conflict is viewed as the latter even if it is unintentional. One useful if not perfect test is to say that legal malpractice is what only lawyers can do whereas fiduciary breaches are what any agent can do. *Vallinoto* **(page 778**) shows what can happen if you assert the wrong theory.

Is Sex With Clients a Breach of Fiduciary Duty? (page 779) This material takes up a developing issue. It has now arisen in quite a few cases, either in damage claims or discipline. *Tante v. Herring* **(page 779**) is one of the damage cases, unusual only because the underlying matter was a social security claim. Note the causes of action: malpractice, breach of fiduciary duty, and breach of contract. The court upholds the fiduciary duty claim on a very specific and fairly narrow ground. Tante used confidential information about Mrs. Herring is psychological state to convince her to have an affair with him. Note, too, that both Mr. and Mrs. Herring had a claim arising out of this breach even though, apparently, only Mrs. Herring was the social security claimant. *McDaniel v. Gile* **(page 781**) goes furthest. These issues most often arise in matrimonial cases although Glenn Close's character did sleep with the criminal defendant she was representing in *Jagged Edge*. That episode and others are addressed in the material on discipline at **page 851**. You may want to reserve extended discussion about the propriety of intimate personal relationships between lawyers and clients until then. Here, however, students should know that sex with clients may result in civil liability as well as discipline. The problem clients have so far encountered is in showing damage. See *Suppressed v. Suppressed* **(page 780**). When should it breach fiduciary duty to have sex with a client? Always? When he or she is emotionally distraught? In *Tante*, it wasn't merely the sex but sex accomplished by use of confidential information that created the claim. An alternative, and expansive, view would hold that sex alone can create the claim if the conduct is particularly outrageous as in *McDaniel* **(page 781**). But we have to worry, don't we, about the state intruding on truly volitional adult decisions?

This question is based on *Flatt v. Superior Court*, 855 P.2d 950 (1994). Flatt had a conference with a prospective client (Daniel) in which the latter disclosed confidential information. Flatt told Daniel that he definitely had a claim against a former lawyer, but a week later returned Daniel's documents, explaining that she had a conflict because her firm represented the prospective defendant's firm "in an unrelated matter." Flatt did not advise Daniel of a statute of limitations problem. The California Supreme Court, in a 4-3 decision, held that even if Daniel was a client, Flatt had no duty to advise him about the statute of limitations. Advising Daniel on the statute would have been disloyal to Flatt's current client. Unlike the Togstads, perhaps, Daniel, knowing the reason Flatt declined the matter, should not have relied on her silence. But the court did not give this reason.

Bart is certainly a client of the inquirer even though he has not fully committed to taking her case. He charged her a fee to do preliminary research at the end of which he is going to give her an opinion. That's a legal service. The inquirer did a conflicts check and discovered that his firm was not representing either Selden or Selden's firm. He then proceeded to do the work and came to a conclusion about Selden's liability. Before telling Bart, however, he learns that his partner, Dorset, had just accepted Selden's firm as a client in a commercial lease dispute, a more attractive matter for the inquirer's firm than is Bart's matter.

Now the inquirer may have made one mistake, but it would be a common mistake. When accepting Bart's matter, even preliminarily, he did not enter her name or the name of the adversary in the computer database. Or if he did, Dorset did not check before accepting the representation of Selden's firm. But even if the inquirer had entered Bart's matter in the database, would he have entered both Selden and the name of Selden's firm? Probably. Both were likely defendants. Then, if Dorset checked the database, the name of Selden's firm would come up.

So the inquirer can be faulted (or Dorset can be faulted) for not catching this conflict. Similarly, the lawyer-defendant in *Flatt* could be faulted for the same reason.

But what now? The firm must reject one of the two clients and prefers to keep Selden's firm as a client. Does it even have a choice? Having told Bart that he would take her case depending upon what the preliminary research revealed – or that is certainly how she would have understood the inquirer's statement – and the preliminary research having revealed a claim, can the firm now drop Bart "like a hot potato" to stay with Selden's firm? I would think not. I especially come to this conclusion if the mix-up is due to the firm's failure to monitor conflicts either because the inquirer did not enter the Bart matter in the database or because Dorset did not review the database before accepting Selden's firm. One or the other seems likely. But if it's the firm's fault, and it cannot drop Bart "like a hot potato," can it drop Selden's firm like a hot potato? It would seem that neither client should suffer. Alternatively, it would seem that whichever client was dropped would have a motion to disqualify the firm from representing the other. The problem, however, is that the firm is not going to represent Selden's firm in the case against Bart so she would not be seeking to disqualify it there. By contrast, if the firm dropped Selden's firm and showed up for Bart in the case against Selden's firm, Selden's firm might seek to disqualify the firm as Bart's counsel on the ground that the firm was counsel to Selden's firm notwithstanding that it withdrew improperly. So from a cost/benefit analysis, the firm in our problem would prefer to drop the client who cannot make the disqualification motion, namely Bart. Would she then have any other remedy? Surely she could get her retainer back, but it is unlikely that she would have any other recourse.

For pedagogical purposes, we can imagine that both cases came in at the same time so that the conflict could not have been detected. What then? Then we might say that the firm has a conflict through no fault of its own. Then we might allow the firm to choose the client it wishes to stay with. If the firm chooses to stay with Selden's firm, what should the inquirer do? Selden's firm now being a client, the inquirer cannot rightly tell Bart she may have a claim against Selden and his firm. So the best course for him would be to tell her that after accepting her matter, he discovered a conflict and cannot advise her. He must return her retainer and any papers she gave him. But does he have to tell her about the statute of limitations? *Flatt* concluded that it was enough to tell the client, after the conflict was discovered, that it had a conflict and could not represent him. The case also concluded that it would be disloyal to the firm's other client to give the plaintiff information about the statute of limitations. A strong dissent concluded that the client (Bart in our question) had a right to that information when the firm withdrew from representing him. The dissent's view was that if alerting the client of the limitations was disloyal to the client it was staying with, that was just tough luck for the firm. It got itself into the mess and it couldn't get itself out by favoring one current client over another. So if by telling the rejected client about the limitations period it was harming its other client, the firm had only itself to blame and had to take the heat.

This theory works if we assume that the firm in our problem is at fault in not discovering the conflict in a timely manner. It may be that it is at fault for that reason. The facts don't allow us to know. If we assume that it is at fault, then we have to choose between the majority view and the dissent in *Flatt* and *Togstad*. *Flatt* can be distinguished from *Togstad* in two ways: the remaining period in the limitations period was substantially longer and the client was told that the firm could not accept his matter because of a conflict, which might have alerted the client to seek other counsel sooner. In *Togstad*, by contrast, the client was told he had no case which could reasonably have lulled her into inaction.

2. Third Parties as "Client-Equivalents" (page 782). A major development since the first edition of the casebook has been the increase in lawyer liability to third parties. Later (page 813), we discuss some of the dominant theories underlying this increase. Here, however, we touch on one theory because of its close relation to liability to clients -- the willingness of some courts in some circumstances to characterize third parties as "client-equivalents." As a result, a lawyer may be held to the same duty of care toward those third parties as he or she must exhibit toward a client proper. Reconciling the cases here is not easy. Opinion letters meant to encourage third party reliance present an easy case **(page 784)**. Some courts are much more willing to impose duties on lawyers to nonclients than are other courts, especially outside of litigation (where, presumably, the "warrior" image holds greatest sway). *Pelham* **(page 783)** is much more begrudging. While we can recognize the court's reluctance to impose duties to nonclients on advocates in litigation, how in the world could it have harmed the wife for the lawyer to notify the insurance company of the requirements of the divorce decree? That is, even accepting the court's sensitivity to divided loyalties, could there have been divided loyalties on these facts? Presumably, the wife has died. Assume she has. Does that mean that no one can now sue for the lawyer's blunder? How if at all would a different result in *Pelham* have muted the zeal of future lawyers in the same circumstance?

3. Vicarious Liability (page 784). The liability of a lawyer's partners for the lawyer's defaults -- or those of co-shareholders in a professional corporation -- is generally assumed if the negligence occurred within the scope of the business of the partnership or corporation. (Many states by statute limit vicarious liability in professional corporations.) What is the scope of a law partnership? The cases here reveal different degrees of tolerance for broad definitions of the word "scope." New York has probably gone farthest with *Grandeau* **(page 786)**. An especially demanding case is *Dresser Industries* **(page 785)**, where partners were held liable for another partner's overbilling to the tune of $3 million. The court had two theories. Overbilling was within the scope of the partnership's business because billing was something law firms do. In addition, the partners were liable for failing to supervise the other partner. See Rule 5.1.

One developing problem is when a law partner serves on the board of a client. If the partner makes a decision as a board member and is later sued for breach of fiduciary duty or negligence, will his or her partners be vicariously liable? One view would answer yes because the decision to sit on the board was obviously in the interests of the partnership. Another view would answer no because the partner's decision as a board member is not something the other partners, who are not board members, can oversee. It's not delegable or subject to partnership control. On the other hand, a partner's decision as a lawyer is, at least in theory, something the firm can countermand. The *Mmahat* case at **page 785** doesn't resolve these questions because the jury there found that the firm partner had made his decisions as an S&L board member in his lawyer, and not in his director, capacity.

The second full paragraph on **page 786** introduces students to the new craze for limited liability partnerships. Interesting angle here: One partner at a major New York law firm told me that his firm had decided not to become an LLP for the following reason. In the event of a judgment against the LLP in excess of its malpractice policy, lawyers who were not personally liable would leave the firm. This is because the firm would be liable and might be paying off the excess judgment indefinitely. That excess payment means that money that would otherwise flow to those lawyers will instead go to the judgment creditor. If those lawyers are large money earners, they lose, compared to what they can earn at another firm, where everything they earn, after ordinary expenses, flows down to the individual partners, including them. By remaining a partnership, and not an LLP, my informant told me that his firm hopes to dissuade business getters from leaving in the event of an excess judgment against the firm because they will not, thereby, be able to avoid contributing to the excess judgment.

B. PROVING MALPRACTICE (page 787)

1. Use of Ethics Rules and Expert Testimony (page 787). I set out here a case permitting the use of the profession's rules of ethics and an ethics expert in establishing malpractice or breach of fiduciary duty. To an extent, this is circular because the rules themselves in large measure are specific applications of common law principles, including principles of fiduciary duty. Consequently, an effort to use the rules to show a violation of a legal duty should not be shocking. On the other hand, what business is it of ethics experts to testify to the meaning of the rules? If the rules are presented as "law," then it is the duty of the judge to interpret the law for the jury. On the third hand, if the rules are presented as illustrative of the minimally accepted level of conduct lawyers in the community observe, perhaps going beyond what the law requires of other agents, then a violation of the rules might be said to be a violation of the standard of care, skill, prudence and judgment established by the legal community in which the lawyer practices. That's a traditional basis for liability. Nor will the jury readily be able to decipher and apply this standard -- as defined by the rules -- on its own.

I chose the *Smith* case (**page 788**) to illustrate the use of ethics rules and ethics experts in malpractice and breach of fiduciary duty cases because (a) it identifies the various state positions; (b) it adopts the majority view; and (c) it permitted use of an expert not admitted in the state and not an expert in the underlying area of law. In the note following, I ask students to identify the possible conflicts in *Smith*. As we see from the first paragraph, the firm represented both the purchaser (Bashor) and sellers (Smith and Murray) of the lots. Further, firm partners were investors with Bashor. The note concludes (**page 790**) by identifying the Restatement section permitting ethics rules to be used in evidence in cases against lawyers and, by implication, ethics experts to interpret the rules for the jury.

Incidentally, you should distinguish between experts who testify to a lawyer's obligations under the Code or Rules -- or legal antecedents to these -- and experts who testify to the standard of care. For example, in a case alleging malpractice in a matrimonial action, a matrimonial lawyer who practices in the community might testify as an expert that the lawyer-defendant did or did not exercise the standard of care exhibited by matrimonial lawyers in that community. Recall *Togstad* (**page 768**). Alternatively, in a case alleging violation of confidentiality obligations or conflict of interest, an expert might testify, based on the jurisdiction's ethics code, that the defendant's conduct violated the standard of care – to avoid conflicts or to protect confidences – in the community.

The Ethics 2000 Commission **(page 790)** proposed, and the ABA has tentatively accepted, a modification of the Scope (in Comment [20]) that would recognize that a violation of the rules can evidence a breach of a standard of conduct.

Ethical Violations as a Basis for Reduction or Denial of Fees (page 791). Even if a lawyer's ethical lapse causes no damage, even if it is not a basis for civil liability, it may still justify a denial or diminution of fee. The theory here is not entirely clear. One court has said that it is not "restitutionary." Another has said the rule is based on "public policy." A third has identified deterrence as the goal and lists factors to weigh in determining how much of the fee to deny. *Hendry* **(page 791)** relies on a deterrent purpose and also on the policy that a fiduciary should not benefit from his or her own wrongdoing. *Hendry* take no position on whether the amount of fee loss should be total or calibrated. The case is unusual in leaving the decision to a jury. The Restatement opts for calibration. The bankruptcy rules separately (and more stringently) provide for loss of counsel fees in the event of conflict. **(Page 792.)** This rule derives from the law of agency. See Restatement of Agency (Second), §469.

Two new cases in this note are *Kirkland & Ellis* **(page 792)**, which says that an ethical violation can serve as a defense to a fee claim even if the client cannot prove damages sufficient to support a counterclaim; and *Image Technical Service* **(page 793)**, which declined to allow a client whose law firm was guilty of a conflict of interest, and so disqualified, to recover the fees the client paid to that lawyer from the client's adversary, under a fee-shifting statute. The law firm's conflict violated its duties to the adversary, not the client seeking the fee.

2. Causation and Defenses (page 794). Here students get introduced to the "case within a case" problem. Causation must be proved and not only where the lawyer's default occurred in litigation. The client who has to prove a case within a case has a double problem. Shouldn't the litigation client be permitted instead to prove the likelihood of settlement rather than the likelihood of victory in court? Probabilities of settlement, and the amount of the probable settlement, could be proved by calling experts in the area of law at issue. We see some movement toward eliminating the "but for" test in malpractice actions and substituting a "substantial factor" test, as in the California, New Jersey, and Maine cases at **pages 795**. These cases do not arise in litigation. When the allegation is breach of fiduciary duty, some courts do not require the plaintiff to prove strict proximate cause, as the *Milbank* case **(page 796)** reveals. But *Milbank*, broadly read, may no longer be good law. Relaxation of the "but for" test even in fiduciary duty cases may be appropriate only when the remedy is restitutionary, to recover the fiduciary's unjust enrichment. **(Page 796.)** I suggest that another way to deal with the causation issue in breach of fiduciary duty cases is to shift the burden of proof on the issue to the fiduciary once the breach is proved, but so far this is only my idea. In Ohio **(page 795)**, the "substantial factor" test has been employed even where the malpractice arises in litigation. I suggest in that paragraph that insisting on a "but for" causation standard in malpractice arising out of litigation in court forces the malpractice plaintiff to agree to a double discount – once for the settlement value of the underlying case and once for the settlement value of the outer case.

Settlements will not generally obviate a subsequent malpractice action. However, the Pennsylvania Supreme Court decision in *Muhammad* at **page 797** held that a settlement did bar a subsequent malpractice action other than for fraud. An allegation of negligence -- for example inadequate factual inquiry -- in the lawyer's recommendation of settlement will not support malpractice. No other court has followed this view and several have rejected it. The court justified its holding on the ground that settlements were favored by public policy and that lawyers would fear to recommend settlements if they were thereafter exposed to malpractice actions based on inadequate legal or factual research. (Isn't that reason silly? Will they fear to try cases on the same theory?) However, the rule is otherwise in Pennsylvania if the lawyer recommended settlement in order to conceal the lawyer's defaults, for example, having let a statute of limitations expire. Post-*Muhammad* cases in Pennsylvania and the Third Circuit have strived to distinguish it **(page 797)**. Its continued validity is in doubt.

The book identifies **(page 797)** contributory and comparative negligence as recognized defenses in malpractice actions and it highlights the Seventh Circuit cases in which corporations sue former counsel for negligence or breach of fiduciary duty. These suits may come through shareholder derivative claims or in an action by new management. They will allege that counsel failed to detect or stop the illegal conduct of former management, as a result of which the entity suffered loss. The Seventh Circuit will allow these actions if former management's illegal conduct made the entity a "victim" of the conduct and not a "participant" to it. In other words, if former management broke the law to enrich the entity, shareholders and successor control persons suing in the name of the entity cannot complain about a lawyer's negligence in failing to discover the fraud. Remember, the lawyer's defaults may have been the same in either case, but in one case the lawyers can defend by asserting that the entity, their client, was "in on it" because former management was breaking the law to increase profits. In the other case, the lawyer will not enjoy this defense because former management was breaking the law to increase its own wealth at the expense of the client. Should so much turn on this distinction?

I cite the *O'Melveny* case at **page 799**. This is the case in which the Supreme Court declined to recognize a right of action under federal common law when the FDIC sued as receiver for a bank. The case was remanded to determine whether the bank would have a claim against its former lawyers under California law where the former management was guilty of fraud. Notice that Justice Stevens suggests that while a state might impute that fraud to the entity in the ordinary case, it might not when "the interests of taxpayers as well as ordinary creditors" -- and not merely shareholders -- "will be affected by the rule at issue. . . ." On remand, the Ninth Circuit construed state law to prevent the law firm from asserting against the receiver a defense that it would have had against the entity client.

"The Law Changed Twice" (page 799)

This case is based loosely on *Smith v. Lewis*, 530 P.2d 589 (1975). The sticking point in *Smith v. Lewis* -- what makes the case interesting -- is the issue of proximate cause. The California Supreme Court did not rule that plaintiff would have been able to establish her entitlement to her husband's federal or state military pension at issue there. The jury so concluded. Compare *Togstad* (**page 768**), where the jury found (as a matter of <u>fact</u>) that plaintiffs would have won the underlying claim. In *Smith*, wasn't the parallel issue a matter of law? Why didn't the California court rule on it? Is it accurate to say that in *Smith* the trial jury was permitted to find as a fact that Mrs. Smith would have been legally entitled to a part of her husband's pension as a matter of law? The state court wrote: "Whether the defendant's negligence was a cause in fact of the plaintiff's damage is a factual question for the jury to resolve." This is curious. What if the next week (or the same day) the state court were presented with the same legal issue (whether a military pension is community property) and held that it was not? How could it then be said that Smith was injured by Lewis' failure?

One argument in favor of the Supreme Court's refusal to look to later developments in the law is this. Had Lewis listed the pension, it could well have been that his client's husband would have settled for a portion of it, given the unsettled state of the law. Because Lewis did not list the pension, it was not even on the table for negotiation. Lewis failed to exercise ordinary prudence when he failed to do the research. The court is prepared to let him pay whatever price the jury chooses to determine Smith would have received. In the nature of things, that can be the full amount (half the pension) or, if permitted, an intermediate sum reflecting the jury's conclusion that there would have been a settlement.

Looking to the facts of this problem, Alice has a case that would go this way: If Adam had made a claim to have the increased inheritance value, given the uncertain state of the law, Madison would have had to negotiate that claim to avoid the risk of losing his argument and having to pay Alice half the increased value. The settlement value of the dispute at the time would have been more than zero but less than fifty percent of the increased value. How much more or less would depend on what the lawyers perceived as the risk that the state supreme court would vote one way or the other. But neither lawyer could predict with a hundred percent certainty. It would therefore be for a jury, not a judge, to predict what a reasonably prudent lawyer for Alice would have been able to obtain given the uncertain state of the law. The jury would of course have to be aided by expert testimony.

A tangential question is whether Adam would escape liability if he had researched the law and concluded that the Supreme Court would rule against making the increased value of the inheritance subject to equitable distribution. Adam might argue that even if other lawyers would come to other conclusions, his conclusion was reasonable and he could make that decision. We saw this issue arise in Chapter 2, when we discussed client autonomy and caselaw at **pages 97-98**. Indeed, one lower court case in California (*Davis v. Damrell*) so held, but its reasoning was rejected by the Nebraska Supreme Court in *Wood*. *Wood* held that because the decision

195

whether to settle is the client's, the client had a right to know about the unsettled state of the law. In the problem as posed, Adam may not have done any research at all and therefore did not exercise reasonable discretion, even if the *Davis* theory applied.

Causation in Criminal Cases (page 800). I preface this material with a "hypothetical" to alert students to the nature of the problem and encourage an intuitive reaction, which I suspect will be to uphold liability. Later, at **page 809**, I reveal the case from which the hypothetical derived. (Note that Adkins brought a collateral attack in federal court but lost after the Fourth Circuit concluded that Adkins speedy trial claim, if asserted, would have failed. Still, that was not the basis for the state supreme court's decision.)

Peeler **(page 801)** and the note following *Peeler* **(page 807)** identify the multiple state responses to this issue. Should it matter whether the lawyer was merely negligent, even grossly so, on one hand, or has consciously sacrificed the client on the other? In *Peeler*, there is an implied allegation that the defense lawyer may have failed to alert Peeler to the offer because of a conflict -- she would have had to testify against another Hughes & Luce client. This is akin to the situation in *Krahn* **(page 808)**, where the court upheld liability. Should the result differ depending on whether the lawyer is guilty of malpractice or some intentional misconduct? I'm inclined to believe so. Consider, as well, the dissent's distinct analysis. It would treat Peeler's case differently because she would have been actually (if not factually) innocent if the offer had been made and accepted. She can prove it. The prosecutor was prepared to give her a "walk." That would have made her "innocent" in the eyes of the law and she would have avoided the consequences of conviction.

Since the last edition of the book, the California Supreme Court has weighed in twice, holding that to recover the plaintiff must prove actual innocence and must also win exoneration either by direct appeal or collateral attack **(pages 807-808)**. Why both? If the plaintiff can show actual innocence, why should he also have to vacate the conviction. The technical answer is that so long as the conviction stands it acts as an estoppel against vindication on the civil claim. But this is a technical answer. Alternatively, if the plaintiff wins reversal of the conviction, should he also have to prove actual innocence in the malpractice action or will the reversal establish his innocence, at least as a matter of law? If the reversal is based on ineffective assistance of counsel in failing to move to suppress incriminating facts, it may be that the plaintiff cannot establish actual innocence but only legal innocence. In that event, we could say that his factual guilt is still the proximate cause of his troubles. The doctrine here lacks clarity and words are used differently in different cases. Alaska's solution **(page 809)** has some doctrinal sense behind it, but may be too complicated. The final paragraph on **page 809** reminds students that the same failure that serves as the basis for the civil claim may also have rendered the lawyer constitutionally ineffective and thereby suffice to vacate the conviction.

A brief note at **page 810** introduces students to the different views taken of the liability of criminal defense lawyers who are assigned to represent an accused.

196

3. Damages or Injury (page 810). Several courts have intimated that they would be willing to allow damages for emotional distress, at least in extreme circumstances. This trend is increasing, as can be seen in *Wagenmann v. Adams* at **page 810**. Wagenmann's recovery against lawyer Healy for his night at the state hospital was $50,000. Judge Selya refuses to limit plaintiff's damages to "purely economic loss." That would leave him "without fair recourse in the face of ghastly wrongdoing." Judge Selya does like those adverbs doesn't he? Note that cases divide on whether a negligent lawyer may also be liable for punitive damages the client is proximately caused to pay or is unable to collect **(page 812)**.

C. BEYOND MALPRACTICE: OTHER GROUNDS FOR ATTORNEY LIABILITY TO CLIENTS AND THIRD PARTIES (page 813)

I have continued to use Justice Pollock's decision in *Petrillo v. Bachenberg* **(page 813)** to illustrate lawyer liability to nonclients. The fact pattern nicely illustrates how a lawyer can violate a duty to a third person who is not even in the picture when the lawyer does the act that creates liability. Also, both the majority and the dissent quote the Restatements of Torts and Lawyering.

What did lawyer Herrigel do to get into trouble? The reports of a prior owner's perc tests on the property showed two passes out of 30 tests, not a great rate although sufficient to satisfy Township requirements. Herrigel had these results because he had represented the prior owner (Rohrer) in its failed effort to sell the land. In October 1988, Herrigel gave Rohrer's broker (Bachenberg) only two pages from the engineer's report on the perc tests. Each page had one perc test passage and some failures. These two pages (called the "composite report") could reasonably be read to say that the property passed two perc tests out of seven tries, rather than two out of 30.

In December 1988, Bachenberg acquired the property in a sheriff's sale. So now it was the owner and it became Herrigel's client.

Bachenberg gave the two pages to Petrillo, a prospective buyer, in February 1989, four months after Herrigel (then representing Rohrer) had given the two pages to Bachenberg. Allegedly in reliance on these results, Petrillo contracted for the land. But after her engineer's six perc tests all failed, she asked for return of her downpayment and the costs of her tests. The question is whether Herrigel could be found to have violated a duty to Petrillo by giving Bachenberg, the broker and later the seller, the two pages of the composite report. The answer is yes.

The key paragraphs are the first two paragraphs on **page 818**. "Herrigel controlled the risk that the composite report would mislead a purchaser." This as so even though he didn't know

197

which purchaser. The court explains how Herrigel could have eliminated the risk. The case would be easy if Herrigel had delivered the two pages directly to Petrillo or her lawyer after being asked about perc tests. But he gave them to his client's broker (who later became the owner of the land and Herrigel's client) months before Petrillo showed up. The court says that a jury could reasonably conclude that Herrigel should have foreseen that Bachenberg, as broker or owner, would give the composite report to a prospective purchaser and that he should have foreseen how it could fool the recipient. See **pages 818-819** for the majority's disagreement with the dissent. The dissent writes at **page 822** that the chain of events between Herrigel's act and Petrillo's receipt of the report is too "attenuated" to create a duty in the former to the latter. The dissent agrees with the majority's analysis except only for the creation of duty, on these facts, to Petrillo.

Some of the most interesting material in the area of lawyer liability is found in this material. The multiplicity of fact patterns that can give rise to lawyer liability to nonclients is astonishing. Unfortunately for lawyers, this is a real danger zone, or at least it has become one in the last few decades, all beginning with the California Supreme Court's decision in *Biakanja* **(page 822)**. Well, maybe not beginning with *Biakanja*, but certainly heavily influenced by it.

The note material at **pages 822-833** identifies some of the more prominent ways in which lawyers can get themselves into trouble. I urge you to cover these pages, even if briefly. I want to call your attention to a few items.

The material on fraud and negligent misrepresentation presents perhaps the greatest area of risk. *Slotkin* **(page 826)** is instructive. A lawyer was held liable to an opposing client after representing his knowledge of his client's insurance limits. He was wrong, but before the mistake was discovered, the opposing client settled. After the error was discovered, the opposing client sued the lawyer for negligent misrepresentation. Even if he believed he was right, nevertheless he was wrong and careless in his mistake. The Second Circuit upheld a jury verdict.

Also worth special attention is the material at **pages 831-832** on the duties of a lawyer who agrees to serve as an escrow agent, which undoubtedly many students will do at least once in their professional lives and most more often. As an escrow agent, a lawyer has an obligation to each of the stakeholders. If one of them is also the lawyer's client, the lawyer can't favor that one over the other. I ask how a lawyer might protect herself from competing claims. The answers are: have the stakeholders agree in the escrow agreement that the lawyer will not be liable for negligence; give the lawyer the right to deposit the money in court anytime the lawyer decides that she no longer wants to be escrow agent because of a dispute among the beneficiaries. These duties should be distinguished from the separate obligation not to convert escrow funds to one's own account. See **page 839**.

Other themes worth noting here are the use of consumer protection laws against lawyers **(page 823)**, the risk of criminal liability for work that is otherwise unremarkable on behalf of a client **(page 824)**, the well publicized $50 million settlement paid by Milberg Weiss for abuse of process **(page 827)**, the material on malicious prosecution and defense **(page 829)**, the responsibility of lawyers for fiduciary duty to the client's beneficiary (**page 829**), and the Restatement's position (**page 832**) which is fairly generous toward recognizing a third party claim.

D. DISCIPLINE (page 834)

1. Purposes of Discipline (page 834) and **2. Sanctions (page 835)** introduce students to this subject. This material can be read at home. Noteworthy is California's efforts to deal with minor infractions through a mandatory one-day legal ethics class (**page 836**).

3. Disciplinary Systems (page 837). This brief note alerts students to the variety of ways that states structure disciplinary systems and the ABA recommendations. The unique California Bar Court is referenced. A brief note introduces students to the phenomenon of private discipline. Increasingly firms have committees that will sanction lawyers who violate firm rules even if the disciplinary committee does not. The use of private sanctioning systems may discourage public discipline if the public authorities conclude that the private sanction is adequate, or so firms may home.

4. Acts Justifying Discipline (page 838). You might pick and choose among these. On the other hand, the whole section is only seventeen pages long. The cases and subjects are chosen with care from the ocean of choices available.

a. Dishonest or Unlawful Conduct (page 839). *Warhaftig* makes the rather dramatic point that some states will disbar for comparatively modest invasions of a lawyer's escrow account and notwithstanding that the client did not ultimately lose any money or that the lawyer would ultimately have been entitled to the money. Warhaftig had an unblemished record. Nevertheless, the court rejected the Board's recommendation and disbarred him. The case offers students an excellent warning about the sanctity of trust accounts. You might point out, too, that in New Jersey, disbarment is forever. There is no right to reapply. Other states do allow reapplication, generally after at least five years.

In *Austern* (**page 842**), we have a rare situation in which a well-intentioned lawyer facilitated a client's fraud. The lawyer closed the deal for a client knowing that the client had insufficient funds to cover his check. The check, for $10,000, was intended to fund an escrow account ensuring the client's performance. Respondent held the worthless check and did not inform his co-escrow agent about the situation. Eventually, the client put up the $10,000. No one lost money. Nevertheless, the respondent was publicly censured. Why did Austern go through with it? The pressure of the moment? An insistent client? His confidence that the client would

199

eventually be able to put up the money? What should Austern have done on learning that the client could not cover the check? Didn't he have a responsibility to his client at that point? It is clear that Austern knew of the check's inadequacy prior to the time the deal closed. He then held the check for nearly two months until his client could cover it. So for two months, the opposing side was under the misimpression that it was adequately protected by the escrow money, when it was not. Still, no claim was made on the escrow money until after the check was covered. Is public censure the right sanction? Too harsh? Too lenient?

Deceit, Dishonesty, Etcetera (page 846). Can we reconcile the discipline in *Warhaftig, Austern,* and *Hess* **(page 849)**? Did Hess get off too easily? He was convicted of a federal felony yet was suspended only. Why is it courts are so lenient on tax cheats? *Wunschel* **(page 846)** reprimanded a lawyer who took advantage of an opposing unrepresented party though he did nothing illegal. The Virginia Supreme Court suspended Gunter after he told his client to tap his own home phone, which was legal **(page 848)**. Pollard, like Warhaftig, took money that did not belong to her yet she was suspended for only one year. And she was an assistant prosecutor at the time! **(Page 849.**) Can these cases be reconciled?

This material contains other authorities on the continuing debate on whether a lawyer may wiretap a conversation with an unsuspecting third party (or ask his client to do so). Some authorities still consider this to be "deceit," even if legal, while others have chosen to allow it. **(Page 848.**) The ABA has flipped here and now finds the conduct permissible. At **page 849** are cases that will not tolerate deceitful acts of prosecutors in connection with their court work notwithstanding the claimed need to engage in these acts in order to catch and convict criminals. Compare *Hammad* at **page 124**. The controversial Oregon opinion in *Gatti* is referenced at **page 850**. See also **page 121**.

There is material here as well on inflating bills or manufacturing false disbursements (an issue that also appeared at **page 165**) and resume padding **(page 847)**.

b. Neglect and Lack of Candor (page 850). This material makes the following points: Neglect can result in discipline no matter how well-intentioned. The discipline needn't come through the disciplinary committee but can come directly from the court. A court may sanction a lawyer for "lack of candor" even though those words appear only in the title, not the text, of Rule 3.3. In *Amstar*, the lawyer deleted language from a quotation. Although the omission was indicated with ellipses, the quote now conveyed a meaning opposite to its original meaning.

c. Sexual Relations with a Client (page 851). A lot of activity here. The material recalls civil actions based on sex with clients **(page 779)**. It's important to recognize that we are not talking about imposition, nor even necessarily duress, at least not those things only.

Tsoutsouris (**page 852**) is new this edition. It arose in a child support matter. The lawyer and client apparently drifted into an intimate relationship. Thereafter the client again hired the lawyer a few years later. The lawyer argued that their relationship did not affect the quality of the work he did. The court rejects this argument, pointing to the risks to the work. The court treats it as a conflict matter where the client wasn't informed of the risks and did not consent. The note at **page 855** asks if the relationship would have been acceptable had the client been informed of the risk. Alternatively, should we say that this is a nonconsentable conflict? Notice, too, that Indiana has no specific rule forbidding the conduct, which is why the court had to rely on the conflicts rule. Students should understand the risks to the client: the privilege might be lost for some conversations; the lawyer's performance as a lawyer might be affected; the fact of the relationship might hurt the client's claim under substantive law. Unlike the Indiana court, other cases cited in the note do not treat the problem as a conflict requiring consent.

Professor Mischler has taken a contrary view of the trend in this area and criticizes cases that discipline lawyers for engaging in sexual relationships with their clients. Focusing on the New York rule, she asks why it limits the prohibition to domestic relations matters. She sees the limitation as both overinclusive and underinclusive.

The Ethics 2000 Commission (**page 858**) would explicitly forbid commencement of a sexual relationship with a client. Where the client is an entity, the prohibition would be against commencing a relationship with a constituent of the entity who supervises, directs, or regularly consults the lawyer. Cases at **pages 855-856** similarly involved no imposition or duress. *Sams* is especially instructive. The client offered to trade sexual favors for legal services, and though the offer was accepted, the act was never consummated. (**Page 856**.) Is there a freedom of association concern lurking here? You might ask students whether, as rulemakers, they would adopt any rule on this issue in their jurisdiction. The types of rules are revealed in the note. Oregon may go furthest while California's does not seem to add anything that cannot be teased out of more general rules.

The quote from *Bellino* (**page 857**), explaining why the conduct was sanctionable, is especially pertinent. The court focuses on the power imbalance in the professional relationship, especially, as here, where the client was a matrimonial client.

d. The Lawyer's "Private" Life (page 859). This material echoes the note at **page 704**, whose focus is use of a bar applicant's private life as a basis for denial of admission. Here presented are examples of drug use and sexual misconduct. Of late, too, courts have treated drunk driving (**page 859**) and domestic violence (**page 860**) as grounds for discipline.

e. Racist and Sexist Conduct (page 861). Lawyers can be disciplined, at least in some places, for either kind of behavior, although a list of the cases would probably fill one side of a small index card. Note the provision (**page 866**) in the 1990 ABA Code of Judicial Conduct,

201

which requires judges to require lawyers to refrain from biased conduct when appearing before them.

Matter of Jordan Schiff (**page 861**) is a useful opinion from a local disciplinary committee recommending that a 28-year-old lawyer's behavior at a deposition receive a public censure, which the court duly imposed. The description of the lawyer's conduct, coupled with the stalled ABA proposals and the Duncan article following, offers several rich avenues for discussion. First, the older lawyer's poor "example of mentoring" is worth noting. Schiff copied Yankowitz. Ms. Mark, by contrast, reacted with caution and dignity. It is hard to believe that a lawyer would actually behave this way on the record. The case can also be used to discuss incivility. Obviously, no one will defend the conduct (but see *infra*), but some may conclude that public censure of this young lawyer was too harsh, especially given Yankowitz's example. A hidden value of the case is to discourage such behavior in others. Another value is to reveal that complaints about this kind of conduct are not imaginary or exaggerations.

In this edition of the book, I add the financial sanction against lawyer Monaghan for mocking an opposing lawyer's accent. (**Page 866.**) *Martoccci* was sanctioned for racist comments. (**Page 866.**) Klayman and Orfanedes sought to disqualify a judge based solely on the judge's Chinese ancestry and were sanctioned. (**Pages 866-867.**)

As the material at **page 865** shows, the ABA has been debating whether to adopt a rule that would expressly make the conduct in *Schiff* improper. Class discussion can center on the two competing propositions. Both were tabled so that the ABA could attempt to generate a single proposal for a future meeting. Nothing happened. However, Richard Duncan's op-ed in the *Wall Street Journal* got a lot of attention (**page 868**) when it was published just before the ABA was to consider the proposals. Mr. Duncan sees them as infringements on freedom and a manifestation of PC. This too, along with *Schiff* and the proposals, should spark class debate. If Duncan is right, is the result in *Schiff* wrong?

At **pages 870-872**, I recount three events in recent years that sparked discussion about racist and sexist conduct in the profession. *Wunsch* (**page 870**) involved a lawyer who was sanctioned for an insensitive (but unethical?) note. The circuit reversed. A female divorce lawyer in Massachusetts was fined for refusing to represent men. (**Page 870.**) A candidate for D.A. in Philadelphia had, a decade earlier, instructed other prosecutors on which minority group members to strike from juries. (**Page 871.**) Each of these events can be used in discussion of the wisdom of rules forbidding racist and sexist conduct in law practice.

f. Failure to Report Another Lawyer's Misconduct (page 872). This note merges the obligation to report another lawyer's misconduct with the duty of subordinate lawyers. Two important points to make here are: First, the change in the rule. The duty to report another lawyer's misconduct under the Rules is suspended when knowledge is confidential under Rule

1.6. Under the Code, the duty was suspended only if the knowledge was privileged. So this duty has been narrowed. It has been further narrowed because not all unethical conduct must be reported under the Rules, only that conduct that raises "a substantial question as to [another] lawyer's honesty, trustworthiness, or fitness as a lawyer." The second point to stress is the Illinois Supreme Court's decision in *Himmel* (**page 873**), where, for the first time in anyone's memory, a court actually suspended a lawyer for violating the reporting obligation. The note material here questions whether *Himmel* is or is not a "plain vanilla" nonreporting case. The facts allow it to be read otherwise, but the court's broad language does not.

One of the video vignettes produced at NYU is a discussion among the members of a law firm executive committee who have discovered that a partner has been, perhaps, inflating his bills and traveling "opulent class" on business trips. In my experience, and if you read the law and popular press, the problem of inflated legal bills seems to be burgeoning. The duty to report another lawyer's misconduct arises in this context. What happens when a partner learns that another partner has fabricated a bill? Is that information a client confidence so that the reporting duty is suspended? I think not (what if a lawyer discovers that a partner has assaulted a client?), but I have heard lawyers argue otherwise. Is the information sufficiently serious to warrant reporting? Often the answer will be yes. Remember, however, that the lawyer has to have "knowledge" of the other lawyer's misconduct. What if the other lawyer has an innocent, if improbable, explanation? How certain does the knowledge have to be?

"Better Late than Never" (page 874)

Students struggle to let Janie off the hook. The bills to clients and the retainer letter tell clients that time is contemporaneously recorded. Yet here is Janie's mentor asking for her time charges across two months so she could reconstruct her own time. Definitely not contemporaneously, as Isadora admits. What to do? The conduct is deceptive, making it not only a violation of the Rules but also a breach of fiduciary duty. Janie not only has a duty to report Isadora to the right authorities (**page 874**, suggesting that her associate status will not remove this duty), she also has to make sure the client – *her* client – is told. What escape? Maybe Isadora has other sources of information that will let her claim that her billing is contemporaneous "in effect." Perhaps, she has a side deal with the client. Perhaps she'll say that she's underestimating so the client is not hurt. Perhaps, perhaps. But perhaps not. Doesn't Janie have to inquire? I think so, hard as it is. Let's face it. If Janie hands over her time sheets knowing what she knows and this blows open, she's in trouble. This is why firms need ombudspersons to protect associates when they must report misdeed of supervisors. But few firms have such protections in any real sense.

5. Defenses (page 875). As its name implies, these paragraphs explain what defenses are available to an errant lawyer. The only one that is likely to work is that the proof does not measure up. If it does, what we call defenses (including psychological and substance problems) are really reasons to mitigate the sanction. Not even the ADA will help.

6. Disciplinary Procedures (page 876). This material can be assigned for home reading, although the notice requirements, and their modification in *Zauderer* (**page 877**), are ripe for discussion. So is the constant debate over confidentiality (**page 879**). The ABA House of Delegates ultimately rejected the Commission's recommendation that all work of disciplinary committees be open to the public from the time a complaint is filed, voting instead to permit public access only after a finding of probable cause.

7. Discipline in a Federal System (page 880) is straightforward. The main points are that reciprocal discipline between jurisdictions is not obligatory although frequent. Further, federal lawyers are subject to state discipline for their work as federal lawyers (**page 880**). Finally there is the question of whether a state can exercise disciplinary authority over an out-of-state lawyer who solicits (or otherwise disserves) clients in the particular state. West Virginia says yes, if the jurisdictional rules are written to allow it. South Carolina agrees (**page 881**). For a recent article see H. Geoffrey Moulton, Jr., *Federalism and Choice of Law in the Regulation of Legal Ethics*, 82 Minn. L. Rev. 73 (1997).

E. CONSTITUTIONAL PROTECTION IN CRIMINAL CASES (page 881)

I hope that the introductory note at **pages 881-884** will give students a global view of the issues that arise in this Sixth Amendment area. It is especially worth discussing the last paragraph on **page 883**. Should we limit our enforcement of the Sixth Amendment guarantee to post-trial review of a lawyer's alleged defaults? Or should we have some kind of pre-trial mechanism for assessing a lawyer's performance? This issue comes up in the discussion of *DeCoster* at page 898. *Strickland* rejects pretrial inquiry.

Strickland **(page 885)** identifies the two issues that must be resolved when ineffectiveness is charged but refuses to define effectiveness beyond saying that it is "reasonableness under prevailing professional norms." **(Page 886.)** (If the norms change, does the constitutional guarantee change?) While the Court then lists "certain basic duties," it disclaims any effort to provide a "checklist." **(Page 886.)** The main concern is for a fair and reliable trial. **(Page 886.)** ABA standards are guides only; the Court is explicitly reluctant to prescribe duties for fear of interfering with the "constitu-tionally protected independence of counsel . . . in making tactical decisions." (Compare the *Decoster* dissent, **pages 898-899**, whose majority *Strickland* cites.) Query whether this does not make it too easy to construe incompetence as strategy. Why not prescribe a checklist which counsel presumptively ought to respect while recognizing that sometimes it may be strategically preferable to deviate? For example, it will almost always be appropriate to move to suppress inculpatory evidence if there is a substantial basis for doing so, although in some rare cases it may be preferable not to do so. Notably, *Strickland* incorporates prevailing professional norms to define the constitutional guarantee. These "justify the law's presumption that counsel will fulfill the role in the adversary process that the Amendment envisions" **(page 888)**. While professional "norms" are not dispositive, they are "guides" in deciding whether the defendant "receive[d] a fair trial." **(Page 886.)** What if "professional norms" become more (or less) demanding?

The determination of effectiveness cannot be made with hindsight, but rather "on the facts of the particular case, viewed as of the time of counsel's conduct." **(Page 887.)** Does this mean that if the judge can identify a defensible strategy to account for what the trial lawyer did, the challenge fails even if the defense lawyer in fact had no strategy or acted out of ignorance? There is "a strong presumption" against ineffectiveness. **(Page 887.)** Can it be overcome if the defense lawyer concedes at the post-conviction hearing that she had no strategy and simply never thought to do what her former client now faults her for failing to do? There is a risk here that defense lawyers will lie to help former clients, isn't there? Does that justify applying a purely objective test and ignoring the defense lawyer's actual state of mind? Under the *Strickland* test, it is not likely that a defendant will be able to establish ineffective assistance based on something her lawyer *did* do. Rather, errors of *omission* are more likely to serve as a basis for ineffectiveness claims and even these, given the two final paragraphs of Part III(A), will be hard to establish.

Two questions it might be worth considering for class are whether the test for constitutional ineffectiveness ought to be the same as the standard for incompetence under the

Code or Rules and whether the test for either ought to be the same as the standard for malpractice liability. If the standards are different, is it because malpractice claims (and ethical charges) usually arise in civil, not criminal, cases? Which way should that cut? If the standards are more lenient one place than another, in which area should they be? Given the reluctance to give criminal defendants the same malpractice redress as civil clients enjoy -- see **page 800** -- perhaps the Sixth Amendment test should be easier so the wronged client can get some relief.

Part III(B) stresses that there must be prejudice. Since the Court is concerned with reliability of the verdict -- can society confidently visit penal sanctions on a person whose counsel acted ineffectively in the way shown? -- it defines prejudice in terms of whether the defendant had "the assistance necessary to justify reliance on the outcome of the proceeding." **(Page 889**.) While prejudice will sometimes be presumed, usually the defendant has the burden of showing prejudice. The Court rejects two formulations of that burden **(page 889)** ("some conceivable effect" and "more likely than not") and opts for "a reasonable probability" standard, which it defines as a "probability sufficient to undermine confidence in the outcome." **(Page 890**.) This test is the same whether the defendant is challenging a conviction or a death sentence.

It might be fruitful to discuss how a judge decides whether there is "a reasonable probability" that, absent the errors, the factfinder would have had a reasonable doubt respecting guilt. What does the standard tell the judge about how to make this decision? Won't the court's decision be speculative, since no one is able to know what the factfinder (unless it was the same judge) could have considered important? But is there any way around this? Presume prejudice in every case? Call the jury back? What are the guidelines? Whether the jury was "out" for days or only hours? Whether the evidence was "close"? Whether expert psychologists agree that the information would likely have affected the judgment of an ordinary person? Or should the judge just decide whether he or she has some measure of doubt about the defendant's (legal) guilt? Forget the jury.

Cronic **(page 891)** applies the *Strickland* analysis in the context of an allegation that a lawyer had inadequate time to prepare. It is worth pointing out that a lawyer who is quite competent may be made incompetent because of a denial of adequate time to prepare. Justice Stevens discusses the Scottsboro Boys case to illustrate a situation where inadequate time to prepare will be presumed prejudicial **(page 892)**.

The following note **(page 893)** identifies some recurrent reasons for alleged ineffectiveness of counsel. *Morris v. Slappy* **(page 896)** shows the limit of the effective assistance right. It does not include the right to rapport. Of course, that is hardly a problem with people who can afford to pay private counsel. Consider the picture from the point of view of an indigent criminal defendant. He or she is assigned a lawyer and will find it hard to get a new one despite a poor working relationship. The lawyer is a member of the bar, of course, and has perhaps been evaluated before being placed on the assignment list. But how long ago was that? Once the lawyer is assigned, the state takes a "hands-off" attitude. *Jones v. Barnes* **(page 87)** gives the lawyer the right to overrule the client's preference on nearly all strategic decisions. If the client is convicted, he or she can raise an ineffectiveness claim, but must meet the high hurdles of *Strickland*, which insists on great deference to counsel's decisions.

The definition of the Sixth Amendment test is especially important as it becomes harder for state and federal defendants to seek redress for federal constitutional rights violation through federal collateral relief. The note on **page 897** emphasizes this fact. As habeas corpus and other collateral remedies narrow, state and federal defendants will increasingly seek to establish "cause" for procedural defaults, or grounds for a new trial, by citing trial counsel's inadequacy. The harder that inadequacy is to establish, or the harder it is to prove prejudice, the less success will habeas and similar petitioners have in getting relief.

In light of all this, a case like *State v. Smith* (**page 899**) is quite interesting. The court held that the method by which the Arizona county fulfilled its obligation to provide counsel to indigent defendants was structurally likely to lead to ineffective assistance. Even though the court could find no inadequate representation "in the instant case," it held that "there will be an inference that the adequacy of representation is adversely affected by the system."

CHAPTER XIV

CONTROL OF QUALITY: LAY PARTICIPATION IN LAW BUSINESS (AND LAW FIRM ANCILLARY SERVICES)

This is the third of three chapters on quality control and my sentimental favorite. I realize that this chapter is not at the core of the course, especially if it is being taught in two credits, but the ways in which lawyers have attempted to exclude those who would "invade" the market for the delivery of legal services (in the profit arena) or those who want to use law to effect social change (in the non-profit arena) tell a wonderful story. (The Preface to the story were the unauthorized practice rules in Chapter 12F.) Obviously, too, the walls are crumbling. Opinion 355 creates a crack in the edifice excluding lay investment (**page 924**). But the arrows point in two directions. Lawyers are seeking business traditionally handled by others. That has created a debate about law firm ancillary businesses, a debate in which victory, so far, has gone to those who would allow such businesses. Since the last edition of this book, an additional part of the story is the rise of MDP, the fight over them in the ABA, and their continuing "threat" to traditional practice under more permissive rules abroad.

This chapter differs from the prior two chapters. Here the focus is on lay management or control of entities that provide legal services. The entities may be operating for profit, for its members, or in the public interest. Traditionally, as we know, the ethical codes looked with deep suspicion on any significant lay involvement in the operation of a law office. The benign explanation for this suspicion was the fear that lay people, not subject to the ethical codes, and beyond the reach of discipline, might encourage or require subordinate lawyers to behave disloyally to their clients. Why would lay people do that? A repeated explanation was financial self-interest. Nonlawyers will sacrifice clients for profit. So we see a rule like DR 5-107(C)), forbidding lawyers to practice in professional corporations for a profit if a nonlawyer has an interest in the corporation or managerial or directorial authority. See also DR 3-102 and 3-103.

Of course, there is a less benign explanation for the refusal to permit lay participation in the operation of law offices. This explanation has it that lawyers wanted to maintain their monopoly on the sale of legal talent. Exclusion of lay investment would hinder large capital formations, and so competition, and would also ensure that only lawyers could sell the services of other lawyers.

The introductory essay (**page 901**) gives students an historical perspective, addresses the effect of limitations on lay participation on the availability of legal services, relates the present material to the material on unauthorized practice of law, suggests questions the student should ask as he or she reads the chapter, and lastly points out that lines can "blur in two directions." Lawyers can also expand to offer nonlegal services, the subject of the final section of the chapter at page 934, on ancillary businesses. With regard to the "unauthorized practice" issue, students should appreciate that although that label is sometimes used to describe entities with lay control or lay investment, in fact such entities do not present the same kind of problem as previously studied. The lawyer who is actually providing the legal service here will presumably be a competent, licensed lawyer in the jurisdiction. The problem arises because of the risk of lay influence. In short, we have a potential conflict of interest. When a lawyer works for a corporation but takes his or her orders from the lay management, conflict dangers arise as well, but we tolerate those. Why the difference?

Legislative History (page 904). This note reveals how hard it was to get off the dime on lay participation in entities that provide legal services. The book traces the ABA's reluctance in some detail, even down to the famous "Sears Roebuck" question at **page 906**. We later double back to ask whether the effort to avoid an affirmative answer to that question ultimately succeeded.

A. NONPROFIT ENTITIES AND INTERMEDIARIES (page 906)

1. Public Interest Organizations (page 906). The first incursion occurred here, with public interest organizations, followed close in time with the activities of another kind of nonprofit entity -- labor unions. *NAACP v. Button* **(page 906)** appears here before *In re Primus* (page 1030), which makes life a little easier for teachers since that is also the chronological order of the cases. In *Primus*, the main issue was marketing (getting the client), not the potential conflict between the lay managers of the sponsoring organization and the clients it seeks to represent. Although, technically, the only issue before the *Button* Court was whether the NAACP could use lay agents to solicit plaintiffs whom NAACP staff lawyers would thereafter represent in school desegregation cases, the Court unavoidably addressed the issue of conflict between the entity's goals and what may be the client's narrower or different objectives.

Button is a difficult case to read (and edit) because much of it is framed in terms of the convoluted interstices of the Virginia statute. Only partly does the majority address the full sweep of the constitutional issue. Still, it is an important decision both historically and conceptually. The framework for the Court's conclusion includes these holdings. Plaintiff's activity was protected by rights guaranteed under the First and Fourteenth Amendments; the state needs a compelling interest to justify its invasion of these constitutional rights; the common law offenses of barratry, maintenance, and champerty are characterized by hostility to "stirring up litigation . . . for private gain, serving no public interest," a circumstance not present where a litigant seeks to use the courts to enforce constitutional rights; fear that a lay intermediary will

210

interfere with "the rendering of legal services" for "pecuniary gain," whatever its validity when "monetary stakes are involved," has not been proved valid here. Using the courts in Virginia to fight segregation "is a different matter from the oppressive, malicious, or avaricious use of the legal process for purely private gain."

The dissent (**page 910**) asserts the "widely shared conviction that avoidance of improper pecuniary gain is not the only relevant factor in determining standards of professional conduct. Running perhaps even deeper is the desire of the profession, the courts, the legislatures to prevent any interference with the uniquely personal relationship between lawyer and client. . . ." What does that mean exactly? Justice Harlan tells a very different story about the plaintiff's litigations. And he anticipates and describes circumstances that may give rise to conflict without regard to monetary interests. Finally, he uses a different burden of proof to validate the state rule. He says that "it cannot be said that the underlying state policy is inevitably inconsistent with federal interests." Harlan has a point. Doesn't history tell us that people are at least as willing to violate rules for political motives as they are for financial ones?

Maintenance, Barratry, Champerty, and Change (page 914). This note describes the overlapping definitions of these three common law offenses and, because the principal case is a little convoluted, untangles it a bit at **pages 914-915.** The note also identifies cases from Massachusetts and South Carolina rejecting champerty and barratry respectively as outdated (**page 914**). They are indeed outdated and can cause much mischief, especially as they may interfere with a person's right to find and support litigation. Their ambiguity makes matters even worse. As the student will see in the labor union cases next discussed, the fact that the NAACP was litigating grand constitutional questions became unimportant. Even the prospect of monetary gain, through fee-shifting statutes, will not necessarily alter the calculus. See *Primus* at page 1030. However, the prospect of income to the lay entity, whatever may be its constitutional right to sponsor the litigation, has caused some consternation. *Miller* at **page 916**, upheld a state law prohibiting the ACLU from receiving a §1988 fee, despite *Primus* and *Button*. *Miller* presented only the First Amendment issue, not the Supremacy Clause issue. Thereafter, however, as noted in ABA Opinion 93-374, which rejected *Miller* (as did the Virginia Bar), a district judge in Missouri enjoined the state from enforcing the holding. *Miller* now seems an anomaly. The D.C. and Eleventh Circuits have also had to grapple with the "fee" problem, but their views have been a tad and a half more enlightened (**page 917**). At **page 915**, I reference articles by Professor Bell and Professor Ellmann, each of whom address the conflicts question to which Justice Harlan alluded in *Button*.

2. Labor Unions (page 917). *Button* could have relied on the fact that the NAACP was fighting for the constitutional rights of its clients. But the labor union cases quickly demolished that possible reliance. As Justice Black ultimately insisted in the third of those cases, *United Transportation Union*: "The common thread running through our decisions in *NAACP v. Button*, *Trainmen*, and *United Mine Workers* is that collective activity undertaken to obtain

211

meaningful access to the courts is a fundamental right within the protection of the First Amendment." It was unimportant that the right the plaintiffs in *UTU* sought to vindicate rested on the Federal Employers' Liability Act and not the Constitution.

The constitutional history leading to *UTU* is discussed at **pages 917-919**. With the advent of the union cases, the stakes become high. Or perhaps I should say "the stake," because in truth there seems to have been only one: money. How else explain that 48 bar associations and the ABA sought rehearing following the Supreme Court's opinion in *Trainmen* (**page 918**), but without success? How else explain the need for three Supreme Court decisions before Justice Black finally said enough is enough in 1971? Justice Black disposes of the states' arguments with dispatch in *UTU*: Bang, bang, bang. If there were any doubt whether the issue is (viewed as) one about money, it should be dispelled by the last paragraph on **page 921** and the first paragraph on **page 922**. If there is any doubt that the First Amendment protects the right of litigants to band together to save money when they petition the courts, it should be dispelled by the second paragraph on **page 922**.

The Supreme Court's decisions through *UTU* required the ABA to modify provisions of the Model Code that purported to forbid conduct that the union cases recognized as constitutionally protected. This modification, reluctant and narrow, is traced in the legislative history at **page 904**. When the Model Rules were debated, the House of Delegates had the Court's rulings before it. Were they given due regard?

B. FOR-PROFIT ENTERPRISES (page 923)

Most recent changes have occurred here. Further, it is interesting *how* they have occurred. The case law provided little support for a right of lay investment in, or management of, for-profit law firms. The legislative history, especially the "Sears" question (**page 906**), showed that the ABA was not inclined to deviate much from the Code's prohibitions. Or so it seemed. But that was before ABA Formal Opinion 355 (**page 924**). I suggest that this opinion means that lawyers will be allowed to work for for-profit law firms in which lay people have invested so long as the law firm is not called a law firm but something else, like a prepaid legal services plan. Of course, not every state will accept Opinion 355. But after it, what is left of the age-old prohibition so far as the ABA is concerned? What we see happening is a movement from a prophylactic and categorical exclusion to a rule that permits the once-forbidden structure but cautions lawyers not to succumb to efforts to compromise their duties to clients and requires appropriate safeguards. However, lest we believe that we have thereby solved the problem, consider the note (**page 934**) on how financial considerations in prepaid *medical* plans may affect the work of doctors employed by those plans. Should we take heed?

The note material following Opinion 355 includes, beyond the critique of the opinion itself, the text of the Washington, D.C. rule, which is apparently the only one that would permit law firms to have partners or managers who are not lawyers but who perform "professional services which assist the organization in providing legal services to clients." There are limitations, of course, but even so this rule is remarkable. Who would have predicted it a generation ago? It allows, for example, a tax law firm to have a tax accountant, a construction law firm to have a civil engineer, a medical malpractice firm to have a doctor, a matrimonial firm to have a psychologist, a criminal defense firm to have a forensic scientist or an investigator, and an antitrust firm to have an economist. Each of these nonlaw professionals can be partners in the firm and participate in the firm's management. Doesn't that make good sense? What would the firm have to do otherwise? It would have to hire the nonlaw professionals as salaried employees. But a salary, even a high salary, will often not satisfy a competent professional's desire to be among the owners of the business in which he or she works.

Not included in this material are the various opinions permitting lawyers to accept assignments from temporary lawyer employment agencies. These opinions raise fee-splitting and conflict issues. See, *e.g.*, ABA Opinion 88-356. I omitted mention of them because I didn't want to introduce the topic in a sentence or two and I didn't want to take the space to address it at great length. By omitting the subject, I preserve it for you to use as a "cold" hypothetical in class or even as part of a final examination.

Multidisciplinary Practice (MDP) is noted at **page 930** with the final recommendation of the MDP Commission at **page 932**. New York State's opposition to MDP proposed, in the alternative, rules that would allow cooperative business arrangements. New York has since amended its code to adopt such rules. The issue is described at **page 933**. Whether and to what extent the New York alternative will be influential, and whether and to what extent the recommendations of the MDP Commission, though rejected by the ABA, will lead to changes in any American jurisdictions (some of which are still considering the issue), is yet to be seen. The impetus for the creation of the MDP Commission was the growing competitive threat of accounting firms that rendered services (viewed as legal by many American lawyers) to clients of those firms. To operate domestically, the accounting firms and the employed lawyers had to claim that the services were not legal, or not only legal; however, the same entities can operate in foreign jurisdictions that do allow MDPs to varying degrees. The final report of the Commission was rather tame. It would have allowed lawyers to share legal fees with non-lawyers in MDPs so long as the lawyers had independence and so long as the non-lawyers were members of recognized professions or other disciplines governed by ethical standards. Non-lawyers could still not render legal services and no passive investments would be allowed in MDPs. **(Page 932.)**

Cooperative Business Arrangements (page 933). The New York proposal allows law firms to have established relationships with professionals from other disciplines so long as there is no fee sharing and the non-lawyers have no ownership interest or control of the law firm. The non-lawyer professionals must be designated as a class by the court and be subject to a code of ethical conduct comparable to the code governing lawyers. There are various requirements for notice to the client. As of late 2001, the New York courts have not designated any non-lawyer professionals who will satisfy the new requirements.

Comparing Medicine (page 934). This little note reminds students that the debate about "non-doctors" having financial interests in the medical profession has often identified the risk of improper influence on the doctor's judgment. Why do we think that will not happen if non-lawyers have economic interests and control over entities that render legal services?

C. MAY A LAW FIRM OWN AN ANCILLARY BUSINESS? (page 934)

Just as others are seeking to capitalize on the sale of legal services, so law firms are seeking to expand into the sale of services not traditionally deemed legal services. At **pages 934-938**, I describe the "battle" of the last dozen years and draw a comparison **(page 938)** with a parallel trend in medicine. I tried to give equal time to both sides of the debate. The opponents of a permissive rule fear that as lawyers expand so might nonlawyers also wish to expand and invade traditional legal turf. The fight has been won by the proponents, at least for now. Rule 5.7 as ultimately readopted after the repeal of its predecessor is no serious bar to the creation of law firm ancillary businesses.

"How Can We Get Together?" (page 940)

This question can be used to address many of the themes in this chapter. Patricia Gumm is an estate planning lawyer, part of a small firm that does only that kind of work plus probate. The firm has wealthy clients who need financial planning. Sometimes that planning is quite sophisticated and beyond the firm's competence. The firm has referred clients to outside financial planning firms and one in particular in which it has great confidence. The head of that firm, Grover Jackson, approached Gumm about some kind of closer relationship, which Gumm thinks would be beneficial to both firms and clients. But she doesn't know how it could be done. She has watched the MDP and ancillary business debate. She asks what arrangements might be possible.

In Washington, D.C., of course, the financial planners can be part of a law firm **(page 929)** so long as the sole purpose of the entity is providing legal services to clients. There is no requirement that the lawyer members of the firm exceed the non-lawyers. But the requirement that legal services be the "sole purpose" of the entity may doom the Jackson-Gumm plan. The merged entity might hope to render (and promote itself as available to render) only financial services to those clients who need those services alone. Jackson may not be willing to give up that opportunity.

The other option is the New York version of the cooperative business arrangement. Assuming financial planners are a profession that satisfies the requirements of the New York rules, including court designation, then Jackson's firm and Gumm's firm can cross-refer clients, but the firms themselves remain distinct. Of course, Gumm's firm can do that now without the New York rules. The effect of the New York rules is to allow her firm to have a contractual relationship with Jackson's firm without fear that someone will charge Gumm's firm with failure to exercise independent professional judgment on behalf of clients it refers to Jackson's firm. The New York rule, although forbidding fee splitting, would allow equitable sharing of costs. However, the New York rule would not allow the close alliance that Jackson and Gumm seem to want.

Gumm's firm could "acquire" Jackson's firm as an ancillary business. But this is not likely to be attractive to Jackson's firm. The advantages work in only one direction – the lawyers get a piece of the other professional entity. Why should Jackson do that?

So the prospects don't look very appetizing. The question can be used to explore why it is that current rules do not let the two firms merge, and form either a law firm or a non-law firm. But whatever we call the new entity, one that can render both legal services and non-legal services with all partners sharing in the profit. The main answers are: threat to the lawyers' indepen-dence if the non-lawyers have the economic clout to importune them; risks to client expectations of confidentiality and privilege when non law work is done for non-legal or even legal clients; and I suppose one might add conflicts of interest between the lawyers' business interest to the merged entity and the lawyers' obligations to clients, although this might simply be a restatement of the first risk to independent judgment. Anyway, this problem can be used to explore whether those risks are real, or real enough categorically to prohibit the merger.

PART V

FIRST AMENDMENT RIGHTS OF LAWYERS

CHAPTER XV

FREE SPEECH RIGHTS OF LAWYERS

The introductory note (**page 943-946**) distinguishes between core First Amendment speech and legal marketing; gives examples of traditional criminal acts, like contempt of court, that can be punished although they are based wholly or mostly on speech; and generally introduces the chapter that follows. At **page 945**, I reference the fact that the First Amendment has also been cited to permit lawyers to dress as they please in court, but not always successfully.

A. PUBLIC COMMENT ABOUT PENDING CASES (page 946)

Publicity about pending cases is not simply a product of the competing strategies of two or more litigants (**pages 946-948**). Whatever might be said about pretrial public relations strategies, we should recognize the existence of the press as an independent player. Significant cases of the last decade were going to be covered in the press whether or not the lawyers talked. Some of these cases are listed at **page 948.** Even lawyers who don't want to talk to anybody and would rather try their cases without the media's glare may have to with daily press coverage whether or not they are willing to cooperate. And if the press coverage really is intense, breathes there a lawyer who will be able to reply "no comment" as day after day allegations against their clients appear on Page One? Breathes there a client who will put up with it? Actually there is one lawyer who says he will not talk to the press under any conditions. Brendan Sullivan, who defended Oliver North, insists that he tries his cases in court and will not talk to journalists. If you can do it in the North case, you can do it anywhere I suppose, but few lawyers will be able to match Brendan's restraint. Journalists I know confirm it. The introductory note also addresses gag orders as an additional mechanism, beyond the Rules and the Code, for limiting extrajudicial commentary by lawyers of others.

Gentile v. State Bar of Nevada (**page 948**). This is a long case and many of us will choose not to cover it in all semesters. However, it is also an important case. It is the first time the Supreme Court has directly and clearly confronted the First Amendment rights of lawyers to speak to the media about their own pending cases. The Court is sharply divided, with shifting majorities. Gentile wins but only because Justice O'Connor finds the rule under which he was disciplined void for vagueness. Otherwise, she sides with the Rehnquist plurality, which would allow the state to limit the speech rights of lawyers about their own cases in ways the government could not limit the speech rights of others. Buried deep within *Gentile* is a fundamental disagreement between the Kennedy and Rehnquist opinions about the role of defense counsel in American law. As emphasized in Question 3 on **page 968**, perhaps the most startling aspect of Justice Kennedy's opinion is his insistence that a defense lawyer's responsibility includes the effort to "demonstrate in the court of public opinion that the client does not deserve to be tried." Did a Justice really say that?

Chief Justice Rehnquist advances the contrary view. The "outcome of a criminal trial is to be decided by impartial jurors, who know as little as possible of the case, based on material admitted into evidence before them in a court proceeding." **(Page 962**.) And: "Because lawyers have special access to information through discovery and client communications, their extrajudicial statements pose a threat to the fairness of a pending proceeding since lawyers' statements are likely to be received as especially authoritative." **(Page 964**.) In the Chief Justice's view, "the substantial likelihood" test of the Model Rules state the proper balance. It "narrowly" tailors the limitations on speech to avoid "two principal evils: (1) comments that are likely to influence the actual outcome of the trial, and (2) comments that are likely to prejudice the jury venire, even if an untainted panel can ultimately be found." **(Page 965.)**

Questions About *Gentile* (page 968).

(1) Gentile won because Justice O'Connor agreed that the "safe harbor" provision on which he relied was vague. She was especially persuaded, I think, by the fact that Gentile researched the issue and "made a conscious effort to stay within the boundaries" of the provision.

(2) No one really knows if pretrial publicity affects the jury. Of course, lawyers engage in it anyway, either on the assumption that it does, or because their opponent is doing it, or because the reporter calls and it is too difficult to resist talking. But if we assume, as courts routinely assume on motions to change venue, that voir dire can cleanse the jury, what are the legitimate state interests in limiting lawyer speech? They are confidence in the impartiality of the jury (we can never really know) and avoidance of the costs of an extended voir dire.

(3) What do students think about Kennedy's willingness to recognize an extrajudicial role for lawyers, in particular the role of talking to the press? And what do students think of the fact that it is *Kennedy* who recognizes this role? The state, of course, has all manner of connections to reporters not just through its prosecutors but through law enforcement generally. Most defendants do not have the resources to hire public relations firms as well as defense lawyers. And unlike the state, defendants come and go. The state is in every case. So for most defendants, it will be their lawyer who will speak to the press on their behalf — at the very least to counter prosecutorial and law enforcement leaks — or no one at all. Does this justify Justice Kennedy's

view? The solution of the amendment to the Model Rules is to add a Rule 3.6(c) which allows a lawyer to make a statement that would otherwise be forbidden by 3.6(a) if "a reasonable lawyer would believe [the statement] is required to protect the client from the substantial undue prejudicial effect of recent publicity not initiated by the lawyer or the lawyer's client." The statement must be limited only to information "necessary to mitigate the recent adverse publicity." Note that the adverse publicity need not have been inspired by the state. A harsh newspaper article will do. For Chief Justice Rehnquist, the answer to this problem is to discipline the prosecutor (see note 6 at **page 967**) where she is the source. Why isn't that sufficient?

(4) This question requires a student to recognize that a majority of the Court, despite Gentile's victory, will afford lawyers associated with matters less First Amendment protection in speaking about those matters than all others enjoy. Justice Kennedy seems to read Rule 3.6 as stating a standard approximating "the clear and present danger test." Chief Justice Rehnquist would read the "substantial prejudice" standard more narrowly. Indeed, it is unimportant to Rehnquist that the statement may not have contaminated the trial. For one thing, the trial may never be held for wholly unrelated reasons. Propriety of the statement should not turn on that fortuity. For another, the state has an interest in avoiding uncertainty and the costs of extensive voir dire.

(5) The answer should be that a lawyer unaffiliated with a case should be as free to comment on it as a nonlawyer. His or her opinions are not then seen as "authoritative" because of special access to information. I actually once testified in a disciplinary case against a lawyer who had made public statements in a case with which he was associated. The lawyer who cross-examined me did a Lexis search and asked about all the public statements I've made about cases. I answered -- and I think it's a complete answer -- that I had no affiliation with those cases so my First Amendment right to comment, after *Gentile*, was higher than Gentile's was. (My views carried no special weight, I said. Alas.)

Defamation Claims (page 969). Over the years, the cases in which lawyers are sued for defamation for statements made in connection with their clients' matters, usually litigations, have increased. The litigation privilege, which absolutely protects statements made in court or court filings against defamation claims, may not protect statements made publicly. That is the lesson of these cases. Sometimes statements made outside of court or court documents will be protected if they are close enough to the litigation itself. But the line is not crystal clear. As the use of the press to advance a client's litigation interests increases, we might expect to see an equivalent increase in defamation claims against lawyers who say things out of court that are seen to defame the opponent notwithstanding that they have said the same things in court.

The Trial of William Kennedy Smith (page 971). The Smith case revealed about as consummate a use of the press as one could imagine (until OJ?). This material offers the students a brief case history. Here we see both the prosecutor and the defense filing papers that would predictably be seen by the press and reported nationwide and, more important perhaps, countrywide. We see as well that the *New York Times* (shame, shame) wrote a long article about the case in which it named the victim and quoted an anonymous source to the effect that she had "a little wild streak." Many suspect that the *Times* article was influenced by the Kennedy family. The reporter who wrote it is based in Boston. However, this has not been proved. The point of the *Times* article is to demonstrate the press's status as an independent player in pretrial publicity wars.

Emotions ran high over the *Smith* case. Many lawyers criticized Prosecutor Lasch for failing to seal her pretrial notice of an intention to use the testimony of the other alleged victims. Lasch had to give this notice under state law but she did not have to file it in a place in which it would be publicly available. On the other hand, nothing stopped her from doing so at the time. The extant gag order did not apply. Should she be condemned? The probability that the testimony would be admitted was very low (ultimately, it was rejected).

For his part, defense lawyer Black filed a pretrial motion that revealed allegations about the alleged victim's mental state. Should he be condemned? Is it possible that one lawyer acted improperly while the other did not? Do prosecutors have a higher duty? (Me: Yes.) If the State of Florida sought to discipline Lasch or Black (not very likely), would *Gentile* provide a defense? Does *Gentile* even apply since the lawyers' "statements" were made in court filings? That's a way around the ethics rule, isn't it? It tends to benefit the state, which is more likely to (have to) file papers containing factual allegations about the crime charged.

What if the Kennedy family did "sponsor" the *New York Times* article? Assume this occurred before the gag order. Could Black have been participant to the publicity effort? Could he have talked to the reporters off the record, given them leads, provided investigative files?

A related theme here is the defense effort to attack the credibility, even the sanity, of the alleged victim. This occurred in a rape case and alarmed many observers because of the view that it would predictably intimidate future rape victims. From Black's point of view, didn't he have an interest, especially given Justice Kennedy's recognition of the role of the defense lawyer, in trying to maintain "spin control" on the story? Black could rightly have feared that if he did nothing the anti-Kennedy forces would take control of the story and Willy would suffer a negative public image that would contaminate the jury. So is this what Justice Kennedy had in mind? Even assuming that Lasch did nothing whatsoever to encourage a negative view of the defendant, didn't Black have a right to meet or preempt negative stories generated by enemies of the Kennedy family or a salacious press?

B. PUBLIC COMMENT ABOUT JUDGES AND COURTS (page 972)

1. Criticizing the Administration of Justice (page 972). The introductory note tells the story of Robert Snyder, whose conduct eventually led to the Supreme Court's opinion in *In re Snyder* (**page 974**). It's a nice story to tell and a necessary one given the Court's opinion. What does the phrase "single incident" at **page 974** mean? What if Snyder did something just like that a year before? Snyder's comments were not about a pending case. He did not even criticize a particular judge personally. He was attacking the system. The system needs an attack now and then, doesn't it? (Snyder's attacks caused change.) Perhaps Snyder's mistake was to be so intransigent. The Eighth Circuit's mistake was to change its mind about what it viewed to be Snyder's mistake. Looking back on this, it is amazing, isn't it, that it could not all have been resolved by the good people of Bismarck? This is a case that never should have happened, isn't it?

2. Criticizing Particular Judges (page 974). Does the *New York Times* libel standard apply when a lawyer is disciplined for criticizing a judge? Must the disciplinary authority prove knowledge of falsity or reckless disregard of truth or falsity? *Holtzman* (**page 975**), tells us that the answer is no, at least in so far as the New York Court of Appeals is concerned. Holtzman's conduct adversely reflected on her fitness to practice law within the meaning of DR 1-102(A)(6). Why is that? Holtzman claimed that her accusation against Judge Levine was true, but the Court of Appeals assumes it was false because the lower courts so found and that finding was deemed binding on it. Holtzman made her "false" statement under circumstances that reflected adversely on her fitness as a lawyer. The court does not say she knew the statement was false. Rather, Holtzman moved too quickly and without checking. She ignored the advice of her staff person (a once and future law professor!), who "counseled her to delay publication until the trial minutes were received." The *New York Times* standard will not apply in lawyer discipline cases because that would "immunize all accusations, however reckless or irresponsible, from censure, as long as the attorney uttering them did not actually entertain serious doubts as to their truth (**page 977**). Is that right? Wouldn't the *New York Times* standard permit a sanction where an accusation is "reckless"? Alternatively, a modified *New York Times* standard could be used, in which the test would be objective, not subjective. What would a reasonable lawyer believe? That's what the *Westfall*, *Ray*, *Yagman*, and *Topp* courts did (**pages 979-980**). See paragraph (5) on **page 978**.

Questions About *Holtzman* (page 978).

(1) In response to the opinion Holtzman said that it was "a blow to those who favor freedom of speech and who care about the treatment of rape victims by the courts." Is she right? Will this discourage others who care about the treatment of rape victims by the courts? Or is it only about Holtzman's own impetuous conduct? You might ask here whether, in light of

223

Holtzman and note cases beginning at **page 979**, judges are too sensitive when it comes to criticism of them, punishing speech that would receive constitutional protection if uttered about any other public official. Is that because judges are truly different in a way that justifies less protection, at least when the criticism comes from lawyers?

(2) Holtzman supporters have argued that her status as D.A. should have given her greater freedom to criticize the courts. Who better than a D.A. knows when criticism is required? An alternative view is that her status obligated her to be more careful about the accuracy of her charge before making it. Which is correct? Holtzman had easy access to the transcript and other sources of information. Others would not have this access. What if a lawyer who happened to be observing the trial from the public section of the courtroom then made the same statement? Would that lawyer also demonstrate his or her lack of fitness to practice law?

(3) *Gentile* ultimately won on his vagueness argument. Holtzman lost under a standard that is surely more vague than the "safe harbor" provision at issue in *Gentile*. Who knows what a court will later determine to be "conduct that adversely reflects on [a lawyer's] fitness to practice law"? Why didn't the decision in *Gentile* influence the court in *Holtzman*? Why didn't the Supreme Court grant certiorari in *Holtzman*?

(4) Anyway, Holtzman had a basis for her accusation. She had a memorandum from a staff lawyer. True, he was "newly admitted," as the court says, but why should that matter? If Holtzman had acted as quickly, based on the same memorandum, but had turned out to be correct, would she still be subject to discipline under the same standard? One would think she would be. Why should the fortuity of whether or not her impetuous comment was correct or incorrect make a difference? As the court says distinguishing *New York Times*, we are not dealing with harm to particular individuals but rather with social harm. Holtzman's conduct either did or did not offend the "minimum level" the court identifies regardless of whether the charge was true or false. But can that be so?

(5) See the end of the discussion in the note on "Criticizing Particular Judges."

Other Examples of Lawyers Criticizing Judges and Justice (page 979). This note identifies a case that, quite coincidentally, was decided in Missouri at about the same time *Holtzman* was decided in New York. Both cases involved prosecutors with political ambition. The Missouri prosecutor also lost, but he at least got a lengthy dissent. Certiorari was denied. Also referenced are a recent censure of William Kuntsler for telling a judge he was a "disgrace to the bench" (this happened in court), the suspension of a lawyer who had wrongly accused a

224

judge of altering the transcript in a proceeding before her, and the discipline of a New York lawyer who, after losing a case, said the trial judge had fallen "in love" with the opposing client, an actor. Most interesting is the case of Martin Erdmann (**page 980**). How is it that Erdmann got away with it where Holtzman did not? Why weren't Erdmann's comments a reflection on his fitness to practice law? If anything, aren't Erdmann's blanket accusations worse than the charge Holtzman made? Holtzman at least had a factual basis for what she said — her assistant's memorandum. Erdmann used gross language to condemn the entire state bench. Two other lawyers who criticized particular judges in offensive ways were sanctioned (**pages 980-981**). But like Kuntsler, the focus of their wrath was a particular judge, not the entire judiciary, as in *Erdmann*.

Yagman (**page 980**) applies the objective clear and present danger test to a lawyer's criticism of a judge where the statement was not connected to a pending matter. The Seventh Circuit rejected that generous protection rather emphatically. *Topp* (**page 980**) also applies the clear and present danger test (or said it did) where the lawyer was not associated with the case about which he commented. *Topp's* result is surely wrong, however. This was a citizen criticizing a judge's motives -- giving his opinion.

C. MANDATORY BAR MEMBERSHIP (page 982)

With the decision in *Keller* (**page 982**) on First Amendment grounds, it is now clear that integrated state bars cannot do whatever they like with the dues state lawyers are obligated to pay. *Keller* identifies "the extreme ends of the spectrum," acknowledging that the precise location of "the line . . . will not always be easy to discern." Aside from this ambiguity, *Keller* gives rise to two questions, one mechanical and one intriguing. The mechanical question is the mechanism that a state bar must adopt to ensure that an objecting member has opportunity to decline to permit his or her dues to be used in those situations in which the First Amendment recognizes the right to object. The Supreme Court almost addressed this issue in *Gibson* (**page 983**), but then dismissed the writ after the Florida Supreme Court clarified its rules. The second and more intriguing question is whether a member of an integrated state bar can object to having the Bar participate in controversial political issues even if his or her dues are not used for those purposes. The argument here is that the member is being forced to be a member of the state bar — that's what it means to have an integrated state bar — and has a constitutional right not to have to associate himself or herself with an organization that takes positions to which the member objects, at least not unless those positions are reasonably related to the advancement of the goal of the administration of justice in the state.

CHAPTER XVI

MARKETING LEGAL SERVICES

How to present material on law firm marketing is always a challenge. Here's the way I have attempted to do it. I divide this chapter into five parts. The first (Part A) defines the "borders" of the debate: the relatively tame ad in *Bates* at one end, and the in-person for-profit solicitation in *Ohralik* at the other. Part B defines the "center" through the nuanced issues raised in *Zauderer*, *Shapero*, and *Peel*. In Part C, I step back and ask what "methodology" the Court has used and should use to evaluate lawyer marketing claims under the First Amendment. I return to the commercial use of legal marketing in Part D by considering particular narrow but interesting issues that have challenged the Supreme Court and state courts. Lawyers who promote the use of their services for purposes other than commercial gain are treated differently, something students will already know if you have assigned the material at Chapter 14A, Part E of Chapter 16 is about the greater First Amendment protection "public interest" lawyers enjoy.

I suspect that most of us do not assign much of this material, if any, especially if we teach the course in three credits. That may be necessary, given other materials that are more important and our expectation that commercial free speech issues are covered in other courses. On the other hand, there is something special about the "lawyer regulatory" aspects of the legal advertising and solicitation cases, and that something echoes other themes throughout the book. That is, when courts review challenges to advertising and solicitation restrictions on lawyers, they necessarily take into account legitimate state interests in regulating the bar, interests that will not appear, at least not in the same way, when the subject of the regulation is a nonlegal activity. In any event, it is possible to assign this chapter in parts. You can assign only Part A (11 pages); Parts A and B (33 pages); Parts A - C, with Part C to be read for background (38 pages); or any of the previous alternatives and Part E (11 pages). Part D is only 6 pages and can be reserved for those semesters, if any, in which you really want to cover the issues, or it can be assigned for background reading. All in all, the chapter or parts of it can be covered in one hour, two hours, or, true luxury, three hours.

A. DEFINING THE BORDERS: *BATES* AND *OHRALIK*

The introductory note **(pages 986-990)** briefly describes the pre-*Bates* era, *Bates* itself(setting out the ad at issue in the case), and the phenomenon of law firm marketing at various strata of the profession. I do not offer *Bates* in full. This saves space. Furthermore, the *Bates* analysis was refined in later cases, especially *Zauderer* **(page 998)**, so students will fully encounter the constitutional theories there. I do, however, provide the reasons Arizona advanced to justify its prohibition on lawyer advertising and the Court's response. I excerpt the court's reasons for rejecting the argument that legal advertising would have an "adverse affect on professionalism." **(Page 989**.) I include this response because the supposed threat to professionalism has been, perhaps, the leading objection to law firm marketing that is not false or deceptive. See the discussion of professionalism at **page 1021**. Also, Justice O'Connor's dissent in *Shapero*, which I find extraordinarily well put whether or not persuasive, relies on professionalism and cites *Bates* as the place where the Court first erred **(page 1012)**.

Bates and the subsequent cases can be seen as presenting an issue of "fit." States can not longer blanketly ban legal ads. They provide information that enjoys some First Amendment protection. The evils Arizona identified may have been evils it could seek to prevent but it had to do so in other, less intrusive ways. A state may ban false or deceptive ads, require disclaimers, and perhaps restrict quality claims because they are hard to verify. *Bates* did not address ads on electronic media.

Students should understand that this is not simply a debate about what single practitioners and small firms serving individuals, especially personal injury clients, will be permitted to do. Law firm marketing has become highly sophisticated. Although large firms do not take out newspaper ads or buy late night television spots, they do search for other genteel marketing strategies. Some are listed at **page 987**. This trend will not disappear, even when the economic circumstance of law firms improves. First of all, competition will be keen for a long time given the increase in the number of lawyers absolutely and in proportion to the population. Second, it is probably impossible to revert to prior ways unless the Supreme Court forces the issue by overruling *Bates* (see below).

Bates was a five-four decision. *RMJ* **(page 1000)** was unanimous. *Zauderer* **(page 998)** was five-three. *Shapero* **(page 1007)** was a four-two-three opinion. Since *Shapero*, Justices Souter and Thomas have replaced Justices Brennan and Marshall. Justices Ginsburg and Breyer have replaced Justices Blackmun and White. So the only member of the *Bates* majority remaining on the Court is Justice Stevens. The three *Shapero* dissenters, Justices O'Connor and Scalia and Chief Justice Rehnquist, remain on the Court. They would revisit and overturn *Bates*. So depending on the views of Souter, Ginsburg, Breyer, and Thomas, or any two of them, we could have seen a demise of *Bates*. States would then be free to impose pre-*Bates* controls on law firm marketing. But they wouldn't have to. As it happens, *Edenfield* (1993) **(page 995)** was an eight-one decision, with only O'Connor dissenting. In *Ibañez* (1994) **(page 1018)**, Rehnquist and

228

O'Connor dissented in part, but *Peel* (1990), on which the majority relied (**page 1018**) was five-four. So this can get very confusing. Who believes what? How persuasively do the facts of the cases explain the different results? The final word is *Went-for-It* (**page 1015**), where Thomas and Breyer joined the *Shapero* dissenters to uphold a Florida rule imposing a 30-day moratorium on direct mail advertising of accident victims or their families. But that doesn't threaten *Bates*, as discussed below.

Ohralik v. Ohio State Bar Association (**page 990**). Commercial speech rights for lawyers do not extend to in-person solicitation of strangers for profit. By "strangers" I mean prospective clients who are not current clients and are not former clients and who have no other significant relationship to the lawyer. Ambiguity in the *Ohralik* opinion left it unclear whether Ohralik would have suffered the same fate had his methods been less offensive. That ambiguity was ultimately removed in *Shapero*. For-profit in-person solicitation can be forbidden as a prophylactic measure. Would the Court have reached the same result if Carol and Wanda were current clients of Ohralik's on unrelated matters? Former clients on unrelated matters? Present or former clients on personal injury matters? Couldn't the state achieve the same result by giving clients who are solicited in-person the right to rescind any resulting retainer agreement, and owe nothing, within say a week after it is entered? (Florida gives contingent fee clients three days to cancel their contracts without penalty.

Looked at as a question of "fit," *Ohralik* says that when a state wishes to address the evils of in-person solicitation of strangers for profit, it doesn't have to worry about less intrusive ways of doing it. It can use a categorical ban. Mr. Ohralik might have been condemned for the manner in which he went about soliciting business from Carol McClintock and Wanda Lou Holbert. Although the Court takes pains to describe that offensive manner in some detail, ultimately he lost merely because he approached them.

"*A Prophylactic Rule*" is the topic of the note at **page 995**. Until 1993, one would have assumed, after *Ohralik* and *Shapero*, that a state could categorically ban for profit, in-person solicitation of strangers by lawyers. That assumption is still tenable. But in *Edenfield v. Fane* (**page 995**), the Court invalidated a Florida rule that prevented an accountant from making cold calls to prospective clients, which were medium-sized businesses. *Ohralik* was distinguished on the ground that a CPA is not "a professional trained in the art of persuasion." (**Page 996**.) If the Court had gone no further, *Ohralik* could still have been read broadly without hesitation. The Court continued, however, pointing out that the CPA's clients were also not as subject to manipulation as the two young women in *Ohralik*. Further, the Court emphasized that the young women were approached "at a moment of high stress and vulnerability."

Finally, the Court defined *Ohralik*'s approval of a prophylactic rule as meaning only that such a rule might prohibit "conduct conducive to fraud or overreaching at the outset, rather than punishing the misconduct after it occurred." *Ohralik* did not relieve the state of the obligation to show that such a prophylactic rule was necessary under the circumstances.

Frankly, I don't think this is a fair reading of *Ohralik*, especially not as characterized later in *Shapero*. But as Justice Jackson did *not* say, "You've only got one Supreme Court and we're it." After *Edenfield*, *Ohralik* can be readily distinguished based on the lawyer's particular conduct and the particular susceptibility of the clients. Perhaps *Ohralik* goes no further than personal injury and similar actions. Or perhaps it survives untouched.

B. DEFINING THE CENTER: *ZAUDERER*, *SHAPERO*, AND *PEEL* (page 997)

1. Targeted Advertisements (page 998). This is the first of three subparts discussing particular issues at the center of law firm marketing. *Zauderer* addressed a state's right to punish a lawyer who placed a newspaper ad that purported to give a particular category of prospective client some level of legal advice. It also contained an illustration. *Zauderer* shows that the division that had appeared in *Bates* and disappeared in *RMJ* has now resurfaced (and will continue). Zauderer's ad appealed to a particular category of potential plaintiff (Dalkon Shield users), seemed to give legal advice, contained an illustration, and failed to contain a disclaimer to the effect that the client would remain liable for costs. Zauderer won on all points but the last. Justice Powell did not participate. All other members of the Court agreed that a state could require a disclaimer in ads that proclaimed "no fee if no recovery." Justice O'Connor, joined by the Chief Justice and Justice Rehnquist, foreshadowing her *Shapero* dissent, disagreed with the majority's view that the First Amendment protected the ad's content. (Zauderer's discipline also raised some procedural issues, one of which concerned a different advertisement, and over which Justices Brennan and Marshall dissented. These issues and that other advertisement are discussed at **page 876**.)

I call your attention to the state's justification based in the fear that lawyers will "stir up litigation" **(page 1002)**. Justice White, rejecting this state goal, quotes Learned Hand's much-quoted observation, "I should dread a lawsuit beyond almost anything else short of sickness and death." But the majority then refused to "endorse the proposition that a lawsuit, as such, is an evil" **(page 1002)**. What are the implications of this statement to the common law offenses of champerty, barratry, and maintenance **(page 914)**? Surely, it limits them.

Zauderer is also a "fit" case. While the state has a legitimate right to prevent deceptive ads, its argument that "it is intrinsically difficult to distinguish advertisements containing legal advice that is false or deceptive from those that are truthful and helpful . . . is belied by the facts before [the Court]." **(page 1003**.) The ad Zauderer placed was "completely accurate." It will be no harder to detect deception in legal ads than in ads for other kinds of products. Acceptance of the state's argument here would afford commercial speech little protection.

Justice O'Connor would apply a lower level of scrutiny. Using it, she would find "a sufficient threat to substantial state interests to justify a blanket prohibition." **(Page 1006**.) She fears that lawyers will use "their professional expertise to overpower the will and judgment of lay people who have not sought their advice" as in *Ohralik*. *Id*. She also fears that targeted ads will "encourage lawyers to present that advice most likely to bring potential clients into the office." *Id*.

2. Targeted Mail (page 1006). The big difference between targeted newspaper ads and targeted mail is that one is public and the other is comparatively private. *Shapero* concerned letters that a lawyer wished to send to individuals known to need legal services in a particular area. Here there would likely be many recipients. But a targeted piece of mail could also go to a single prospective client. Would Ohralik be in practice today if he had sent McClintock a letter instead of talking to her in person?

The *Shapero* plurality, only one of whose members (Kennedy) remains on the Court, using the "fit" analysis and relying on *Zauderer* and distinguishing *Ohralik*, concludes that the harm the state anticipated ("overreaching and undue influence") was not so great as to tolerate a blanket prohibition. This case was not "*Ohralik* in writing;" rather, "the mode of communication makes all the difference." **(page 1009**.) Mail solicitation presents a lower risk of coercion. A letter can be ignored. Privacy invasion is nil or nearly so. Less restrictive means are available to the state. Lawyers can be required to file solicitation letters with state agencies. Justice Brennan rejects the argument that these agencies lack resources and expertise to review such letters. The record showed "no evidence that scrutiny of targeted solicitation letters will be appreciably more burdensome or less reliable than scrutiny of advertisements." **(page 1010**.) The state agencies might have more work, but the constitutional interest in "the free flow of commercial information is valuable enough to justify imposing" these costs. **(page 1010**.)

Justices White and Stevens, concurring, would leave to the lower courts the decision about whether Shapero's letter was deceptive or misleading. In her dissent, Justice O'Connor approaches the legal marketing debate from a rather different perspective, which is discussed in connection with the note at **page 1018** below. All three dissenters are still on the Court.

The Response to *Shapero* (page 1014). After *Shapero*, the ABA redrafted Rule 7.3, which had theretofore prohibited targeted direct mail advertising. In the new rule, adopted in February 1989, lawyers are forbidden, with minor exceptions, to engage in in-person or live telephone solicitation. Rule 7.3(a). Written or recorded solicitation is permitted so long as the contents satisfy the requirements of Rule 7.1 and the solicitation does not involve coercion, duress, or harassment. A prospective client can also inform a lawyer of his or her desire not to be solicited by the lawyer. Rule 7.3(b). The emphasis on "live" telephone contact means, it appears, that telerobotic machines are acceptable. See Maryland Opinion 85-17, which is in

231

accord. Those machines dial all telephone numbers within a particular vicinity and give a brief recorded message about the lawyer's practice.

Rule 7.3(c) now requires that all "written or recorded communications from a lawyer soliciting professional employment from a prospective client known to be in need of legal services" — the facts in *Shapero* — "in a particular matter, and with whom the lawyer has no family or prior professional relationship, shall include the words 'Advertising Material' on the outside envelope and at the beginning and ending of any recorded communication." Any challenge to this requirement would seem unlikely to prevail. Does "prior professional relationship" mean only an attorney-client relationship? Does a brochure describing a law firm sent to the CEO of a Fortune 500 company constitute the kind of mailing that requires the designated words on the envelope? No. What about a letter offering antitrust counseling to a company continually in need of such counseling if the letter does not refer to a "particular matter"? Probably not.

Some jurisdictions went much further than the ABA. The Florida, Georgia, and Iowa rules are described at **page 1015**. Whereas the ABA requires targeted mail ads to have the words "Advertising Material" on the outside envelope and at the beginning and end of any recorded communication, Florida requires all ads, targeted or not, to have the word "Advertisement" printed "in red ink" on the envelope and *each page* of the communication. Only regular mail may be used. No faxes. Georgia specifies a type size. Iowa requires a warning. State variations can work havoc on a national ad campaign.

Went-for-It and lower court cases in light of it are discussed at **pages 1015-1017** *Went-for-It* is the only lawyer marketing case to put every current Justice on the map. The two surprises are that Breyer voted with the Shapero dissenters and that the court relied on very flimsy evidence (discussed at **page 1021**) in crediting the state interest in protecting the bar's reputation. Efforts to expand the holding have failed in lower courts. On the other hand, *Went-For-It* is a narrow opinion and indirectly endorses even the precedent where Justices in the majority dissented (the price of Breyer's vote?). It even acknowledges the availability of advertising on the electronic media, a subject the Court has never addressed.

3. Claims of Special Expertise (page 1017). I treat *Peel* as a note case. It is most intriguing to me because it has a potential for encouraging private organizations to accredit lawyers and thereby assume a function traditionally performed by the state. Of course, the lawyers will have to have been admitted to practice somewhere, but once admitted, *Peel* seems to permit private groups with legitimate standards and subject to reasonable state regulation to further credential the admitted lawyer. Unlike state licensure, these efforts would be subject to antitrust regulation, but that should not be particularly inhibiting. As competition increases, along with the levels of specialization, I think we will see more groups like the National Board of Trial Advocacy. Will states try to regulate them out of existence, despite *Peel*? Or will they welcome them? Stay tuned. The amendments to Rule 7.4 (see **page 763**) will encourage this trend. One version of Rule 7.4(c) now envisions that organizations may be accredited by the ABA to certify lawyers as specialists in an area of law. If so, a lawyer who lists the certification need not add a disclaimer that the lawyer's jurisdiction does not have a procedure for such certifications. Further, the Supreme Court's decision in *Ibañez* **(page 1018)**, recognizing the lawyer's First Amendment right to list her status as a Certified Financial Planner and a CPA in her Yellow Pages ads and on her business cards will also advance the trend toward private certification.

C. DEFINING THE METHODOLOGY (page 1018)

Some of the material in this Part will have filtered into class discussion even before you reach it. But much of it will extend discussion. The whole section is three and a half pages. I thought it worthwhile to "take a moment out" to talk about how the court analyzes lawyer marketing cases. Doing this is especially appropriate given the intriguing perspective of Justice O'Connor.

How Does the Court Know Things? (page 1019) What is the Court's source of empirical information? To the extent that the court is "overruling: a "legislative" judgment about a likely harm, it is making a judgment of its own about the likelihood of the particular harm and the availability of other means to guard against it. Or is it just saying that given the First Amendment dimension, the state has a higher burden? Of course, this assumes that the harm is one the state can seek to prevent. How does the Court know if a state has carried its burden? The book contrasts the Court's empirical analyses in *Ohralik*, *Shapero*, and *Schaumberg v. Citizens for a Better Environment* **(page 1020)**. In *Schaumberg*, the Court struck a village ordinance that barred certain door-to-door and on-the-street charitable solicitations. I contrast *Schaumberg* and *Ohralik* in particular because both involved in-person invitations. Why did the First Amendment protect the charitable solicitors but not the legal ones? And of course in *Edenfield*, the Court saw no risk sufficient to tolerate a prophylactic rule. How does the Court know that the risks in *Edenfield* are lower than the risks in *Ohralik*, sufficient to justify a constitutional distinction? If a state, after *Edenfield*, wanted to prove, empirically, that that perceived danger of overreaching is greater than the Court now seems to believe, will it be allowed to do so? Or is the empirical conclusion true as a matter of law?

At least in part, the basis for the assumptions of some members of the Court seems to be their view of the affect of money on behavior.

Professionalism and Money (page 1021). Here is where I talk about Justice O'Connor's *Shapero* dissent. O'Connor assumes, first, that professional membership "entails an obligation to temper one's selfish pursuit of economic success" and second, that "fairly severe constraints on attorney advertising" will help do that. Justice O'Connor is willing to allow states to forbid marketing, even the ad in *Bates*, in order to create a climate that will discourage lawyers from focusing on acquisition of wealth. She is willing to do this even if it means that fees will go up.

What do students (some half of whom will graduate with massive debt) think of O'Connor's view that professionalism entails a commitment to reduce one's interest in money? This view is widely shared. Should professionalism be defined as a willingness to subordinate the interest in the acquisition of wealth? If so, states, in fostering professionalism, can legitimately pass rules that make it harder for lawyers to get clients (and money).

The jurisprudential question here is: Absent proof of a causal relationship between marketing and professionalism as Justice O'Connor defines it, to whom should the Court defer? Should it defer to the state's perception of a connection? Or should it defer to the purported First Amendment interest? As regards the state interest, should the Court accept the state's claims at face value? On intuition? Or should it be cognizant of the possibility that a state's limitations on marketing may reflect the interests of powerful lawyers who fear that marketing by others will interfere with their own acquisition of wealth? Even if there is a relationship between pervasive legal marketing and an interest in wealth, as a policy matter is that so bad? From one perspective, it is a lawyer's interest in money that encourages him or her to help others vindicate their rights. Why can't we use acquisitiveness, even greed, toward that end? But this would be an "ends" argument for state rulemakers, not the Supreme Court. Tempering greed is a legitimate state goal.

D. DEFINING THE RULES (page 1023)

Part D can be assigned for home reading, discussed in class, or omitted. It hops across three current issues in the world of lawyer marketing. None is momentous. All are controversial. The first is whether the First Amendment protects legal advertising on the electronic media (**page 1023**). *Bates* specifically did not address that question but *Went-For-It* seems to accept it. But regulation is extensive in some states. The Model Rules permit television and radio advertising as do most jurisdictions, but Iowa, Florida, and New Jersey impose severe restrictions.

A brief note alerts students to the use of Internet to advertise (**page 1025**) and the only instance so far of a lawyer who was disciplined for his manner of advertising. I have a feeling that this note will grow in future editions.

The next note asks whether states can require disclaimers on legal ads (**page 1025**). Surely they can after *Zauderer*, at least within reason. Sometimes a required disclaimer can make an ad effectively useless, as in *Daves* (**page 1027**).

Last is a brief review of the law regarding solicitation of other lawyers' clients, which may be forbidden under substantive law **(page 1027)**.

"I'm Back on My Feet" (page 1028)

This problem asks whether an ad may properly use an actor to impersonate a client. Literally, the actor is misrepresenting himself or herself. But doesn't everyone know that? In addition, if television is going to be effective, and to a lesser extent radio, doesn't it have to be dramatic? In my view, actors should be allowed and the focus should rather be on the content of what the actor says. The content of these two ads seems to be acceptable, that is there is no real danger that a viewer or listener will reach inaccurate conclusions based on the content of the ad. The ad seems to make no promises other than that the speaker managed to keep his house and most of his savings. Should that be forbidden? What if the bankruptcy law would enable the firm to achieve the same result for virtually all clients? New Jersey forbids televised dramatizations (ones on radio are allowed). Is that rule constitutional?

E. SOLICITATION BY PUBLIC INTEREST AND CLASS ACTION LAWYERS (page 1029)

Public interest lawyers do not work for profit and that has made a difference. Class action lawyers have to be able to reach their clients or potential clients and that has also made a difference. The special treatment public interest lawyers get also arose, in a different context, when we discussed lay participation in, or control of, public interest organizations that provide legal services. (See Chapter 14A.)

The pedagogically convenient aspect of *Primus* **(page 1030)** is that it was decided the same day as *Ohralik* **(page 990)**, a fortuity that gave Justice Rehnquist an opportunity to ask some pointed questions about the two **(page 1037)**. For the Court, the absence of a profit motive makes a great deal of difference. Why should that be? While it is true that throughout history we have many examples of people who are motivated by greed to act improperly, as remarked earlier, we also have many examples of improper conduct motivated by political aspirations. Which motive has worked the most evil?

Or is the Court simply saying that when the motive is political — when the courts are used to achieve a political or associational objective — the First Amendment, for better or worse, provides greater protection than when the motives are purely financial? So a prophylactic remedy will be allowed (or a lesser "fit" tolerated) in the latter situation, but not in the former one.

It bears pointing out that today Primus's letter would be protected under *Shapero*. But that was not clear then and so the case turned on Primus's purpose. Under Model Rules, would Primus have to write "Advertising Material" on the envelope? Rule 7.3(c), read literally, says yes if done for "pecuniary gain" (and reading Rule 7.3(a) and (c) together).

A side issue in *Primus* concerns the unaddressed behavior of Dr. Pierce's lawyer, who was present when Mrs. Williams signed the release. The impetus for Mrs. Williams to do so was an obvious wish to have Dr. Pierce care for her child. Did the doctor's lawyer behave improperly in permitting Mrs. Williams to sign a release when the doctor was counseled and she was not? See Model Rule 4.3 and DR 7-104(A)(2).

Analyzing *Primus* from the perspective of "fit," we see that the Court says that South Carolina's action must "withstand the 'exacting scrutiny applicable to limitations on core First Amendment rights. . . .'" **(page 1035**.) This is because when "political expression or association is at issue," the Court will not tolerate the "degree of imprecision that often characterizes government regulation of the conduct of commercial affairs." With that kind of standard, of course, Primus had to win. Indeed, could a state forbid a "public interest lawyer" to solicit clients <u>in person</u> so long as she did not overreach or mislead? I think not. Rule 7.3(a) would not apply because it specifies "pecuniary gain" as a motive.

Communication with Class Members (page 1037). This note identifies the special First Amendment protection that might be afforded in class action litigation, where counsel needs to speak with potential members of a legitimate class. Although *Bernard* **(page 1038)** does not rest on the First Amendment, it flirts with it. *Kleiner* **(page 1039)** shows that *Bernard* is not equally available to the defense seeking to speak with potential plaintiff class members as to the plaintiff seeking to do the same. The *Gates* case **(page 1038)** can be seen as a clash between the no-contact rule and first amendment rights. The trial judge enjoined the ACLU from contacting members of a prisoner class for whom the trial judge had already appointed class counsel (with whom the class members were dissatisfied). The Fifth Circuit reversed, 2-1, relying on *Bernard*.

"I Need to Make Contact" (page 1040)

Max is in private practice. He takes cases for profit. So is he more like Ohralik than Primus? But the cases he takes are very much in the public interest (what does that mean?) and his fees come from the opposing side (like the ACLU's "fee" in *Primus*). So is he more like Primus than Ohralik? Max is desperate to meet his potential clients, but his letters go unanswered. Must he label them as advertisements? Can he ask an intermediary to solicit their interest in a lawsuit? *Ohralik*, literally read and as reinforced by *Shapero*, would seem to say that a state can categorically forbid Max's in-person efforts. Is that wise? What if Max knows no one who works at the hospital? Can he approach a stranger who does work there and offer to "compensate" her for her "time" in making the inquiries? This question exploits the uncharted territory between *Ohralik* and *Primus*, as Justice Rehnquist did in his *Primus* dissent. Profit motive does not automatically end the analysis.

"The Letter Was Dumped" (page 1040)

This question raises the in-person solicitation issue in the context of a private practitioner willing to work for free. It can be seen as the converse of the prior question. Max considers himself a "public interest lawyer" who is prepared to work without a fee from the client although he will seek one from the court. Gloria is a private practitioner who works for a fee but is prepared to represent a prospective client for free for what we might charitably characterize as public interest motives. After *Ohralik*, it is clear that a state may forbid in-person solicitation of clients for profit. If a lawyer is willing to handle a matter for free, may the state nevertheless categorically forbid in-person solicitation of the client? I think not. Remove the profit motive and you should enjoy greater First Amendment protection. But what if the lawyer's motive is publicity, expecting that publicity will lead to paying clients?

In each of the two prior questions, what is the effect of *Edenfield*? It is possible, in both, that *Edenfield* will serve to enable the lawyer to make the contact or cause the contact to be made. In the second question, of course, Gloria only wants to write a letter that will not be designated as an advertisement. (Can she go further and telephone?) This is much less intrusive than the cold call permitted in *Edenfield*, although the prospective client is under greater stress. In the first question, Max wants to get someone to talk to the prospective client. That gets closer to *Ohralik* and the clients are not like the business people in *Edenfield*. Yet neither are they as vulnerable as the two young women in *Ohralik*.